GRANT TEAFF WITH THE MASTER COACHES VOLUME II

Other Books by Grant Teaff:

I Believe (Grant Teaff with Sam Blair)

Winning (Grant Teaff with Louis and Kay Moore)

Seasons of Glory (Grant Teaff and the Baylor Bears)

Coaching in the Classroom (Grant Teaff)

Grant Teaff with the Master Coaches (Grant Teaff)

A Coach's Influence: Beyond the Game (Grant Teaff)

Audio and video tapes:

The Master Motivator

The Christian Family with Grant and Donell Teaff

Winners without Drugs

The David Principles

GRANT TEAFF

WITH THE

MASTER COACHES

VOL II

Presented by

The **Foundation**®

American
Football Coaches

ISBN: 978-0-9885459-1-5

Convention photos and executive director portrait photos provided by the AFCA. Master Coach photos courtesy of Sports Information Directors at the coach's former or current schools. Dick Vermeil photos courtesy of the Kansas City Chiefs.

Dedication

This book is, as the first was, dedicated to all Master Coaches I had the privilege of interviewing.

Secondly, I would like to dedicate this book to my great team at the AFCA and the American Football Coaches Foundation.

When I took over the American Football Coaches Association, right after the 1994 AFCA Convention, I found myself not so much coaching my new team (Sandy Atkinson and Mel Pulliam), but more picking their brains and learning how an organization that I had been a vital part of actually worked. The three of us moved the Association to Waco, Texas, and we worked hard each day to reach the 20 goals I set with the Board of Trustees in 1994. Following the move to Texas, Janet Robertson was added to our staff. As the Association grew, we added more staff and created The Foundation.

No head coach is any stronger than the members of his staff. Over the years, we added staff members who were great leaders in their own right, and they joined me in the important mission of the Association and The Foundation. Through their efforts, the AFCA educational venues have changed and grown.

The AFCA and The Foundation associates to whom this book is dedicated:

Gary Darnell, Associate Executive Director
Adam Guess, Managing Director of Finance & Operations
Janet Robertson, Director of Conferences & Events
Vince Thompson, Director of Media Relations
Kevin Morgan, Director of Information Technologies
Tai Brown, Director of Education
Amy Gilstrap, Convention Services Manager
Amy Miller, Executive Assistant
Jordan Slentz, Membership Staff Assistant
Rhonda Martindale, Membership Staff Assistant
Sara Schindler, Finance & Foundation Staff Assistant
Genee Ordones, Foundation Staff Assistant
Will DeWitt, Media Staff Assistant
McCall Parrish, Media Staff Assistant
Stacy Sirkel, Coordinator of Publications
Carlos Cabrera, Information Technologies Staff Assistant
Josh Davis, Graduate Assistant
Jonathan Hill, Graduate Assistant
Isaac Gittens, Graduate Assistant
Donell Teaff, AFCWA Liaison
Kelly Smith, AFCWA Convention Coordinator
John Lisk, Marketing
Butch Gardner, Convention Exhibitor Manager
Dennis Poppe, Liaison to the NCAA
Mike Bourland, Jeremy Pruitt, and Graigory Fancher, Legal Counsel

Special recognition to Mel Pulliam and Sandi Atkinson, who became the bedrock of a great staff.

Acknowledgments

This book, like the first, would not have been possible without those who, on that special occasion, served as Master Coaches, allowing thousands of members to sit at their feet and learn.

2006 Don Nehlen
Bowling Green State, West Virginia

R.C. Slocum
Texas A&M

2007 Bobby Bowden
Florida State

John Gagliardi
St. John's

2008 Terry Donahue
UCLA

John Robinson
USC, UNLV, Los Angeles Rams

2009 Tom Osborne
Nebraska

Joe Paterno
Penn State

2010 Lou Holtz
William & Mary, North Carolina State, Arkansas, Minnesota, Notre Dame, South Carolina, New York Jets

Dick MacPherson
Massachusetts, Syracuse, New England Patriots

2011 Barry Alvarez
Wisconsin

Fisher DeBerry
Air Force

2012 Lloyd Carr
Michigan

Tubby Raymond
Delaware

2013 Phil Fulmer
Tennessee

Dick Vermeil
UCLA, Philadelphia Eagles, St. Louis Rams, Kansas City Chiefs

2014 Marino Casem
Alabama State, Alcorn State, Southern

Bill McCartney
Colorado

2015 Bill Curry
Georgia Tech, Alabama, Kentucky, Georgia State

Jerry Moore
North Texas, Texas Tech, Appalachian State

Ken Sparks
Carson-Newman

The institutions listed are the ones at which that coach had his greatest impact. For more complete information on their coaching careers, see their biographical sketches at the end of the book.

Table of Contents

Foreword

Many years ago when I entered the coaching profession, I attended every clinic I could afford. I took very thorough notes, asked as many questions as I could and, after returning home, I studied them extensively. No matter how much I sought knowledge from successful coaches, I could not satisfy my appetite to learn how to be a successful coach. Consequently, I learned many things by making mistakes and I guess you could call it the trial-and-error method. Had Grant Teaff's book, *Grant Teaff with the Master Coaches*, which is the Bible for all coaches who have a desire to succeed, been available when I began my coaching profession, it would have saved me money, time, and losses.

No one in my lifetime has done more for the coaching profession than Grant Teaff as the Executive Director of the American Football Coaches Association. What some people don't realize is that Grant was an excellent football coach. I know this first hand as our Arkansas teams played Baylor for seven consecutive years when Grant was head coach. I tell you sincerely, his team was well-coached, disciplined, and played with great class. They were normally a Top 20 football team. I can honestly say that when Grant was on the opposite sideline from me, I knew we were going against the best.

Typical of Grant's unselfish attitude, he has interviewed many great coaches and put their thoughts on various subjects in a "must have" book. While Grant has done so much for the coaching profession in general, I feel this manuscript may be his greatest gift to all coaches.

As I read the first volume, I thought "Boy, I wish this book was available when I was coaching!" as it contains so much valuable information. There you can enjoy the contributions of several coaching legends such as Darrell Royal, Eddie Robinson, Frank Broyles, Paul Dietzel, Charlie McClendon, Bo Schembechler, Vince Dooley, Tom Landry, Bill Yeoman, Don Shula, and many others.

After reading this book, I promise you will refer to it constantly over your career. It will never go out of date. This book and it's predecessor are what I refer to as significant manuscripts because they will help others be successful. This describes Grant Teaff: always trying to help other coaches be significant.

Thank you, Grant.

Lou Holtz

Preface

An amazing idea, like a plant adaptable to the climate, nourished and watered, will grow into something useful or beautiful or both. That's exactly what happened when the simple idea to bring back the great coaches of the past to the AFCA Annual Convention. It allowed the coaches of today to receive the wisdom, knowledge, and expertise from those who had gone before. Instead of just the standard interview, the decision was made to ask each Master Coach the same questions.

Now, with the publication of *Volume II*, coaches will have two reference books to find out exactly what the Master Coaches thought about the pertinent issues coaches deal with, no matter the decade. The books, *Grant Teaff with the Master Coaches* and *The Master Coaches, Volume II*, are a treasure trove of wisdom from those great men who have successfully coached our game decade after decade.

With each interview, my heart was warmed by how deeply those Master Coaches cared about their players, their staff family, their own family, and the great game of football. That trait ran through each of the Master Coaches. It was a blessing for me to have the opportunity to spend time talking with each of them.

I think it is also appropriate, as I have concluded my tenure as executive director of the American Football Coaches Association, to say to those coaches whom I have had the privilege of working with as members of our Board of Trustees of the AFCA and The Foundation, thank you for your service to our game. These men care so deeply about the importance of our game, particularly in America today, that they give endless hours serving, without pay, to make sure generations of coaches are educated properly and understand the importance of teaching values and a strong work ethic as they teach the game of football.

America needs our game, but for it to remain viable, those who coach must understand that they, through the American Football Coaches Association, are the guardians of the game. We must always be diligent to make our game safer to play, as well as seizing every opportunity to teach "beyond the game."

In our profession, we all stand on the shoulders of those who have gone before us. My prayer is that each of us who stood on those shoulders will be willing and worthy for others to stand on ours.

G.T.

Chapter 1

The Value of Effective Planning

A few weeks prior to my father's death in 2002, he was in the hospital in our hometown of Snyder, Texas. He was quite ill and delirious. My daughter, Tracy, and I were with him in his hospital room. He had been sleeping, then all of the sudden he opened his eyes, looked at me standing to his left, raised his right arm and pointed to the portable heart monitor sitting at the foot of his bed. He said, "Grant, take that to the third floor, because they need it up there." I replied, "Yes, sir," then walked to the end of the bed and took the handle in my left hand and rolled it around behind his bed where I thought he could not see me or the heart monitor. I was wrong. He was not fooled. Dad looked at Tracy and said, "You know Grant can't do anything unless he has a plan."

I confess that he was right. Somehow, at a very early age, I came to the realization that I needed to come up with a plan if I wanted to accomplish the things I had in my heart. Many things did not come natural to me, so the idea of planning, then executing that plan, became vital to my success.

The definition of a plan as found in the Merriam-Webster dictionary is "a detailed formation of a program or the action or method of achieving an end." The business dictionary definition reads: "A written account of intended future course of action aimed at achieving specific goals or objectives within a specific time frame. It explains in detail what needs to be done, when, how, and by whom, and often includes a best case, expected case, and worst case scenarios." I would say that description is elaborately defining.

During my sophomore year of high school, I became a goal setter. As a junior, I realized in order to reach my goals I must plan to reach them. I set a goal to be a head football coach in the Southwest Conference at that point. Near the end of my senior year, the school yearbook came out and had a page of predictions for our senior class. Being one of those seniors, I quickly looked for the prediction prepared by the yearbook staff. My prediction clearly stated, "Grant Teaff will be the head football coach at the University of Texas." I have often said jokingly, "I only missed it by 100 miles." (Baylor University in Waco is 100 miles from Austin and the University of Texas).

I knew if I were to have any chance of reaching what many people might have seen as an extreme goal, I needed to figure out what it would take to get there. I outlined the following:

1. Graduate and find a way to go to college to receive an education (this was fundamental).
2. Play football, earn a scholarship, work a job that would help me become a good leader.
3. Master communication techniques.
4. Use my plan of success from high school to develop a positive attitude while being willing to give total effort in every endeavor, and work every day to become a self-disciplined individual in control of my own actions and life.
5. Develop a capacity to really care about my own development and about others.

Later, having met and married a beautiful Texas Tech cheerleader, I was determined to bring her into my world of goal setting and planning. I did and she bought in. We set plans to reach goals in every segment of our life: spiritual, physical, family, financial, and, of course, football.

Interestingly enough, your goals and plans are based on the knowledge you have. I took the head track and assistant football coaching jobs at McMurry University shortly after we were married. My beginning salary was $3,000 a year. However, we were to live in the men's athletic dormitory (an old wooden structure on the McMurry campus), which provided free rent for us. We also ate in the school cafeteria free of charge. Wow, we were rolling in dough!

Being named the head track coach at McMurry was one of those oh-by-the-way-you're-the-new-head-track-coach moments. Based on my mentality at that age, and not knowing anything about track except that you turn left and hurry back, I set a plan by which I could be knowledgeable and build a successful program.

In 1957, I was a 23-year-old head track coach, and knowing nothing, I realized I had a gold mine in the state of Texas. Track is very big and important in Texas, at every college and university there was an outstanding track coach. My plan was simply to learn to coach track from renowned coaches in the state of Texas. For instance, at Howard Payne University (about 70 miles down the road from Abilene, where McMurry is located) there was a wonderful man by the name of Cap Shelton who had extraordinary success in the distance races. Jack Patterson at Baylor University had amazing success in the sprints, the quarter mile, and, of course, all the relays. The coach at Abilene Christian University was a great sprinter coach, as well. The coach at North Texas specialized in field events, and the coach at Southwest Texas did a marvelous job with hurdlers.

I called each coach to ask if they would spend three hours with me talking about their specialty in track. They all accepted and by the end of the week I had a notebook full of notes about every track event with the exception of the long jump. I found a book that had been written about the long jump 30 years earlier, and from that I learned the fundamentals to teach that great event. Later, I was coaching two of the top long-jumpers in the world. The next part of the plan was to recruit the best athletes I could find. Remember, I had no money; however, I was given 15 scholarships. I had read about a miler from New Zealand named Ian Stud and I decided to write him a letter to offer him a scholarship. I knew he was close to a four-minute mile, which in those days was very, very good. Ian accepted my offer and made his way from New Zealand to Abilene, Texas. No one on the Division III level could come close to beating him. I basically recruited sprinters who could run the quarter-mile. John Dale Lewis from Coleman, Mike Stell from Fort Worth, Bill Miller from Winters (40 miles from Abilene), and Bruce Land from West Texas. They were four of the best sprinters in the country at that time. They made our 440-yard and 880-yard relays formidable in any track meet.

After three years as the assistant football coach and head track coach, at age 26, I became the head football coach at McMurry. Interestingly enough, becoming a head coach in college was part of our first three-year plan. In actuality, I became a head track coach immediately and three years later I became the head football coach.

Fairly early in my career, I learned a valuable lesson: sometimes, one can have the best plans, execute them well, and reach a measure of success, yet sometimes the goals of others will interfere with you continuing to reach yours. For example, after taking over McMurry football, I had three straight winning seasons and continued to coach the winning track program. Without my knowledge, the administration had a plan of their own. They decided to go non-scholarship in athletics (which would parallel today's Division III where grants and aids are used). After three years of planned success both in track and football, I was faced with either leaving the program as it was going downhill, or staying and trying to re-establish scholarships. For some reason, I have never been one to jump ship. I had a choice – be prudent and go to SMU where I had been offered an assistant job, or stay at McMurry and fight. The faculty representative at McMurry at the time, Dr. Bill Miller, came to me and asked if I was willing to stay to work with some of the Trustees in order to restore scholarships. I agreed to do so because I felt it was the right thing to do. However, I had no idea of the impact that the canceling of scholarships would have on the athletes I had recruited. Frankly, most of them left to go to other places where they could have full scholarships. Though our record in football suffered for three years, scholarships were finally restored by the Board of Trustees and the President.

J.T. King, head football coach at Texas Tech University, had offered me a job as an assistant coach on a couple of occasions. After the scholarships were restored, I decided to join Coach King and his staff. This meant going home to West Texas for Donell and me. Those next three years at Texas Tech were years of personal growth. The athletic director and Coach King told me they wanted me to become the head coach at Tech when Coach King replaced the retiring AD, Polk Robertson. They were not sure of the exact date, but they felt it would be within the next two or three years. At the end of my third year at Tech, Angelo State University made me an offer that was extremely hard to turn down. Angelo State, after all, was my junior college (at that time it was called San Angelo College), and I looked forward to coaching where I had started. Also, after my experience at McMurry,

I was confident I could build a successful program anywhere, under any circumstance. When I talked to Coach King and Coach Robinson about leaving, they both thought it would be a very good move. I could go to Angelo State and get more experience, then return to Tech as the head coach. I liked the idea. The appealing thing to me was that Angelo State had never had a winning season as a senior college. I wanted to change that. Plus, Angelo State promised I could build new facilities.

I have learned in life that even the best laid plans sometimes fail to materialize, because other factors change. My original plan was to go back to Texas Tech as the head football coach. That plan was disrupted when J.T. King stepped up to take over as athletic director. It was reported to me that the selection committee made a decision not to hire any assistant on the staff, nor any previous assistants. I was eliminated, and they hired an outstanding coach named Jim Carlin, who coached from 1970-1974.

In my own life, the definitely unplanned, and not even suspected, coaching position at Baylor University fell into my lap. The reason it fell into my lap was that nobody else in America wanted the job. I didn't even want the job. However, I believe that God has a plan for each of us and that His plan was for me to end up at Baylor. It's an interesting story how I got there, but this chapter is about the importance of planning. I didn't plan to be at Baylor, but when I accepted the job, I took over a program that had only won three games in three years, hadn't won the championship in 50 years, and had very poor facilities. There was a large 50,000 seat stadium that was supposed to have real grass, but that had disappeared a year or so before. It also had wooden bleachers with splinters all over them, no practice field, and no weight room. After I took the job, I came up with a plan to restore the downtrodden program.

The simple plan was to create a positive attitude, instill belief that winning was possible at Baylor, improve the facilities, and surround myself with a staff who believed in the plan. Then, it was time to roll up our sleeves and execute that plan.

During our first spring training in 1972, 33 scholarship players came to my office to tell me they no longer wanted to play because I was demanding too much from them. So be it. I shook their hands and wished them well. Our staff dove in taking the young men we inherited, added positive recruits, developed a team that was highly conditioned and highly motivated, and, interestingly enough, expected to win. In just three seasons, our team accomplished the feat known as "The Miracle on the Brazos," but I made it clear to everyone that it was no miracle. The so-called "miracle" consisted of beating Texas, the perennial champion in the Southwest Conference, then going on to win the conference outright for the first time in 50 years. As a part of my plan, I planted the seeds of confidence in those who lacked it – on the athletic field, across the campus, and with the alumni. On one remarkable Friday night in 1972, at a pep rally behind the student center, I boldly made a promise to the freshmen, "If you will get behind your team, remain positive, and believe Baylor can win against anybody, I promise you that before you graduate, we will be champions of the Southwest Conference." Two years later, the Baylor Bears became the champions of the Southwest Conference.

The short-term plan was working, but we needed to secure the future by recruiting top athletes in Texas. In order to do that, we had to improve our facilities dramatically and use the fact that we were playing the Who's Who of the Top 10 in non-conference games as a recruiting advantage.

We explained to recruits and to our own players why we mostly played non-conference games on the road. We played Kentucky,

Nebraska, Air Force, BYU, Georgia, Ohio State, Michigan, Missouri, Colorado, Oklahoma State, Florida State, Oklahoma, Auburn, and South Carolina. The schedule and the facilities in general made it tough to be on top year after year. Also, the road schedule took its toll physically, some years more than others. Injuries in the non-conference games would leave us shorthanded in the first part of the conference schedule. We promoted the concept to our players that the tougher our non-conference schedule, the tougher we would be in conference play. That theory became the truth and we proved it year after year.

Prior to the 1992 season, my plan was to finish my coaching career at Baylor, then use my contacts as athletic director to make sure Baylor landed in a strong conference, because it was clear the Southwest Conference was going into demise. When Arkansas left to join the Southeastern Conference, it was another sign that the end was near for the Southwest Conference.

Another unexpected event in my life occurred during the 1992 football season. I had already announced that it would be my last season to coach, so the Board of Trustees and the selection committee of the American Football Coaches Association put on a full-court press. I had been on the AFCA Board for many years and served as the chair of the Ethics Committee, so I knew every member of the Board and they knew me. My intention was to stay at Baylor as the athletic director, but throughout the 1992 season, members of the AFCA Board of Trustees made it clear I was their only choice to be the new executive director. That, combined with a couple of things happening at Baylor, gave me a solid reason to succeed Coach Charlie McClendon who served as executive director for twelve years. I have loved every moment of my twenty-two years of service to our game and profession. According to my personal belief, going to Baylor was part of God's plan; I felt the same way when I left Baylor for the American Football Coaches Association.

My plan for the AFCA is well-documented, so I only mention it because we are talking about the importance of planning.

At the time I took over, the AFCA had three employees (including the executive director), there were just shy of 3,000 members, and the office was two rooms in a strip mall in Orlando, Florida. The assets overall were small, but I looked at the AFCA as one of the most important organizations in America serving our game, our profession, and the young people our coaches influence on a daily basis.

While presenting to the Board at the AFCA Convention in Anaheim, California, in January 1994, I laid out 20 goals to make the AFCA viable in every segment of the football community. I must say, the great board members and the individuals who have caringly served as our presidents throughout my years, combined with our amazing membership, make the AFCA what it is today. I believe the opportunity to be heard is important for any segment of an organization. Therefore, our Board of Trustees is extremely inclusive and they serve as conduits to all the different constituencies. Plan to succeed, execute the plan with a positive attitude, and it will happen!

As an example, one of my major goals was to change not only the delivery of our educational system – including the publications and the now-thriving AFCA website – but also to make sure that everyone could see and hear at the AFCA Convention. I also wanted to ensure that a high percentage of all presentations would be video recorded, then transcribed, so that all members, even those not attending the AFCA Convention, would have access to the educational opportunities offered.

This book and the previous one, *Grant Teaff with the Master Coaches*, the Master Coach Video Series, and the extraordinary sessions at the AFCA Convention came about because of a plan. The first step of the plan was to make our former coaches an important and vital resource for current coaches. I wanted to start the series with two of my favorite coaches, and two great Hall of Famers: Darrell Royal and Eddie Robinson. From the first Master Coach session in 1995, we have had the Who's Who of former coaches, most of them Hall of Famers, and all who love our game and coaching. So the plan was to bring them back, two at a time, at each AFCA Convention and ask everyone the same questions every year. The rationale for this was that whenever the Master Coach Series stopped there would be a treasure trove of knowledge from these Master Coaches. The first *Master Coach* book had 22 amazing coaches who shared their wisdom. This book has 21. There is a special reason for having 21 in *Volume II*. One of the best coaches in the history of our game, Coach Ken Sparks, has been in a battle with cancer. He has courageously continued to coach, inspiring his team and his peers. Ken's guarantee for successfully overcoming cancer is not assured, but he fights on. I wanted Ken and his amazing testimony, as well as his inspiration, to be available to coaches now and in the future. I felt the opportunity to share his wisdom and his faith would be a blessing to Ken, however, the blessing was for the one who asked the questions that day and for the thousands who heard, and will now read, the answers.

My plan and my goal is to present *Volume II* to all the coaches in attendance at the 2016 AFCA Convention in San Antonio, Texas. There was talk about our Association creating a nice medallion commemorating my years as a coach and as executive director. I felt most coaches had a drawer full of medallions and medals, but I wanted to give something to our coaches that could be meaningful and motivational. Instead of giving our coaches a medallion, Donell and I, along with the American Football Coaches Foundation, wish to give another book to those in attendance. For the coaches who were unable to attend the AFCA Convention, like we did with *A Coaches Influence: Beyond the Game*, we will allow any active member to receive a book by only paying the small shipping fee.

Over the last 22 years, I have asked some of the greatest coaches in the history of our game to answer prompts that are pertinent to successfully coaching football. Somewhere around 40,000 coaches have listened and learned from these Master Coaches. I have had coaches repeatedly ask, "When are you going to answer the questions you ask the Master Coaches?" Well, the time is here and now.

First of all, I am honored that coaches would consider my answers worthwhile, as it has been 22 years since I coached a game. However, the whole idea of this book is to get an array of opinions from different successful coaches as to how they deal with each of the key issues that are pertinent to a successful head coaching career. So for those who asked my opinion, and for those who may find my answers useful, I have added my answers to the end of each chapter as a bonus to you.

On page 251, there is an official biography of each of the Master Coaches in *Volume II*, however, like in *Volume I*, I have personal things to say about each one of the Maser Coaches.

Don Nehlen

Don Nehlen was an extremely successful football coach at the University of West Virginia, and he is absolutely one of the finest men I have ever known. Don was the epitome of integrity while becoming one of the great coaches in the history of West Virginia.

The Nehlens and the Teaffs experienced something that none of us had experienced before or after. Don invited Donell and me to spend a long weekend with him and his wife, Merry Ann, and speak on campus. Then, we drove to the FBI headquarters, which were not far from Morgantown, as Don had set up a meeting with the FBI to promote the AFCA's Child Identification Program.

After I spoke to a large gathering, the Nehlens and the Teaffs were on our way out to dinner. Don and I were in the front seat, with Merry Ann and Donell sitting in the back. As we pulled up to an intersection, we were broadsided by another vehicle. Fortunately, no one was hurt, but, interestingly enough, the individual who ran into us sued Don because he was a noticeable figure in Morgantown. I remember doing depositions from my office in Waco. Don was terribly embarrassed I had to go through that, but the good news was the lawsuit was dropped after the deposition.

R.C. Slocum

I consider R.C. Slocum a very close friend of whom I am indebted. When we instituted the American Football Coaches Foundation, I needed someone who cared about the game and was willing to serve our coaches by assuming a leadership role in The Foundation. I asked R.C. to serve as president of The Foundation and he has done so since its founding. He has also served as the Master of Ceremonies at The Foundation's CEO Coach of the Year award dinner.

R.C., at heart, is a defensive coach. He gained success as a defensive coordinator at Texas A&M University before taking over as the head coach. His success as the head coach of the Aggies made him an icon for all time at that great university. His leadership and his character brought great respect to Texas A&M's football program and he was inducted into the College Football Hall of Fame in 2012.

Bobby Bowden

Bobby Bowden and I have been long-time friends. Early on, we established a close relationship because of our Christian faith and our love of the game of football. For years, we both have helped raise funds for the Fellowship of Christian Athletes.

Several years ago, Bobby asked me to come to Tallahassee to speak to his coaches and his team. I was happy to do so, because not only did I admire Bobby as one of America's great coaches, but also because I liked him as a man.

The Bowdens and the Teaffs have traveled thousands of miles together on Nike Coaches' outings, which we were privileged to be a part of. In those relaxed times, we had many discussions about our philosophy. In 2013, I asked Bobby to do the foreword for my book, *A Coach's Influence: Beyond the Game*. His first sentence in the foreword was, "I believe Grant Teaff and I have as much in common as any two coaches in America."

Bobby's coaching record is one of the best in college football. He has received just about every award related to our great game. Yet to me, the kind of father, husband, and caring man that Bobby is, is his most important achievement.

John Gagliardi

In 2006, John was inducted into the College Football Hall of Fame and then in 2009, received the American Football Coaches Association's Amos Alonzo Stagg Award. In 2012, John Gagliardi announced his retirement from St. John's University.

John was a head football coach for 60 years. At his retirement, he was the winningest football coach in the history of college football. He coached longer than any other coach in history, including Stagg.

While John was still coaching, and well after he had received the AFCA's Stagg award, I had the opportunity to do something special for him. At the time, the AFCA was sponsoring the Hula Bowl and, of course, we were providing the coaches for the All-Star game. When I called John, he was taken aback when I told him I wanted him to serve as one of the coaches for the Hula Bowl. He readily accepted and told me it was one of the best weeks of his life. He got to coach with some outstanding coaches, and I can tell you the All-Stars on both teams fell in love with John. He was a strong influence, even though he was with them for only a week.

Terry Donahue

Coach Donahue's tenure as head coach at UCLA netted him the most conference wins of any coach in the Pac-12 Conference. He won 98 conference games and compiled a record of 8-4-1 in bowl games. Terry became the first coach to win a bowl game in seven consecutive seasons. He won three Rose Bowls, won or shared five Pac-10 conference championships, and his record was 10-9-1 against USC.

Many coaches have gone into broadcasting after their coaching careers. Terry did so, as well, and he became the lead college football analyst for CBS Sports from 1996-1998. In the early 2000s, Terry spent four seasons as the general manager for the San Francisco 49ers.

One of my fondest memories of Terry is when I asked him to serve on the AFCA Ethics Committee. He apologetically turned me down. For years, I would jokingly harass him about joining the Ethics Committee the very next year. Like most of us, Terry didn't feel worthy of judging his fellow coaches, but there is no doubt in my mind that he was thoroughly qualified and would have been a great member of that committee.

John Robinson

John holds a unique position among football coaches in America. He is one of the very few who have coached at one institution during two different tenures. John was the head football coach at the University of Southern California from 1976-1982. In 1983, he became the head coach of the Los Angeles Rams. Then in 1993, John returned to USC through 1997.

While at USC during those two tenures, John was a four-time Rose Bowl champion and captured a share of the 1978 national championship. When I called John to ask him to serve as a Master Coach, he was extremely gracious and excited about the opportunity.

John's appearance as a Master Coach was so well-received by members of our Association that I had many ask if I could have him back for a second interview.

Tom Osborne

Can you imagine coaching at a major college from 1973-1997 and never have a season with fewer than nine wins or without going to a bowl? Tom Osborne did just that at the University of Nebraska.

When I first arrived at Baylor in 1972, there was no weight room, thus no weights, and even worse, no way to get bigger and better. I finally raised enough money to build a concrete block weight room under our stadium with enough money left over to get some fire-sale weights and equipment. However, there was no money for a strength coach. I had spoken at a coaching clinic in Michigan and, unbeknownst to me, a young high school coach was in attendance. At that clinic, he decided he wanted to work for me at Baylor.

In early summer 1972, that same young man drove up in front of my office with all of his possessions and his family in tow. When Bob

Fix walked into my office to tell me he had come from Michigan to work for me, I was stunned and said, "I don't have any openings." He said his wife would get a job, he just wanted something to do and would work for free. I told him that the best I could do would be a volunteer position working with our strength program. I saw Bob's willingness to learn and his intention to serve me and our program successfully. I named him our strength coach and sent him to Nebraska, who I thought had the best strength program in America at that time. Tom Osborne and his staff welcomed Bob with open arms. He came back to Texas loaded with information. In two short years, Baylor, with Bob Fix, developed one of the top strength programs in America.

Thanks, Coach Osborne, for helping a struggling program develop a meaningful weight program. Your kindness and generosity should not surprise anyone. Certainly, the caliber of your leadership as a football coach, a Congressman, and an athletic director for Nebraska is a standard for all aspiring leaders in those categories.

Joe Paterno

I first met Joe in person when we both carried teams to the Cotton Bowl in 1975. His reputation, of course, had preceded him and I found him to be very warm and open to a young up-start coach whose team was attending its first bowl game in 11 years. Later, through Nike, Donell and I got to know Coach Paterno and his wife Sue extremely well.

Here's a little insight into Joe based on what happened at the Cotton Bowl. Baylor took the lead at halftime and in the third quarter Penn State had caught up. Midway through the fourth quarter, they went ahead. Two scores could win for Baylor, so we drove the length of the field to score a touchdown. With minutes remaining, we lined up for an onside kick which, if successful, could have put us in a position to win the game. However, it was not only not successful, it proved to be quite unsuccessful. The onside kick sailed high, caught in the wind, and fell short behind our coverage team. A Penn State player ran through our coverage team, picked up the ball, and ran it back for the touchdown that sealed the victory for Penn State.

My wife and daughters were my and Baylor's four biggest fans. Layne, our youngest daughter, who was nine at the time, was furious with Penn State that they scored on our kick. She proclaimed to her mother and anyone else who was listening, "Joe Paterno ran the score up on my daddy!" Pausing she looked directly into Donell's eyes and said, "I am going to find a rock and hit him with it." She immediately took off out of the stands heading for the field just as the game was finished. Donell looked high and low for Layne and finally found her close to the Penn State dressing room. She had somehow found a rock and was poised to chuck it at Joe when he emerged. Fortunately, Donell found her before Joe came out, so a possible disaster was averted.

Fast forward to early spring, Baylor had a dinner honoring our 1974 conference champions and Baylor's first football conference championship in 50 years. Joe Paterno was invited to speak and he graciously accepted. The day before he was to fly down for the dinner, I called him and explained Layne's anger at the game earlier that year. Although we had made it clear to Layne that he had not run up the score on Baylor, I wanted him to be forewarned about the situation.

The night of the dinner, Joe was picked up at the airport and delivered to our house along with his son, Jay, who was fairly close to Layne's age. (Jay later became a college football coach, as well.) When they arrived at the house, I opened the door and as Joe came in, he said, "Where is Layne?" I pointed to her sitting in the den. Joe went straight to Layne with a huge Nittany Lion under his right arm and several Hershey chocolate bars in his left hand. Joe said, "I want to apologize for that score. We were very lucky to win the game, but I was not trying to run up the score. Can you forgive me?" Then he handed her the gifts he brought. After the dinner, we took the Paternos to the airport, and I asked Layne if she was okay with Coach Paterno. She said, "He's a very nice man, and I appreciate the gifts, but I still think he ran up the score."

Years later, when Layne took over the production of the AFCA Convention, she and Joe would have many laughs about that game and his night in Waco, Texas.

Lou Holtz

Coach Lou Holtz and I have competed against each other as coaches, but we have been friends since the first day we met. My feeling of friendship for Lou is probably not exclusive to me, as Lou has the capacity to make everyone he meets feel like a friend. I have admired him as a man, as well as a football coach.

Lou was elected into the College Football Hall of Fame in 2008. Everyone is aware of his distinguished career as an analyst and his unique ability to brighten his colleagues' and his viewers' day. My fond memories of Lou are the times we competed as opposing coaches on the football field – he at Arkansas and me at Baylor. We had some head-knocking football games, and each won our share, but Lou would surprise me every now and then.

In 1978, we played Lou on the road and our defense evidently impressed him. The day after we played, he called to ask for permission to speak to my defensive coordinator; he said he wanted to hire him to work at Arkansas. I laughed, assuming he was passing a compliment to my staff. I thanked him and said, "No, you cannot speak to him."

Another strong memory I have of Lou was during a game in Waco in 1980. The winner would take the lead in the Southwest Conference. Prior to that season, I had a redshirt freshman who broke his neck in a scrimmage game and instantly became a quadriplegic. The story of Kyle Woods is well known, but what many people may not know is how opposing coaches care about all players, not just their own.

Kyle was back at Baylor to see his first game since his injury. When Lou saw Kyle on the sidelines prior to the game, he came over to spend a few minutes visiting with Kyle and encouraging him.

I asked Lou to do the foreword for this book. Obviously, he said yes, and I am most grateful for that.

Dick MacPherson

Dick MacPherson had a distinguished coaching career. He has coached on both the collegiate and the professional levels, as an assistant and as a head coach. Dick's overall record in his collegiate accomplishments placed him in the College Football Hall of Fame in 2009. I have had many conversations with Coach MacPherson and always held him in high esteem. He is clearly a man of integrity, and had a very positive relationship with all of his players.

I remember when Dick received the American Football Coaches Association's Coach of the Year honor in 1987. Although he had had an outstanding year, I remember clearly that he gave credit to his staff and his players.

Barry Alvarez

Similar to many Hall of Fame coaches, Barry Alvarez started coaching at the high school level in Mason City, Iowa. His team won the 1978 class 4A state title. My longtime friend, Hayden Fry, hired

Barry as an assistant at the University of Iowa. From there, Barry would work with Lou Holtz at Notre Dame. In 1990, he became the head coach at the University of Wisconsin. His legendary record includes being the winningest coach in Wisconsin history and will stand for years to come.

I always appreciated the fact that Barry was a very natty dresser. Being from West Texas, I had never seen anyone who wore shoes without socks. I certainly never expected to see a prominent coach who did not wear socks with his loafers. Barry didn't, but he made it seem okay to my very conservative eyes. I think in the long run that has been one of the very appealing traits of Barry Alvarez – he has always been his own man.

Fisher DeBerry

Like many successful college head coaches, Fisher started his career coaching in high school, then stepped onto the collegiate scene as an assistant coach. He was hired by Ken Hatfield at the United States Air Force Academy. When Ken left for Arkansas, the obvious choice to succeed him was Fisher DeBerry.

Fisher and his wife, LuAnn, have also been longtime friends with the Teaffs. When I stepped away from coaching, but remained as the athletic director at Baylor, Fisher invited me to the Air Force Academy to speak. He knew the Board of the American Football Coaches Association was trying to convince me to assume the leadership role of the organization. Fisher took time during my visit to present a clear and persuasive argument. I knew then why he was so successful at recruiting. His main point was, "Coach, you always said you wanted to make a difference – and you have as a coach – but I believe you are the individual who can make a difference in our Association, thus making the difference in the lives of thousands of coaches who will make a difference in the lives of hundreds of thousands of young people across America."

That trip, and Fisher's words, were the defining moment in my decision-making process. Thank you, Fisher. You made a difference in my life.

Lloyd Carr

Lloyd Carr became the head football coach at the University of Michigan in 1995 and served as the leader of the Wolverines for 13 years. Coach Carr had a great record of 122-40. He won or shared five conference titles, and his 1997 team was declared a national champion by the Associated Press. His record against Top 10 teams, 19-8, is outstanding.

I very much like Coach Carr's infamous quote "If you are a leader, you're going to be criticized, you're going to be second-guessed, betrayed, ridiculed, castigated, and those are the good things. You have to make up your mind that you're not going to be distracted from what you came to do."

The very first game Coach Carr served as the interim head coach, the University of Michigan played the University of Virginia. Michigan was down 17-0 with less than 12 minutes left in the fourth quarter. Lloyd's quarterback, a redshirt freshman named Scott Dreisbach, had not been successful in the game. When Coach Carr put him back in the game, both he and Dreisbach were booed. Dreisbach proved the booers wrong and his coach correct. He brought the team from behind, sealing the deal with a 15-yard pass to the end zone with four seconds left on the clock. Michigan won the game.

Tubby Raymond

Coach Raymond is among the Master Coaches for good reason – he is considered the father of the Blue Hens, the University of Delaware's football team. For 36 years he roamed the sidelines, earning 300 wins and three national titles.

Few coaches in American football history have a stadium or a field named after them. Coach Raymond, like many coaches who are very successful for a long time at any specific university, is loved and admired by his former players, coaches, student body, faculty, and fans.

Coach Raymond is also an outstanding artist. He is a true portrait painter. I love the headline that described Raymond's other talent, "A Coach's Brush with Fame: Tubby Raymond is the University of Delaware's Longtime Football Coach – and Resident Artist." Since the mid-1960s, during the football season Coach Raymond would paint a portrait of at least one senior every week, and then he hung the portrait in the team's locker room on Thursday.

When the national headquarters of the American Football Coaches Association was completed in 2001, Coach Raymond called me and volunteered to do portraits of all of the AFCA executive directors. Since 1922, there have been four of us, and I have held the position longer than any other. I was overwhelmed by Coach Raymond's generous offer and I readily accepted. The four portraits have hung in our boardroom since their completion. I consider it very special to the history and tradition of our great Association. (See the portraits in the photo section located in the center of this book.)

Phil Fulmer

Phil Fulmer coached the University of Tennessee Volunteers from 1992-2008, compiling a record of 152-52, and he was inducted into the

College Football Hall of Fame in 2012. Phil Fulmer was a great football player at the University of Tennessee and was an All-Southeastern Conference offensive guard. Fulmer helped Tennessee to a record of 30-5 from 1969-1971. After a long stint as an assistant coach at Wichita State University and one year at Vanderbilt University, he returned to Tennessee as the offensive line coach, then assumed the role of the head football coach. His accomplishments in that capacity led him to the 1998 National Championship Game. The winner of the National Championship Game receives the No. 1 spot in the Coaches Poll, thus receiving the Coaches' Trophy (aka the Crystal Ball). The Bowl Championship Series commissioners were gracious and allowed the Crystal Ball to be presented along with the BCS National Championship Trophy.

Phil has the credit of setting the pattern for all coaches who received the Crystal Ball after him. Phil, with his team up on platform out in the middle of the stadium, walked over to receive the two trophies. He reached down and took the Crystal Ball off its base, raised it above his head, lowered it, kissed it, and then passed it around to his coaches and teammates. His actions set a tradition that is now a part of any team receiving the Coaches' Trophy.

Phil served on the AFCA Board and introduced the American Football Coaches Association to the Jason Foundation, an organization that works with coaches to help prevent teen suicide. Phil's support of the Jason Foundation created a partnership with the AFCA that our Association, our Board of Directors, and our membership are very proud to be a part of.

Dick Vermeil

Coach Dick Vermeil is known by most as the head coach of three NFL franchises: the Philadelphia Eagles, the St. Louis Rams, and the

Kansas City Chiefs. However, Dick was named Coach of the Year on four different levels – high school, junior college, NCAA Division I, and professional football. I daresay that record stands alone.

Coach Vermeil was a great football coach, and he is very interested in life. A very popular movie was made about Dick and his idea of having an open tryout to add someone to the roster of the Philadelphia Eagles. He discovered and signed Vince Papale, the inspiration of the blockbuster movie *Invincible*.

Dick also owns Vermeil Wines, a small family vineyard in Napa Valley. To me, Dick Vermeil is a Renaissance man.

Marino Casem

In 2003, Coach Casem was inducted into the College Football Hall of Fame. He earned that great honor by being an outstanding football coach at Alabama State University, Alcorn State University, and Southern University. Coach Casem compiled a career record 159-93-8. His Alcorn State Braves won four black college national championships and seven Southwestern Athletic Conference titles. He was known as "The Godfather," because of the great respect he had from both former players and coaches alike.

Bill McCartney

Coach Bill McCartney is one of the most unique coaches and men it has been my pleasure to know. First of all, he was a terrific football coach at the University of Colorado from 1982-1994. He compiled a record of 93-55-5 and won three consecutive Big Eight championship titles. His 1990 team was crowned national champions by the Associated Press, sharing the title with Georgia Tech. He was inducted in the College Football Hall of Fame in 2013.

Of all of Bill's accomplishments as a football coach, his legacy was the creation of Promise Keepers, a ministry for men. The ministry had a huge impact across America for several years.

The Baylor Bears played Bill's teams three different times, once in Colorado, once in Waco, and once in the Bluebonnet Bowl in Houston, Texas.

Coach McCartney won five Coach of the Year awards in 1989 – the American Football Coaches Association's Coach of the Year award, the Eddie Robinson Coach of the Year award, the Walter Camp Coach of the Year award, th Big Eight Coach of the Year award, and the Paul "Bear" Bryant award. Through coaching and Promise Keepers, Bill and I became solid friends, and I, for one, stand amazed at all the good he has accomplished in his life.

Bill Curry

Bill Curry is a two-time Super Bowl champion and played in two Pro Bowls for the amazing Vincent Lombardi. Bill also played for other great coaches, such as Don Shula and Bobby Dodd. His teammates included Willie Davis, Art Star, and Johnny Unitas. Coach Curry was an outstanding broadcaster for ESPN, is one of the finest speakers of any profession, and is highly thought of by his coaches everywhere.

Bill was a member of the AFCA Ethics Committee when I was chairman. Before each meeting, I would give a little encouraging talk to all the committee members stating that if they were going to serve on the committee they had to adhere to all rules of the NCAA and the American Football Coaches Association's Code of Ethics. At a break, Bill walked up to me and said, "Coach, you don't mean *all* the rules?" I looked at him and answered, "Yes, Bill, all the rules." Bill has told that story many times, and it is true, not only for members of the Ethics

Committee, but for all coaches. We must be an example to our players and to other coaches.

Jerry Moore

Jerry Moore was inducted into the College Football Hall of Fame in 2014, and is nationally recognized as one of the great coaches in the history of our game. Everybody in the nation saw Appalachian State University's spectacular win over Michigan in 2007. However, many have forgotten that he was also the head football coach of North Texas and Texas Tech with a career record of 242-135-2.

From a personal standpoint, it is obvious he was a great football coach, but his Christian faith and stand for Christ wherever he coached was a shining example for all Christian coaches. Those who Jerry coached got a lot more than just instruction on how to play the game and win. They saw in Coach Moore, and in his staff, how to be real men, as well as real football players. It is very interesting how all of the great Master Coaches I interviewed over the past 22 years have many of the most important characteristics: integrity, drive, leadership, and the capacity to really care.

Ken Sparks

This year, Ken Sparks embarked on his thirty-sixth season of coaching at Carson-Newman University. As of the writing of this book, he is the sixth winningest coach of all time, behind Glenn "Pop" Warner and fellow Master Coaches John Gagliardi, Joe Paterno, Eddie Robinson, and Bobby Bowden, with a record of 334-92-2. Ken Sparks is a proven winner on the football field, but he is much more than that. He is a consummate leader who teaches young people how to live life abundantly. His own courage and his example of living life bravely and successfully inspires his team, as well as thousands who have followed his career.

In all my years of doing the Master Coach series, I have never invited three coaches in one year. The last Master Coach series was held at the 2015 AFCA Convention in Louisville, Kentucky. The Master Coaches that year were Ken Sparks, Jerry Moore, and Bill Curry.

Ken is one of the most courageous men I know. He carries on his coaching responsibilities while fighting cancer. The prognosis has not been good, but Ken carries on. I wanted very much to have Ken as a Master Coach, not only for his accomplishments on the football field, but also because of his faith and his inspiration to all of us.

Chapter 2

Describe your philosophy in relation to your players.

Don Nehlen

The number one thing I wanted to make sure my players understood was the fact that we had an open-door policy. They knew they could come and see me, or any of my coaches, at any time. They could call our secretary and have access to our coaches at any time. If players are going to come out to the football building to see one of the coaches, then they have a problem. If that coach is not available, that problem can fester and it can hurt your football team. I told our players, "Hey, if the president calls or the athletic director calls, I will tell them to take a message. I'll call them back after the meeting. You can see us at any time." All of our players had access to our home phone numbers, and we felt very strongly about that. I think the most important aspect a head coach can have, or any coach, is honesty. I don't think you can have a great program if the head guy is not completely honest. Your players may not always want to hear what you're going to tell them, but as long as you're honest, they're going to respect you. If you're honest, fair, and consistent, you're not going to have many problems with your players with an open-door policy.

R.C. Slocum

Well, I agree with what Don [Nehlen] said. It's important for the players to be able to come anytime and have access to the coaches, to feel like they can come and talk to you. I never thought my role was to be their buddy. I always thought that I should be a father figure, someone they could come and sit down with. Like Don said, you don't always tell them what they want to hear. The player has to think you have his best interests at heart. We get guys, unfortunately, who have not had the benefit of having a strong father figure. They never had anyone who said, "You can't act like that, son. That's bad for you. You're disgracing your family, this program, and yourself." Part of being a man is growing up. Your reputation is something you make. A lot of guys we'd get would have NFL aspirations and I would tell them, "When they come calling in four years, all I'm going to do is relate what you've done and what I've seen, as honest as I can. If you've been dependable, honest, and a hard worker, I'm going to tell those guys." I believe, as football coaches, we will be held accountable. I go into homes and take parents' most prized possessions – their sons – and they entrust them to my leadership. That's a huge responsibility. I think someday, the good Lord is not going to ask me about how many games I won or lost, but He will hold me accountable and say, "I gave you a bunch of kids over the years that I put under your leadership. I was counting on you to teach them the right things and lead them in the right direction. Let's talk about how you did." I always try to keep that at the forefront of my relationship and, as a head coach, pass it down to my assistants. We bring a player into our program, not just to teach him how to play cover-two or how to backpedal, but also how to become a man. We give them lessons that will help them be better people, better citizens, better husbands, and better fathers.

Bobby Bowden

I can say it in one word, availability. To make myself available for my players is probably the greatest thing I can do.

John Gagliardi

You know, I don't know about philosophy. I like being around these college guys. Ever since I left college I've been with 18- to 22-year-old guys. The nice part about it is that until I look in the mirror, I think I'm still 18 or 22. As a matter of fact, when we won our last national championship a couple of years ago, one of the reporters said, "Wouldn't this be a good year to retire? You just broke the all-time collegiate wins record and won another national championship." I was up at the dais with a couple of my ball players and I said, "What? Do you want me to leave these 18- to 22-year-old guys and go find a park bench and play checkers with some old guys? They can't hear what I've got to say and aren't a bit interested." I said, "I'm going to stay with these guys here." We do have an open-door policy, that's for sure. We're always available. It's no chore for me.

Terry Donahue

First, everybody who coaches wants to be respected by their players. Being a head coach or an assistant coach means players have a certain level of respect for you. I think it's important that coaches earn the respect of their players. Coaches need to understand that players are going to respect you first because of who you are, the rest of it you have to earn.

You earn it by your knowledge base, by the way you conduct yourself in crises, by the way you handle yourself outside of football, and by the way you're perceived by your players as to what kind of a person you are. I'd much rather be respected by my players than liked by my players. I'd like to have both, but if I had to select, then I'd certainly select their respect before I would their affection.

Secondly, it's important to be honest and forthright with players and yet, at the same time, be somewhat diplomatic. You can be brutally honest, but that doesn't accomplish what you want to get accomplished. At the same time, I think it's very important that you're honest. Players deserve to know [the truth]. They deserve to have their questions answered properly. It would always strike me when a player would come in and say, "I was with Coach So-and-So, and Coach So-and-So said this..." It would dawn on me that Coach So-and-So and I weren't on the same page. When that happened, I visited with the assistant coach and tried to figure out why we weren't on the same page. In the end, I always wanted to get back to the player so that he could have an honest appraisal and an honest answer from me.

The third thing I would say about relationships with players is, when you're coaching, you're trying to stay employed. Winning is one of the most important things. It's your lifeblood. It's how you support your family. It's how you build your career. It's the things you do. When you get away from coaching, as you get older and move farther away from it, you come to understand that what is important are the relationships you've built with players. You hope that in some small way, you have imparted some education and experience on players as they go forward and become successful.

At one time, I was more concerned about how many games I won. At this point in my life, I'm more concerned and much more proud of the guys who played for me, guys like: Ron Caragher, who [was] the head coach at the University of San Diego; Rick Neuheisel, the [former] head coach at UCLA; Karl Dorrell, the former head coach at UCLA;

or Cormac Carney, who is a federal judge. Those things are much more meaningful to me. Those are the relationships with players that mean a whole lot more to me today than the games we won or lost.

John Robinson

The initial part of your relationship with your players is football. That's what brings you together. You're not there as a head coach or an assistant coach for any reason other than football. So when you create a relationship with them, you have to be willing to talk football with them. You have to get them to the point where they are comfortable talking to you about their position, the team, and your ideas. If you are the type who is always riding them about their performance rather than discussing things with them, then I don't think you ever get past the first phase of the relationship.

Since I've retired, I've been stunned by the number of players who have approached me to talk about the role that I had in their lives. I'm sure that the same is true with Terry [Donahue] and everybody else. It's a bit stunning. I think to myself, "Was that really that important?" It must have been. We impact these people dramatically. Your relationship has to grow from football, in the beginning, to something more meaningful. It's important you find time to be around a player other than on the football field. As your relationship grows, you need to find some way you can see him in a different environment.

When you bring a player into your program; you bring him in because he can play football. You also bring in his baggage. If he's been a poor student in high school or he is rowdy, then you inherit those traits in that kid and you should be willing to work over time to get that out of him. You can't bring him in and say, "Okay, you're here. Now you have to be this perfect student." He's not going to be. If he cuts class in high school, he's going to cut class in college. It will take time for you to begin to change him, so it is important that you know as much about him as you can. Be sure to recognize where the problems are and have your assistants focus on those problems. Over time, you can change the 17- or 18-year-old who comes into your program. Before he leaves as a 22-year-old, he's a different person and you've affected that change to a large degree. The times that we fail are when we don't get to know or understand the player, or we are just too busy to pay attention to him.

Tom Osborne

I like to treat the players pretty much like I'd want somebody in my family to be treated. Once you've had a son who has played – maybe high school or college football – and you go through that, you begin to realize there are some major differences in coaches and how kids are treated.

I remember one time Lou Holtz called me. It was during the season, and he was down at Arkansas at the time. He said, "I'd like to come up and visit you for a couple of days." I'd never had a coach do that during the season. I was kind of surprised. I said, "Well sure, Lou, I'd be glad to have you come." He was there for two days and he sat in the meetings and watched practice. Before he left he said, "You know, the one thing that really struck me, and the thing that jumped out at me, was how positive your coaches were." I'd been around it for a long time and hadn't thought about it much.

Sometimes we equate coaching with criticism, with catching somebody doing something wrong and criticizing or punishing them. Yet the best way to move the needle, to get somebody from here to here, is to catch them doing something right and reinforcing it. As much as you can, I think it's important to be positive.

Some of you may not understand this, but I never really felt it was necessary to use profanity. Coaches have the ultimate authority, and if they don't do what you want them to do, they don't play. I think it's really important that you explain very clearly what you want, and that you have high but reasonable expectations. Then you don't have to rant and rave. So often coaches coach as they were coached. At one time, there was a pretty heavy dose of what you might call a boot-camp mentality where you humiliated people and you kind of ran them in the ground. I don't know that that's really necessary. I think you can get the most out of them if you treat them with respect, treat the fourth-team player with equal dignity as you would the first-team player. Even though they're not going to play on Saturday, let them know that, as a person, they are as important to you as the guy who is starting.

Joe Paterno

Well, I think all of us have to understand that play doesn't include everybody. You have some kids who have certain problems and other kids who have certain problems. I think the hardest job is that you have to get to know the kids before you can really start to handle them.

I think the hard part is when you get a kid who's just not quite in it with you. How do you go about molding him? How do you give him a little more confidence? I'll go back to my coach, Rip Engle, who I think was one of the great coaches of all time. He coached at a high school in Waynesboro, Pennsylvania. In the 10 years he coached at that high school, he only lost 10 games. He left to become an assistant coach at a college, and they didn't win 10 games the next 12 years. I asked him what happened with the situation. He said, "Well, the head coach never gave himself or the kids a chance to get to know each other." He said,

"I never cut a kid. If a kid wasn't doing well, or if I couldn't make contact with him, I'd try to get somebody, whether it was a teacher in the high school, or somebody else that might have had a little better feel for the kid, try to help me get to know him." I've tried to keep that in mind when I've been with kids who just don't respond right away. In our situation where we recruit kids, a lot of them will come in and they have the world by the tail, nothing-I-need-to-know type of attitude. The first time you kick them in the rear end and tell them, "Hey, you have a long way to go," then somebody's got to build them up a little bit.

I think every kid's a little different, and for me to get up here and say, "This is the way we deal with every kid," that misleads you. Sometimes you get a kid from a one-parent home, no father in the home, with no discipline. He doesn't quite understand the role that a coach is going to play in his life. You have to work your way into that.

I think the big thing is to get to know the kid, and don't give up on him. Give him a chance to have success. If he has a little bit of success, I might make a big fuss in a squad meeting. He may have made a good catch. He may have dropped 10 in a week. He makes one good catch and I might say, "Hey baby, you're as good as your clipping said you were." You have to be a little bit of an actor with kids, I think.

Lou Holtz

Well, first of all, I explained to them the first day they arrived on campus, "You come here to become us. We're not going to become you. I don't care how you wore your socks in high school. I don't care how you practiced. You will become us. I'm going to make certain assumptions. I'm going to assume you want to win. I'm going to assume you want to graduate. I'm going to assume you want to be successful. I'm going to assume you want to make a contribution to our football team."

The very, very minimum every player should expect when he comes to your school is the very best coaching in the country. That's your obligation. I also feel that the players are going to have obligations. They're going to have responsibilities.

The difference between athletes today and 30 years ago? Today everybody wants to talk about their rights and privileges. Thirty years ago people talked about their obligations and responsibilities. If you want to feel you have the right to failure, you do not have the right to cause other people to fail. It's important as a leader to make sure they understand the obligations and responsibilities they have. They will have a role on this football team, and they'll determine it by the role they earn in spring practice and the winter program. Maybe their role is to cover kickoff. They may say, "I don't want to cover kickoff. I want to run the ball. I want to throw the ball." So you tell them, "I understand that, but that's not your role. You must do your role to the very best of your ability so you don't jeopardize our goal of winning."

I think players have to know what you expect from them and exactly what they can expect from you. I always felt they don't need a friend. They need a leader. They can name you the head coach. They can name you the assistant coach. Those titles come from above. What they cannot do, they cannot name you leader. Leaders will come from below. You can only be a leader if you have a vision where you want to take the program. You have a plan of how you're going to get there, and you hold people accountable. I think it's especially important for players to understand what we expect from them and what they can expect from us.

Our priorities will always be our faith, number one. I have a strong faith in God, and I'm proud to say it. Too many are embarrassed by it in this politically correct society, and that's the nice thing about being my age. I personally don't give a darn. I'm so old I don't even buy green bananas anymore.

It's going to be our faith, one. It's going to be our family, two. It's going to be education, number three. It's going to be football, number four. I want them to understand that the last thing is going to be their social life. Wherever you are today – good, bad, or indifferent – is because of the decisions you make. Life's a matter of choices. You choose to drop out of school, you choose to do drugs, you choose to run with the wrong people, you're choosing to fail. You choose to goof off in school, you're choosing to flunk out. Understand that whatever decisions you make, you're going to be held accountable for them. That's the main thing I try to do in a relationship with a player – [help them] understand what I expect from them, and what their obligations and responsibilities are.

Dick MacPherson

The players are going to make us or they're going to break us. I would tell my players, "The most important thing that I want you to know is that you are the most important thing on this football team. On the way, I promised your parents that you're going to get a degree from this fine institution. So if you work your butts off on the football field and in the classroom, everything you believe is going to happen is going to happen. You have to make sure that you understand that where you play is the greatest institution in the world, and we're going to find a way to win. We have some coaches who are going to help with this outfit here. We're going to have a heck of a team, I promise you."

Barry Alvarez

Well, the one thing I always tried to do was make sure my players understood I was approachable. I wanted them to know they were always welcome, I always had an open door, and we could have a conversation. I wanted them to feel comfortable. When I hired assistant coaches, I always wanted to listen to their feedback during the interview process, about how they get close to their players. I wanted to hire assistant coaches who got close to players and built a relationship with those players.

I also made it a point with the leaders of the team. I went specifically and spent time with them and got to know them. It got to the point where they felt comfortable with me, because I relied on them. I always wanted to know what the voice in the locker room was. I wanted to know, and get a feel of what they needed from us. It's not written in any book whether a team needs to be pushed, whether you need to back off, whether you have to get after someone or pat someone on the back. It's not written anywhere. That is what a coach has to do. They have to have that feel, so I've relied on the relationship and the feedback I had from the leaders on the football team.

Fisher DeBerry

Since I've retired, I've had a little bit of time to sit around and think a little bit about the game, and there's no question in my mind that it's not about the wins and losses. It's not about the awards you've acquired. It's about the relationships you make with your players. There's no question about it. Our program at the Air Force Academy was built on one thing, and that was family.

It's amazing what you can accomplish if you can develop a situation where the players love the players, the coaches love the coaches, the players love the coaches, the coaches love the players, and where the wives love the wives. That was something we worked really, really hard at. I wanted my players to know I trust them.

I grew up in a little old country town in South Carolina called Cheraw. I know many of you have been there in your worldly travels. We had a couple brother combinations in that community. If you ever got in a fight with one of those brothers, you knew you'd have to deal with the other.

I have always adopted that. Brothers are hard to beat. Our whole thing was, we didn't want to let our brother down. We tried to build that accountability among our players.

I'd ask them all the time in meetings and out on the field, "You are your brother's keeper. Are you taking care of your brother?" So, we had a little ritual after the game every Saturday. As soon as we got our pads off, we'd go around the room before we did anything else and we'd hug each other's neck. We would look each other in the eye and say, "I appreciate what you did today for me and for this team," whether we won or lost. We tried to live the core values of the Academy, which are integrity, first, above all; certainly, service before self; and excellence in all that we do. That was really the foundation we tried to build. We didn't allow profanity in our program and we didn't allow fighting. I felt that if you allow fighting on the field amongst one another, it destroyed the family concepts you were trying to build.

We had one rule and one rule only. I think you can have too many rules, but we had only one rule, and that was to do what's right. If you do what's right, you're going to be all right.

I also wanted them to know I was totally committed to the total development of the complete person. I expected them to be outstanding students. We were going to do everything as coaches to help them be the very best football player their God-given talents would allow them to be. We wanted to create social opportunities for them. I felt a real responsibility for their spiritual growth, also. But bottom line,

I wanted them to understand fundamentals are the key to the game. Our ability to block and tackle is going to ultimately determine our success. I always wanted to have somebody come in to talk to them about alcohol and drugs, who it had a negative experience on. Having someone who has really had that experience can make an impression. Our philosophy was basically the three Fs: faith, family and football. I found out very, very often if you get those out of order, you can really screw things up.

Lloyd Carr

I spent every day I was in that office trying to develop a culture that was essential to being successful. The three cornerstones of that culture began with the word respect. We had a football team of players from all over the country: different races, different religions, different socio-economic backgrounds, and different views of life. Michigan is a great public university, 50,000 students, and every one of those people have a right to be there, a right to be respected in terms of the way they see the world.

The first thing that we talked about was being in a football team, that in our building, when we traveled, wherever we went, we were people who respected each other's differences. Secondly, we talked about trusting each other. I always told them as a football coach, they could trust me to tell them the truth, as I perceived it to be.

The last cornerstone we talked about was family. Essentially, in a football mode, that means that we care about each other. I always told them that I care about how they do academically. I want them to graduate. I care about them when they have personal issues at home. We care about each person in that building. Who is having a bad day? Who is having problems in life or problems in his career? We cheer for those guys who are having success, who are doing well, and have things that are going well for them. If we can have that kind of culture, we felt like that was what was conducive to being successful.

The last thing, as a football coach, I don't think you can do anything more than to be fair to your players. If they trust that you are fair, then you are going to have a good relationship with the guys on your football team.

Tubby Raymond

My relationship with the players begins with the recruiting. I always wanted them to know that I had great expectations for them and they in turn could have great expectations for their coaches, a mutual movement. It is one of great respect and to create a mutual respect. I'll believe in you, you believe in me, until you prove that you can't be in that situation. That is about it.

Phil Fulmer

I think all of us have a background that we come from of some sort that develops us early. I was so fortunate in Little League, middle school, high school, and even in college, as intensive as it was Tennessee, to have really positive influences and coaches who cared and didn't mind kicking my butt when I needed it. They also didn't mind hugging my neck. I've thought about that a lot as I was planning and hoping to one day be a head coach; never really imagining at the University of Tennessee or anything like that, but I knew I would have my opportunity somewhere.

I wanted to be a positive influence for the players. I've seen a lot of my former players last night and today. I've also seen a number of my coaches when we did get an opportunity. I saw a lot of good head coaches. You know, Doug Dickey and Bill Battle were both my coaches, and Coach [John] Majors was under [Dickey when he was AD at Tennessee]. There are a lot of ways to do things.

When I got my opportunity, we wanted to be a family in every way that it could be. Not all family members are going to be perfect all the time and you had to manage yourself within those, but we wanted it to be a place that parents felt good about their sons being there. We used the philosophy of "Every day go get better as a player, as a person, as a student, or spiritually." We were one of the first schools to have a team chaplain, James Mitchel, who I'm sure is probably sitting in here. You know those kinds of influences that were well beyond football. We went for the best players we could, particularly those big, ugly guys in the defensive front who you knew were going to be outstanding stoppers. To build an attitude and staff, and, fortunately, my staff – the core of us – stayed together for a long time, and those kids were able to experience that. It was about the players. It was about the attitude that we did it with, and also coaching them hard on a daily basis to be the best that they could be, whether in the off-season program or pushing them academically. All of us can count kids who would have never made it if it hadn't been for their position coach or head coach making the difference in their lives.

Dick Vermeil

First off, regardless of what level you're coaching, you're coaching people. You're coaching kids who are playing football, and I approached my whole career that way, regardless of whether it was high school or at the end with the Kansas City Chiefs. You coach people to play football, you don't coach football. I really never changed my approach to working with young kids in any way, all the way through. Now, I learned to coach better, smarter, for a lot more money, and have a lot better players, but the overall approach was always about making the individual player the best he could possibly be, regardless of whether he's a first-string player or third-string player. If you're the third-string right guard, I wanted you to be the best possible third-string right guard you could be. We approached everything that way. What I really enjoyed, probably most in all my coaching, are the relationships with my players. People say you can get too close to them in the NFL – and yes you can – and it can negatively influence decisions, but it never negatively interfered with the true feeling you had about some of the people you coach. It doesn't happen with an entire roster, but it does happen with a big percentage of the roster. Mike Jones, the guy who saved my rear in the Super Bowl, made the tackle on the last play of the game, is sitting right here in the stands. I enjoyed the personal side of the relationship with my players as much as I did the physical side.

I sometimes forced them to work harder than they wanted to work, because it was my responsibility to help them be the best they could be and provide them the time, the environment, and the coaches to help them be the best they could be; whether it be high school, junior college, college, or anyplace else, and for the most part it worked. You forget a lot about your X's and O's, but you don't forget those people.

Marino Casem

This is the greatest profession in the world. The first thing in how I relate to our ball players? There's a fine line between love and hate. That fine line is respect. I tell them, "You have to love somebody. It doesn't have to be me, but love somebody. Love your mama, your daddy, your brother, your sister, your position coach, or your assistant coach. Love somebody, because they're going to do what I want them to do – play for them. You don't have to play for me, play for them." First of all, I have to earn their respect. They have to trust me and I have to earn their trust. I have to be fair and friendly, but firm. I tell them the truth all the time, even though they might not want to hear it. If he is a poor ball player, I tell him he's poor, but tell him there's a way to improve himself. I tell him the truth and I'll tell him what nobody else will tell him. Nobody else will tell him what he is, but he [should] expect the truth from you. You have to earn their trust. You have to listen with care and really care. Don't just invite him to your office bring him in, and talk to him for 15 or 20 minutes, then say "I have an open door," then rush him out and bring the next one in. You have to listen and know and understand what his problem is, what his issues are, and really, really care. Because the one thing about it, if you don't deliver your best people to the field on Saturday, you can't win. You have to deliver the product. He has to care. He has to play for you, for the University or for somebody, but he has to believe that what he's doing is good for him, and you have to make him believe that. We have a saying, a local one, "We work so hard, we work harder than everybody else." Everybody would try to catch us working wrong and all that kind of stuff. We were working hard. We told our guys, "If you stay, you'll play and we'll win championships." You know it's all about recruiting, retention, and graduation. That's the name of the game.

Bill McCartney

It's been 20 years now since I coached, so coming here I had a measure of anxiety and anticipation, hoping I can relate to you guys who are currently coaching this great game. Everything rises and falls on leadership. Every family, every business, and every team is a direct reflection of the leadership. A quote that I like is from the famous Bill Parcells, who says, "Disunity will kill you quick in football. One maverick can capsize the whole team." In football, he goes on to say, teamwork is the key ingredient. Every player, from the quarterback to the special teams players, are interdependent. He had a sign in the locker room that said "Individuals play the game, but teams win championships."

In August, the team would report for the new season and we hadn't practiced yet, but there's energy, there's excitement in the room. They're bonded, but they've probably been apart over the summer. I would always start that first meeting and say, "Men, we need to answer three questions: Who are we? Where are we going and how are we going to get there? What's our identity, what are our goals, and what is our strategy?" In Colorado, we might answer those three questions this way: "We're the Colorado Buffaloes. We're in the top 20 all-time in victories in college football. We take great pride in our tradition here and those who came before you paid a great price. We take pride in playing the nation's toughest schedules." The year we won the national championship, our schedule was ranked as the most difficult. We look for the maximum challenge. Now where are we going? Bo Schembechler would have said something like this: Big dreams create the magic that stirs men's souls; the most competitive guys play the most competitive games. Here at Colorado, we subscribe to the psychology of high expectations. Think big and you will be big. Think small and you'll be small. I learned this from Coach Schembechler and, from that time on, it became a part of our coaching philosophy.

Here's how we would do it. We'd have the seniors in front, the juniors next, and the sophomores and the freshman would be in the back of the room. We would tell them, "Each one of you guys needs to look up here at this coaching staff and you need to genuinely say from your heart, 'Coach me. Please coach me and take me beyond myself. Take me where I can't take myself.' Now, if you're thinking like that, we can do this. T-E-A-M. Together Everyone Accomplishes More." So from the very first meeting we continued to emphasize that you have to submit to authority. A lot of these kids are from single parent homes. Maybe there's just mom there, and she loves him with all her heart, but she's not giving him the tough love. So for the first time, he's in an environment where he's going to be challenged to put the team first. It's a whole new way to live and die. When I was listening and watching Coach Saban [when he spoke at the AFCA Convention], it seems like they have mastered that at Alabama. They monopolize it at Alabama. It's about the team.

Bill Curry

I think football coaches, college and high school, are the most important people in our culture. I think we are the last line of defense in teaching discipline and ethics, and the right moral fabric in a way that's understandable to all young people. Whether they like football or not, it's hard to dodge the reality of the huddle because my philosophy is this: we can recruit a child from South Central Los Angeles and another one from the hills of East Tennessee, and we know full well that our culture has taught them to hate each other's guts; they come into training camp with that expectation, that they're going to fight, and they're going to be snarling and angry at each other, but put them in the same color shirt and make them run, make them sweat, make them bleed sometime – not intentionally – and they will build a relationship that lasts forever.

When you take a bunch of children and subject them to the kind of discipline that's required to do what we do in football, they learn a couple of things. The most important thing they learn is, sweat smells the same on everybody. Then they find out the person they thought they hated, they love. The next thing you know, you have guys inviting each other home for Thanksgiving, and the family is transitioned because it's hard to be a racist with a 17-year-old who loves your Thanksgiving cooking. When those guys learn to love each other, it lasts the rest of their lives. To me, that's why football really matters in our country.

When I was 15 years old, my high school coach asked me if I wanted to be a day camp counselor, and I did it for all the wrong reasons. It was big bucks. It was $15 a week, and that was a whole lot more than I could make sacking groceries at Harris Food Town. So, at College Park Recreation Center I became a day camp counselor. I had eight little snot noses I was responsible for, and I was not looking forward to having them with me all day, every day. But within two weeks, I knew what I was going to do with my life.

I was informed from within and from above, you're going to be a coach. You're going to love young people every day. I love all the players I ever coached, all the people I ever worked with, and I commit to them for life. One of my great joys, at age 72, is that I hear from some of them just about every day. Caroline, our children, and our grandchildren come first in my life, and they know that. But these folks are right after.

Jerry Moore

It all starts with recruiting, and I think you know what you want when you go out looking for a player. You don't want any surprises for them or yourself. You want them to know what to expect. They're going to get coached. Everybody in this building wants a guy who wants to get coached. They want you to make them better. That's been our approach. Ken [Sparks] and I have never really talked about this, but we do the same thing. We had a doctor in town who gets a Bible for those kids at Appalachian State University, and they have access to that for the rest of their lives. The most hard-nosed guy, I think, was Jesus Christ.

Ken Sparks

It's very important for you to present the truth to your players about what life is about. My number one emphasis: We can do it the world's way, or we can do it God's way. If we do it God's way, the last time I checked, He's undefeated. If you do it the world's way, there's a cliff out there that we fall off of. The main thing I have always concentrated on is to make sure that I tell them the truth, because truth is truth, it doesn't change.

That's the way we present it to them. I think the thing that gets tempting sometimes is to get in the world's system in order to get something. In other words, do God's thing my way. God's thing my way doesn't work. God's thing, God's way works. We don't apologize for it, and, hopefully, when we're recruiting them, they understand that.

We can't live your life for you. That's not our privilege. You have to live your life. You have to make the choices. We want to make sure that – based on God's word – we present the truth. We give them a Bible on their first day. We give them an FCA *Competitor's Bible*, and we give them an Eagle Way Notebook, which is something we wrote several years ago, and update every year, to try to make sure they understand where we're coming from.

Grant Teaff

Theodore Roosevelt said, "People don't care how much you know until they know how much you care." Based on my own personal feelings about how I wanted to be treated, I developed an approach to life that has served me well. Foundationally, I treat people the way I would like to be treated, and that included my players, staff, family, alumni, students, and eventually my AFCA staff. In short: positive, encouraging, honest, and caring. Those are four human characteristics you can't fake very long. The key for me was, as a young person, God evidently instilled in me the way I wanted to be treated, so then I correlated that into the way I treated others. Don't misinterpret treating others well for a lack of discipline, mental and physical toughness, or high expectations.

As I became a head coach very early in my career, I did the things that seemed natural, trying to adhere to the basic way I wanted to be treated and treat others.

One example was given in an article written for the *Livestock Weekly* under the heading "All About Ranching" by Dennis McBeth. Dennis was a student at Angelo State University while I was coaching there. Here are quotes from his column:

Having told this story hundreds of times, it is likely past time for it to be written and give credit to whom it is due. Dennis explained that in high school he made the decision not to play football because he was raising and showing livestock . The high school coach taught the required physical education, and Dennis did not feel he was treated fairly in that class, probably because he did not play football. His opinion of the high school coach was very low.

Moving on to college with a negative opinion of football coaches, McBeth says, "There was a required PE class in bowling that happened to be taught by the football coach at Angelo State. I was not favorably impressed because of my demeaning treatment as an Ag student by the high school coach. My involvement in Ag led me to be a member of the judging team, and we were scheduled to compete in the Fort Worth Livestock Auction Show. It was necessary to inform all instructors whose classes I would miss that week. I agonized about telling the football coach that I would not be in class the following week because of what I had always experienced in high school in these situations. When I told the coach where I was going, his response shocked me. He smiled and responded by showing excitement that I was on the team, we were competing and representing the college, and he wanted us to go to Fort Worth and win it all. One hundred percent positive and probably the greatest pep talk I had ever received prior to any type of competition. Maybe this is one reason the college coach later became one of the outstanding coaches in the nation. I know it is one reason why I have always appreciated Mr. Grant Teaff."

For football players specifically, I made certain I had some contact with every player each day, which included scout teamers and walk-ons. During warm-ups, I walked around speaking to players individually, and during practice I made sure I made eye-contact, giving a nod of approval, or even voicing disapproval of an effort or action.

It was required by every coach on my staff to go into the dressing room after practice to say some positive words to each of their position players. Our staff demanded a lot in practice and we coached hard, so I wanted the players to know it was business, not personal. I also had coaches in the dormitory every night, so the players would know our presence would be around, but also to give the players the opportunity to talk to one of the coaches should they have a problem or issue.

A truth I learned from my parents was simple: say what you mean, and mean what you say. In other words, make it clear to everyone what the rules and standards are, make it clear what the penalties are, and then fairly enforce those penalties. I think the most important truth, whether it be in a marriage, in business, or on a team, is trust. A head coach must stand up for their players and assistant coaches, sometimes at the coach's own peril. Honesty builds trust. I can remember on several occasions where I told the squad about a set of circumstances that were not in their best interests, decisions that the administration had made. Though we did not like those decisions, we had to stand by them. It was important for the players to know I was fighting for them to make things better.

I never wanted to get too close to individual players, but I was unafraid to do so when it was necessary. Now, some of my closest friends are those who once played for me. A few of my former players now call me Grant, but not many. I take no offense being called by my first name by men who are in their sixties. I believe in teaching life's lessons at every turn, using the game, the practice, and even discipline issues, to hammer into players the basics of getting along in the world and succeeding in life. There were some players who I thought never heard a word I said, yet as we have reunions I hear those players saying the same things to their children that I said to them years ago.

My basic rules related to my players.

- Be firm.
- Be fair.
- Show a true interest in them as young people and students.
- If you make a promise, keep it.
- Teach leadership and encourage the students' growth as leaders throughout their careers.
- Demand personal responsibility, class attendance, proper eating and sleeping habits, and completing daily homework. I encouraged each player to be the strongest link in the chain of team success.

Chapter 3

Discuss your relationship with assistant coaches.

Don Nehlen

In dealing with my coaching staff, I tried to [make them] feel like they were associates. I never hired anybody that I didn't think was a good person. He was going to have money to go out and recruit and represent West Virginia University. I wanted a good guy to start with. He also had better know his Xs and Os. I very seldom ever hired a coach without talking with his wife. If I didn't see her personally, I talked to her on the phone. I told her what kind of job her husband was going to be offered. If Mama is happy, chances are, Papa is going to be happy. If that coach goes home and Mama is all upset because he's got to be there until midnight every night, then you have a problem. I think it's important that a wife knows exactly what his schedule is. I think that it's important that the coach knows what his schedule is.

There are coaches out there right now who think that they have to monopolize assistants from 7 a.m. until midnight, and I think they're wrong. If this game is so tough that your guys can't come to work at 7 a.m., or whenever you want to start, and get home at a decent hour, you're doing something wrong. When I first started to coach, it would take us until Wednesday to figure out what somebody was doing because we had to cut it up and stick it on the wall. Now, all you have to do is push a button on a VCR. These guys have enough information on Sunday to formulate their game plan. They don't have to have [assistants] at the office until midnight every night. I really believe that. I wanted a coaching staff who couldn't wait to get out on the field and be enthusiastic. I didn't want a bunch of guys who've been getting five hours of sleep every night for the last two months. I wanted an enthusiastic, energetic coaching staff. Now, when we had work to do, we needed to do whatever was necessary to get it done.

I also talked to my coaches about their relationships with the players. I never wanted to see any of my coaches in the coaches' locker room until at least 20 minutes after we left the practice field. I said, "You spend that time in the locker room talking to your kids and the other players." For example, let's just say that R.C. was the linebacker coach and he walked off the field with a defensive back. R.C. would say, "Hey, Johnny, how'd you do today?" "Oh, I didn't have a very good day." R.C.'s response would be, "Hey, Johnny, don't worry about it, you play for a great coach. Coach Smith is a super secondary coach. He'll have you flying tomorrow." If, on the other hand, that kid says, "Oh, I had a great practice." Coach Slocum says, "Hey, I knew you would because Coach Smith is a great coach." In other words, I tried to have the coaches build up each other with players, rather than the linebacker coach always being with the linebackers or the running back coach always being with the running backs. I think it's important that the kids get to know all the coaches, not just their [position] coach.

R.C. Slocum

The first thing would be, I wanted good men. When I interviewed a guy, my biggest concern was not how much football he knew, but what kind of guy he was. Is he a team player or someone who cares about kids? What's his motivation for coaching? I'd always ask, "Why do you coach football?" Whatever success I had, it's because I had a bunch of great assistant coaches. They were all good men. I gave them the opportunity to do their jobs, but I made it clear what I expected from them in terms of their behavior, then I gave them the support and opportunity to do it. I created an open door atmosphere with my staff because I wanted them to feel like they could come tell me anything. As assistant coaches, you have an obligation – if there's something going on, if there's something you think that we can do better – to come and tell me that. Now, once you've brought that to me, I have an obligation to listen to you with an open mind. Once you've done that, your obligation is over. As a head coach, you may get two or three different angles coming at you, and you have to take all of that in and make a decision on what's the best direction for the program.

You're wrong as the assistant coach if you tell the head coach what you think is wrong, but then if he doesn't do it like you want it done, you become a clubhouse complainer with the other staff. I would tell my coaching staff, "There's not a problem we have that we can't solve in this room with us. If there's a problem, we need to get together and we need to work it out." If you have an assistant who confides in friends or his wife about what is going on and how they think something is wrong, and they go and tell other people, that will kill a coaching staff and a program. If I had guys taking work problems home, I would ask them, "Are you part of the problem, or are you part of the solution?" The solution is coming to me. Your wife can't do anything about it. I can do something about it. You're obligated to bring that to me. Let's sit down as a staff and get it worked out. We have to handle it within house.

I have another point about the relationship with coaches. I always felt like I had every right to be demanding as a head coach of my assistants. However I wanted something done, I had every right to demand and to explain, "This is how I want it done." I never felt I had any right to be demeaning to my assistants. I don't know where this all started, but I've seen guys who get a title [and feel] that gives them the right to be a jerk to anybody. If you're not in a good mood that day, you don't have a right to treat him in a way that – if you were not the head coach and he weren't working for you – he'd probably whip you for, if he were big enough. I've seen guys do that with assistants, and I've seen assistants do that with players. I think that is fundamentally wrong. If you use your title as a coach to handle players in a demeaning manner, or if you, as a head coach, talk to your assistants in a way that is not respectful of them, that is wrong. If you don't like how they're coaching, be a man, get them in, treat them with great respect, and tell them, "I'm not pleased with how you're doing this. This is what I expect." You have no right to start cursing that guy and sometimes you can talk in a demeaning way without cursing. Recently on television, I saw a head coach turn around to one of his assistants and almost slapped him, but the guy jumped back. If I'm an assistant, I'm a professional and you're going to tell me to be a professional and do a professional job, but you're not going to treat me like a piece of junk. I think it is fundamentally wrong to treat your coaches or your players that way. You better be hugging those guys and trying to make them think they're special.

I used to use an example with my coaches. I'm not worth a flip as a golfer. I am hitting golf balls and you are going to be my golf coach. I'm hitting and all of a sudden, you start cursing me out and say, "You sliced it again." "Coach, I know I sliced it. Tell me what I can do to keep from slicing. Don't stand here and yell at me. Tell me what I can do to get better. I want to be good."

Bobby Bowden

Well, naturally my delegating has shifted in the years that I've been coaching. I've never separated myself much from the assistant coaches. I think some head coaches are way up here [holds hand high in the air] and their assistants are down here [drops hand near the floor]. They don't try to get close at all. That used to be the way it was. I've always been pretty close with my assistants. I would say that if there is a style now, it is that they do all the coaching. All I want them to do is let me know what they're doing. They're going to do all the coaching. My job is to solve problems. That's all I'm good for is to try to solve a problem.

John Gagliardi

First of all, one of my top assistants is my son, so I have to treat him a lot differently. The other guys are former players of mine. I like that because I don't have to convince them that what we're doing works. They know what we're doing. We do things so differently that a lot of people wouldn't understand it. In Division III, we have assistants who do more than coach football. One is a head baseball coach. Another one is a track coach, and another assistant is a head wrestling coach. So, they have a lot of duties. When I started, I was not only the football coach, but the basketball coach, the baseball coach, the trainer, the equipment man, and the custodian. When I started getting a couple of coaches, I didn't know what to do with them. It's kind of nice. I feel like I'm retired with all these guys I can delegate something to. What I want to be is a figurehead. Let these [assistant] coaches take over and [I] just show up. That would be nice.

Terry Donahue

I have a couple of thoughts on that subject. When I first left UCLA as a player, I was very lucky. I went to work for a fellow named Pepper Rodgers, who is a great personal friend now and was a quality football coach. I was 23 years old. Pepper spent a lot of time recruiting a big defensive lineman out of Arkansas named Karl Salb who was one of the best shot-putter/discus guys in the United States. He was all of 6'5" and 285 pounds, and he could run a 4.7. He was one of those beautiful guys who was a high school football player and track star. He went to the University of Kansas, but he didn't play football, he was a track guy. Finally, after recruiting him for a year and a half, Pepper Rodgers got him to come out for football.

I was a 23-year-old, first-year defensive line coach for Pepper. He had given me the opportunity of a lifetime. We were out in the hot Kansas sun during two-a-days. It's 100 degrees outside and the humidity is high. I'm working out the defensive line hard like all defensive line coaches work players. We're going over bags, recovering fumbles and we're busting their chops. All of a sudden, Karl Salb went over the bag and didn't show much effort while doing it. I told him to get back and do it again, and do it right. He did it about half-way through again. I got him to do it one more time, then he started running for the gate. He went right out the gate. I'm yelling at him, "Be sure to shut the gate."

Like a lot of young coaches, I didn't blink. I just kept right on coaching. I was coaching Orville Turgeon, who was about 5'9", 185 pounds. He could read ahead and play five-technique better than Karl Salb anyway. When practice was over, we were in the locker room and Pepper Rodgers said to me, "Terry, how did Salb do in practice today?" I replied, "He didn't do very good, Coach. He quit. He doesn't have any heart." Pepper said, "Listen, after you shower, come on up to my office." I showered up and went up to Pepper's office. He was sitting behind his desk and he taught me an invaluable lesson about being an assistant coach. He leaned forward and said, "Terry, do you know how long I recruited Karl Salb to get here?" I said, "Well Coach, I know you recruited him, but I don't know how long." He said, "I spent a year and a half recruiting that guy to be here. Do you know how many 6'5", 285 pound defensive linemen who run a 4.7 there are in the state of Kansas and around the country?" I said, "Well, I'm sure there's not very many." He replies, "You're right, there's not very many of them at all. Do you know how many 23-year-old defensive line coaches there are in the country? I expect you to get Karl Salb back on this team." I went and got Karl Salb back on the team and kept my job. Pepper Rodgers taught me a really important lesson that I never forgot. He taught me that it was his program. He was the head coach and my responsibilities as an assistant coach were to him, to do what he wanted me to do and not necessarily what I thought I needed to do or what I wanted to do.

Every coach recognizes that their staff is their lifeblood. If you don't have the right quality people and the right guys at the right positions, then you can't survive in football. It's equally as important as recruiting. Your staff is everything, but there is an obligation for assistant coaches to realize that someone is the head coach and someone has to make decisions. The fur can fly and there will be disagreements, but eventually everybody has to accept the chain of command and do what you're required to do to make that staff function effectively.

The other thing I would mention is that in hiring coaches, you can look for a lot of qualities in people, but the most important quality to me was integrity. I always felt that from integrity, everything else flowed. If you have integrity as a person, then you'd have loyalty.

You'd understand work ethic. Commitment wouldn't be a problem for you. So integrity was something I really wanted to search out in the coaches who worked with us at UCLA.

The last thing is to make sure that you get the smartest assistant coaches you can. As a head coach, I knew I had certain weaknesses, areas I wasn't as knowledgeable in, but somebody else out there was. I wanted to bring quality coaches into our program who knew more than I did and who could help me be successful. I didn't care how smart they were or how much notoriety they had received. I just wanted to make sure they were working for us at UCLA.

John Robinson

A lot of my best friends were guys who coached with me. When I started at USC, most of the coaches I hired were contemporaries. We were in it together and we saw each other as contemporaries. It was clear I was the boss in the head coach sense, but there was a friendship. As you get older as a coach, you begin to hire coaches who are younger and have not shared the mutual assistants' jobs.

The first thing you need to do is hire guys who want to be there. The coaches that are shaking your hand, but looking over your shoulder at the next job, are not going to work out very well. You need guys who want to be there. You have to explain the role you want them to do. I think we all want to let coaches have freedom for their ideas. Once you get in that meeting room, yell and throw erasers at each other, and you decide on Plan A, it is absolute treason for a guy to want to stay with Plan B. If you'll allow a man to express himself with passion on his idea, then you have to make sure he abandons that idea if you go the other way. The same applies to you. If you accept Plan B, then you have to be ready to go with it.

Assistants need to be loyal to each other. For example, if an offensive coach is saying, "How in the hell could we do it when they couldn't stop them?" That kind of thing is also treachery on a staff. It is important that you give your assistant the sense that if he does his job for you, then you'll help him get his next job. It's not disloyal for him at the end of the year to come in and say, "I've got a chance to get with Terry Donahue at UCLA. Can I interview with him?" You should do everything you can to help him get that job. I'm really proud of the coaches I've coached who have gone on and had great success. Most of them feel that I had some role in it. There is a wonderful relationship between the head coach and assistant. I think that as I got older, I was probably neglectful to some of the young assistants in spending time with them and trying to teach them what I knew. I think I could have done a better job of that.

Tom Osborne

First of all, I think it's really important that you let [assistants] coach. Sometimes you hear about a head coach who'll go around and watch coaches conducting drills, maybe jump into the drill and say, "That's not the way to do it." I really think it's important that each assistant be given an area of responsibility, make sure it's clearly delineated – they know exactly what they have to do and what they're responsible for – and then let them do it. If you have anything to say to them, do it in private. Don't criticize them in front of the players. I think that's number one.

The other thing I thought was important was that we tried to get input from everybody. We would – usually on Sunday – talk about our approach to the next game, and everybody had a say. Of course, at some point you can't debate anymore. At some point the head coach has to say, "Well, this is what we'll do, and this is what we won't do." I really think it's important to value the opinions of those guys. Because if you put them down and you don't listen to them, pretty soon you're not going to hear anything from them, and there's some pretty good input that comes from people who aren't necessarily the coordinators.

One thing that has really been a problem in our country, and you may have thought about it a little bit, is exceptionally high executive pay. You see guys running a company into the ground and leaving with a $50 million golden parachute, yet the average rank-and-file people don't make much money. So, I thought it was important that the assistants be paid well. I always made sure they got shoe money, camp money, those kinds of things, because I didn't think it was fair for me to get 10, 15, 20 times what the assistants did. I tried to let them know they were appreciated. I tried to be concerned about their families. As a result, we had a lot of continuity on our staff. The average Division I coach leaves after three years, so that means on an average staff you have two or three guys leave a year. We'd lose about one every three or four years. I know Joe [Paterno] has had great continuity, too. Believe me, that helps you. It helps you in recruiting, it helps you in communication. The staff I had was probably 90 percent of whatever success that I, or anybody, had at Nebraska.

Joe Paterno

I couldn't agree more with what Tom [Osborne] said. I think you have to respect your coaches. You shouldn't have them on your staff if they can't have some input. I think Tom's point about how little they make compared to what we as head coaches make [rings true] – you always have to do things for your staff. They have families. They have obligations. If you're not paying attention to them, you're not going to get any input. Everything Tom said would be pretty consistent with what I think we do at Penn State. Hopefully we do it as well as Tom.

Lou Holtz

My personal belief is that coaches are more important than players and I want to tell you why. You cannot win without talent, but you can lose with talent. I've seen a great assistant coach take a poor player and make him average; take an average player and make him good; and take a good player and make him great. Poor assistant coaches will take a great player, make him good; a good player, average; an average player, poor; and a poor player, gets you fired.

I prepared this book called "The Gamecock Bible." It has everything about my philosophy, about dealing with coaches, dealing with players, how we win, and how we practice. There isn't an offensive or defensive thing in this book. When I hired an assistant coach, the first thing I did was give him the book and tell him, "You read the book, and I want you to understand this is what I believe. If you have a difference of opinion, I want to know now. I'm not going to have you come in and say, 'No, I want to do it this way or that way.'"

You have to have great coaches. That's your obligation, and you'll never have a problem – I never had a problem with a coach. I had disagreements. There's a difference. A problem is if you and the assistant coach have two different objectives. If both of your purposes are to make sure they graduate and they win, you might have a disagreement about how to reach that, but you'll never really have a problem.

I wanted my coaches to understand that they will be held accountable. I have three basic rules. I can sum up everything I believe about life and about coaching in three simple rules, and this is what I put on the coaches as well. Number one, do right. Just do what's right and avoid what's wrong. If you have any doubt, get out the "Bible". Rule number two, do everything to the very best of your ability. Rule number three, always show people you care. That's it. Because every player and every coach has three questions: One, can I trust you? Without trust there can be no relationship. The only way you trust each other is to always do the right thing. The second question everybody asks: Are you committed to excellence? That's the answer if you do everything the best. The last thing they want to know: Do you care about me?

I've been blessed to have some great coaches: Monte Kiffin, Pete Carroll, Urban Meyer, Charlie Strong, my son Skip, Houston Nutt, and the list goes on and on. There can only be one philosophy and it has to be mine. Before you join our staff, I want to make sure you read that book and understand it thoroughly.

Dick MacPherson

I think the greatest ability anybody can have is to select men of ability, and I think one of the great things I did was surround my football players with a bunch of great assistant coaches. They went on to great success all over the place. I had a lot of fun coaching over the years at both UMass and at Syracuse because there's nothing like being the head coach, because you set the agendas and have a lot of fun.

By the way, I want everybody here to know that I paid my dues. I worked long and hard to get to where I was, and I enjoyed the heck out of it. I think that the biggest thing all of us have to remember is loyalty to the team and to yourself, and everything is going to be fine.

Barry Alvarez

When I was an assistant coach, I was fortunate to work for Hayden Fry and Lou Holtz. They allowed me to do what I wanted to do, which was coach. That is what I wanted to do with my assistants. It's important you have good communication with them and they understand exactly what their role is and what their responsibilities are. Let them coach, but set the parameters. I made sure there were parameters they understood I wanted and how we expected to play and win the game, but I wanted them to coach. I did not want to micromanage. If I saw something I wasn't sure of, then I would correct it.

As far as off the field, I think it's what you feel comfortable with, but I was fortunate. A number of my assistant coaches and I worked together as assistants at other places. So socially, we did a lot of things together. Our wives did things together. My wife is the classic coach's wife. She did a lot of things for the families. We wanted to have a family atmosphere, so it was a very close-knit group.

Fisher DeBerry

I wanted them to know from the outset what my philosophy was football-wise, and that was to win championships. I believe you have to have great defense, you have to have the kicking game and you have to be able to run the football. I wanted them to understand that I felt they had the best coaching job in America. I used to tell them, "Hey, if you don't feel that way, and if you're not excited to be here every morning when you get up, come to work, be with the type of guys we have here and do what you can do for our young people, then let me know and I will do everything I can to help you find that job." At the same time, as we know, there are no utopias in football.

I used to tell our staff all the time, "Hey, if you see a turtle sitting on a fencepost, you know one thing for sure – he didn't get there by himself, someone had to put him up there." That's so true in coaching.

The head coach is only as good as his assistants, and I wanted them to know how much I appreciated them. I wanted them to know this was their team. It wasn't my team. I wanted them to have ownership in the team and be able to make suggestions they thought were good for the team. We did an awful lot together. We look[ed] for opportunities to be together and do things together as a staff.

Lloyd Carr

I tried to show my appreciation for my coaches financially. I always told our coaches, "When I look out there as head coach on Saturday afternoon, what I see is who I am as a coach. If that team is undisciplined, if that team is unprepared, if that team is sloppy, if that team is not executing, that is me." As an assistant coach, if you are the secondary coach and that is the way your unit is playing, that is you.

We are responsible and when we see things we don't like, we better change it because if we don't, somebody else is going to take advantage of it. I think it is critical, on a coaching staff, that you have great cohesion and that you get along. If you don't have great cohesion as a staff, how can you have great cohesion as a team? The one thing we tried to hang our hats on, when that game was over, there was going to be no finger pointing. We were going to try to figure out why we lost and get better for the next week, but we were not going to point the finger at a player, the offense, or the defense, because those things will cause you to self-destruct.

Tubby Raymond

I was head coach at Delaware for 37 years; we would act like we were family. Consequently, most of the assistants I hired over that period were men who played for us. They were already part of the family.

I don't think I ever hired a guy for what he knew. I figured we could borrow things that he didn't know, but you can't borrow the ability to communicate, a passion for football, and the ability to get along with and trust people.

We did a lot of other things, too. We gave them assignments in the off-season with respect to our opponents so they could be involved in the process of creating the schematic for the following fall. I think that helped them, they enjoyed that.

Phil Fulmer

It's obvious just from the relationships that were built that you were looking for men of character, men that you wanted your family to around, and men whose family you wanted to be around. For the most part, we had very low turnover while I was at Tennessee and that's a good thing. We made sure that we went out and studied people. We really worked at not getting stale. Fact is, when Dick [Vermeil] would come in from his broadcasting to get information from us, we would spend hours picking his brains about offensive and every time we would find out something statistically about ourselves that we didn't know offensively or defensively. So, it can come from a lot of places.

You wanted guys who were professionals. You wanted guys who could manage themselves in all settings. At Tennessee, we had to go a lot of places to recruit and be in a lot of different kinds of environments. If they can handle themselves well there, but most importantly when they got that young man under their wing, they were going to be his father away from home and a positive influence. I did expect them to be an extension of me to [the players] and from [the players] back to me. I wanted them to know what was going on in their lives, academically, and in every other thing.

I was very fortunate, David Cutcliffe and John Chavis were my coordinators for long, long time. Both of them are still out there just doing great, David as a head coach and John at LSU as a defensive coordinator. [John is now the defensive coordinator at Texas A&M.] That's probably a perfect example right there. I took over in 1992 and had a coach who was a defensive coordinator who left right away. I was getting all this pressure from all over the place to go outside and hire the greatest of the guys – the gunslinger who is out there who has the name – and here I had worked as an assistant with John Chavis for all those years, across the hall. If I had a question about something I was trying to fix offensively, I'd go to him. We ran together, we worked out, I knew the man as who he was. I took a lot of criticism at the beginning, but it has turned out that he's been [named] assistant coach of the year a couple times. [He] had great, great, defenses, and should be a head coach. Same thing with David. David came up as a graduate assistant. He was a high school coach, had to sell his bass boat and his Cadillac. He was the head coach of Banks High School in Tampa, at 26 years old he came to Tennessee and started at the lowest-of-low positions, then became the coordinator, and is now the head coach at Duke and doing just fantastic. There are more stories than that. Men of character, men of great work ethic. I didn't want to be the one who was turning the lights off every night. That's a problem sometimes, too, and early in the morning, but I had Steve Caldwell, Dan Brooks, and just a lot of really solid, solid coaches and solid men.

Dick Vermeil

I feel pretty much like Phil [Fulmer], to me it was all based on what kind of person you were. When I was in high school, I had one assistant. When I was in junior college, I had one assistant. Then all of a sudden I'm at UCLA, then coaching for Chuck Knox and the Rams and we're in the playoffs, and I get the UCLA job. They'd been winning. I'd been on their practice field, spring practice, I knew these guys could coach, I watched them. I felt the smartest thing for me to do was keep as many of those guys as I could and keep them recruiting. It's still players who win games, not coaches. I wanted to make sure they could keep recruiting for the month I'm going to be coaching pro football. I hired seven of those guys and all seven were outstanding beyond my expectation They're lifelong friends.

What I tried to do in the NFL was always try to hire a person to coach a position who knew more about it than I did. So, after spending a year with him, I can maybe qualify myself as being able to coach that position as well as he could. Going into '81 and '82, I really felt that it was the first time in my life I could coach any position on offense, defense, or the kicking game, and do it well. That really gave me confidence as a head coach; to evaluate what was going on and how to improve our process so I could provide an environment and an atmosphere in which the assistant coach could do a better job, then I could critique and make constructive comments and seek information from others. I hired Sid Gillman [when he was] 70 years old. I called six different people about Sid Gillman. I had met him once at a football clinic in Reno. We were listening to Vince Lombardi speak; it's the only time I had ever met him and only two people told me to hire him – Al Davis and Jack Pardee. I hired him. He didn't coach football as much as he coached coaches. He does not get enough credit for being a quality football coach. This guy was a teacher! He made every one of us, especially on offense, a much better football coach. From the fundamental standpoint, the drilling standpoint, the concentration on technique, [he] took us way beyond. I thought I was a halfway decent offensive coach; he improved me 60 percent. He improved everybody and the scheme and everything. A ton of stuff all you people as coaches watch in the NFL on Sunday originated with Sid Gillman. It really did. He was an amazing guy. The whole theme is hire somebody who knows more than you do, then provide him an environment where he can be the best he can be and make you look pretty smart. I did a little more of that when I came back out of coaching. Mike Martz [was a] brilliant football coach. Without Mike Martz we wouldn't have won a Super Bowl. We're a pretty darn good football team, because we'd spent two years building it. Take Peter Giunta, who's now secondary coach of the Giants, and John Bunting who was head coach at North Carolina and who played seven years for me, and you put these packages of a very knowledgeable guys together and it's amazing how much smarter you look as a head coach.

Marino Casem

First of all, although it's recruiting, retention, and graduation with the players; it's recruiting, retention, and growth with assistant coaches. You have to get a guy who is hungry and who has a mind like a sponge – he wants to soak up all of the knowledge he can get. He has to be loyal. At the end of the day, regardless of how we disagree, we have to coach the same group, and we have to be on the same page. You have to have a guy who is flexible enough to be able to do that. That's the kind of guy we want. I want a guy who wants to be a head coach someday, but I don't want him to want my job. I tell them they have to understand that from day one. I'm a dictator. I hope I'm benevolent, but my vote is 51 percent all the time. Regardless of what they can come up with, at the end of the day my vote is worth 51 percent. I want a person who wants to be a head coach and I want him to be a guy who can make adjustments under stress. You may have a game philosophy about what you're going to do, but then you [kick] off. Your philosophy might change right there. You have to make an adjustment and that adjustment has to come from within, and we have to be able to do that. He has to be flexible, but he has to be a very knowledgeable person and be able to work under stress.

Bill McCartney

I think the thing that's important when we look at our staff is, how do they act when the pressure's on? In other words, we can be very congenial, but under pressure, how do your values compare? Do you have the same set of values? Will he submit to your authority? Some guys don't want to be corrected. They're very competitive. They're super charged, but they can't take correction. What happens when you disagree in strategy? What happens when you're in a meeting room and you have different opinions, and yet, you're the head coach? I think game plans are an imperfect science. Nobody has a monopoly on always coming up with the right game plan. I had a guy who coached at Colorado. What I would do, as the head coach, is go into the various meeting rooms and I would see how good of a communicator each assistant coach was. I would watch him as he would introduce new material to the players at his position, because I wanted to know if this guy was getting all the information across, or if we had to cover him. Some guys have different strengths and weaknesses. I went into this guy's room, and he was coaching our quarterbacks. I was in there about five minutes and I found myself taking notes. I mean this guy knew a lot more about quarterback play than I did. As a head coach, I like to make decisions, but I realized this guy was better at [quarterback play] than I was.

I think there's a lot of humility in working with staff, honoring them, empowering them, and submitting to their authority. Yet, the bottom line is – when you have an assistant coach, is he a true team player or is it more about him? If it's more about him, it won't work. It will undermine the morale of the team at some point.

Bill Curry

I feel the same way about assistant coaches as I do with players. I expect them to be role models, especially for our players. I take it as a personal responsibility to teach them what I expect in terms of our attributes and our value system. I believe very strongly in unbendable ethics. That does not mean I always live up to them. I certainly don't. I fail every day. There are five basic virtues that the Institute for Global Ethics has established that all cultures accept: fairness, honesty, respect, responsibility, and compassion. I expect my coaches to be those things for the players, and we work on it every day.

Jerry Moore

I think it borders on the same premise as the players. They better know what's expected. I think loyalty's a huge part of any success. The last thing I'd ever want to do is jump on a coach or embarrass a coach in front of the players or other coaches. I think that destroys the very first thing I talked about, being loyal. I think if we work hard enough, and we spend enough time with each other, that we all know what's expected. It's no different than any other organization. There are going to be times you stump your toe, or you may say something and you really didn't intend for it to hurt, then you get it corrected. Either you go to them or they come to you, "Coach, how are we going to get this fixed up?" I think you have to communicate.

Ken Sparks

I've been very fortunate through the years to have an unbelievable group of men. At one time, there were five of us who were together for over 25 years. That's unheard of nowadays, because everybody seems to be climbing the golden ladder to go somewhere. The staff we have now is a great combination. We have five coaches who have young children, and we have a couple of granddaddies. To see the granddaddies, which I'm one, and to see those young coaches raise their kids – and which we try to have [the kids] in our building as much as we possibly can – then watch them pour into their players is unbelievable. How can it get any better than that? Most of our players are from single-parent or no-parent homes, and they're looking to see what a daddy looks like. We're on one page as a coaching staff, because I found out a long time ago that the ground is pretty level at the foot of the cross. If we have disagreements, or if there's something that's going on with us, all we have to do is go to the foot of the cross. I have coaches who have coached in Division I. I have coaches who have played in the NFL. I have coaches who have been All-Americans in the SEC. To see how they are on the same page, as far as being a daddy to kids, it's exciting to watch and see the results of that. All the players want to know is, do you care enough about me to really love me? I'm so excited about our coaching staff and the way they buy into the ministry of doing something worth something for eternity.

One question I would ask the audience is, do you micromanage your staff, or do you all agree on certain aspects and let them do their coaching and handle their business? In the spring, we have every one of our coaches write down what they think is their gift package, how God has gifted them to do certain things. How we fit together is the key to the coaching staff.

If you have a guy who grabs his turf saying "This is what I want to do and this is how I want to do it," then before you know it, somebody else is going to grab his [own] turf. Then you have a bunch of turf-grabbers, and that doesn't work on a coaching staff. In the spring, I have them write out the responsibilities they want on this coaching staff and the things they think they are not gifted to do.

I don't micromanage on the field. I don't micromanage their off-the-field responsibilities, because they don't need it. If you're having trouble doing what I'm asking you to do, please let me know so I can help you. We'll make sure we do this together. When you get all the parts fitting together and nobody's standing out, it's a beautiful thing.

Grant Teaff

For me, there are certain attributes I looked for when hiring college football assistants. They must be able to believe in and see our university and our philosophy. They must be able to evaluate talent and develop strong relationships with high school coaches, administrators, and parents. They must always represent our program and university at the highest level of integrity. I preferred family men as top assistants, but, of course, it was not as important for graduate assistants.

An assistant coach must have integrity, be honest and forthright in their recruiting, and never cheat. Sometimes you can do a great job in hiring, yet, for whatever reason, that individual does not work out for your staff. However, I can say for my staff that every coach whoever left got an equal or better job. One of my tests in the hiring process was to have Donell join me, the coach, and his wife for dinner. It is a more casual environment to get to know someone, and Donell's instincts were so amazing when it came to reading people that I can honestly say I never hired an assistant coach and his wife unless Donell gave me the positive nod.

When I took over at Baylor, I purposefully hired several high school head coaches I had come to know and trust over the years. Our quick success at Baylor can be attributed to the evaluation of potential players by our assistant coaches, as well as the confidential recommendations from the high school coaches who trusted me and our staff.

I believed in a family environment for our staff and team a long time before it became prominent and talked about as it is today. I wanted our staff and their children to feel like they were a vital part of our plan for success. Our coaches' families were important and we made extra effort to involve them. We were one of the first staffs to have Halloween and Christmas parties for our families, as well as making sure the wives were able to travel on at least one road trip. Donell only made the flights the other staff wives made. She would drive like the rest of the families or take a commercial flight. Our coaches knew we trusted them, expected them to recruit within the rules, and if our program was rewarded, they would be rewarded.

One year, we won seven games and were invited to a bowl game, yet our administration turned it down, because it might have cost them a little bit of money. We, of course, were not able to do anything for our team who missed the bowl, but Donell and I took our coaches and their wives for a weekend cruise off the coast of Florida. We had to borrow money from the bank for the trip, but it was worth the effort and the cost – our coaches and their wives deserved it, and it was the right thing to do.

My leadership methods are very simple. Give someone a job, the authority to do it, and then expect very successful results.

Chapter 4

Discuss your defensive philosophy.

Don Nehlen

I was always the offensive coach, but when I went to Bowling Green State, they made me the defensive coordinator and that was a shock. I was taught that you win football games by not making mistakes. You don't get beat deep and you don't do dumb things. I wanted our defensive football team to know that the offense was not going to dictate to us. They could come out in any formation they wanted to, we were going to do what we wanted to do. I wanted our kids to understand that, if we happened to guess right, we would have 11 guys running like crazy to the football. I used a zone concept in the secondary. Now that doesn't mean that I didn't play a little man-to-man, but we were going to know how to play a zone, both two-deep and three-deep. Up front, we wanted to line up nose-to-nose now and then and punch them in the nose. We were going to angle and slant up front. With all the spread offenses now, I think it's more important than ever. I grew up in Ohio. Woody Hayes played the Oklahoma defense. The strong safety always went to the wide side of the field. He had some principles I lived with, but now, with all these spread offenses, if you don't play fives and nines out there I think you're in real trouble. I don't think you can let a quarterback read the backside guy, make the tackle on the cutback, and have nobody outside there because he will be off to the races.

If I were coaching today, I would play two-fives, two-nines or two inside linebackers so I have the ability to bring four, three, two, or none. I'd drive them crazy because if they're going to spread you all out, you can get to the quarterback pretty quick. I'm going to hit him a lot. Now, if he's going to throw it, he's going to throw it right now. I'm not going to let him read the tackle. If that tackle's squeezing, I'm going to run around him. I'm going to have another guy sitting there.

The big thing with defense is having a philosophy and selling it to your kids. Another thing about defense that I think is really important is that you have to sell physical conditioning. Defense is reactionary football and you have to be running all of the time. Those kids have to understand that great defensive football teams are in great physical condition because they have to be chasing that ball all over the field. Defense is fun football! Get them excited about playing defense!

Get some coaches who are young and enthusiastic. You don't need to do a lot of things. So many coaches have eight and nine coverages. Teach fundamentals. How do you take on a block? How do you get off a block? How do you tackle? Spend time doing that, not on 10 different coverages. I think we have a tendency to get carried away with all of these X's and O's. You have to teach them how to play football. They have to be able to deliver a blow, and they have to be able to get off that blow and run to the football. They have to be able to do the things you want them to do. Don't let them dictate to you.

It's obvious that I think Bo Schembechler was a great coach at Michigan. He gave a speech one time and talked about success and sticking to basics. Schembechler said he went to a clinic one time and the title of this guy's speech was, "The New Evolution of Defense." He sat there and listened to this guy. The person giving the speech said, "I have 10 stunts this way and 10 stunts that way. We have eight or 10 different coverages that coordinate up front." Schembechler said some fellow in the back raised his hand and said, "Hey, I've seen your teams play and you give up about 465 yards a game. How can this be the new evolution of defense?" The guy giving the speech said, "My guys couldn't tackle." Bo said, "I went up to that coach and said, 'Coach, I'm going to save your job. You take eight of those coverages and throw them out. You take most of those stunts and throw them out. Teach your kids how to shed and tackle. You might win some games.'" I think that's really important.

R.C. Slocum

The "Wrecking Crew" actually came from the kids. Our style on defense was reckless. One of the kids said something about wrecking offenses and it stuck. So, we started talking about wrecking things and that's when they became the Wrecking Crew. The first time someone printed that, I thought it was a pretty catchy title. It was the kids taking pride in wrecking other offenses. From that point on, it was a concentrated effort with the coaches. I said, "We can talk about it when people in an interview ask you about our defense. Instead of talking about our defense, we can say 'Well, I think the Wrecking Crew is going to show up and do this and that.'" We had good players and good schemes to make the title stick. The players built upon that and took pride in "the Wrecking Crew." I thought it was another way of making it a special thing. We got to a point where we had Wrecking Crew caps made. Who would get one of those caps? It was a pride thing, whether you got a Wrecking Crew cap or not.

My philosophy was always speed over size. If I had to sacrifice one or the other, I would rather sacrifice some size to have more speed. If you can't line up and have a base defense that you feel good about, then you are in trouble. A lot of guys want to stunt. Kids are always wanting to stunt and blitz. It's an awful thing to get in the game and think you have to always outguess the offense. You have to be able to line up and have a scheme. If we will line up and execute what we're doing right, and [regardless of] whatever they do, we'll be okay. We won't give up a big play, and we'll have a chance to hold them to a reasonable game. If you can start with that and get to where you can play base technique, when you do move you can have some effect with it. When you get the offense hunkered down, trying to come off and block your base defense, then your movements have effect. I never was smart enough to guess right all the time.

I see defenses where they'll have that other team for a loss, but the next play they give up a 40-yard play. It's just trading back and forth. I was never willing to give up the big plays. I wanted to play a sound defense and gang tackle to keep the plays to a minimum. Have some flexibility within your scheme, but keep it as simple as possible. I think most coaches over coach. I agree with Don [Nehlen], people have way too much defense sometimes.

If we're making a motion adjustment, you can get on the board in the office and figure out, if they do this kind of motion, we'll do this. You can do that on the chalkboard or in the meeting room, but when you get on the field and it is happening in the heat of the game, I wanted adjustments that may not be quite as good, but we can get it every time. We wanted to get lined up with a sound defense, minimize the big plays, and not beat ourselves. Defense should be reaction. I've thrown out a million stunts and a million motion adjustments over the years. It makes more sense to make this guy do this, but if you're not careful, you'll have two or three packages. In this package you do this, in this package you do that, but for that kid, he is also on the punt team, he's got assignment on the punt return team, and when he learns all of that stuff, he is loaded down. I was conscious as a head coach of trying to say, "We're giving him too much. We have him on the punt team, punt return, and the nickel package. He has too much stuff." I wanted to give the kid information where he would feel total confidence to line up, so when the ball turns over, he's ready to go somewhere, and go somewhere fast.

Bobby Bowden

The style we're seeing more of nowadays – zone blitzing – fits my philosophy pretty well. I like the idea of attacking, but I hate to give up that big play. I think the zone blitz has helped solve that. I think the best defense ever would have a seven-man blitz and seven men dropping. There have been years where your defense is built around pressure, then it's built around dropping players in coverage, then a mixture of the two. Now it seems like we see more zone blitz. Again, I like it because you can put pressure on the passer and get some good penetration, yet not give up the big play.

John Gagliardi

We think defense is incredibly important, because the offense is not always going to be able to go. We like to think if we can't move the ball, let's punt it down there and see what they can do with the thing, then we play good defense. I think the most incredible part of our defense is that we never ever make a tackle in practice. Since maybe 1955, we haven't made a tackle on our practice field, but we play pretty good defense. I feel that, if you line up in the right spot, you beat the blocking scheme and get the guys to the ball carrier. You could be the best tackler in the world, but if you can't get to the ball carrier, it's kind of tough to make the tackle.

So, all we do in practice is work on getting to the ball carrier, but we don't ever bring him down. We're always in shorts or sweats and that's it, since the last time we hurt our star player. In the 1950s, we had an assistant coach who was also the athletic director. He would say, "Oh, we have to hit. We have to hit." Well, we hurt our star ball carrier, a guy named Jim Lehman, who is the father of Tom Lehman, the great golfer. Jim Lehman led the country in scoring, so getting him hurt was kind of tough.

As an aside, Tom was a good quarterback and he was supposed to come to St. John's. His dad called me and said, "Tom has decided to go to the University of Minnesota." I said, "To play football?" He said, "No, he is going to play golf." I said, "Oh, what the heck kind of future do you think he has in golf?"

Terry Donahue

At UCLA, one of the things we always believed in, defensively, was quickness and speed over size and strength. That stems from way back when Red Sanders came out to the West Coast. It was bred into in every UCLA player. As a coach at UCLA, you were always going to try to utilize your speed and quickness. I grew up in a background that said you never sacrificed your speed and quickness in any position for size or strength.

We had some great defensive coordinators in Bobby Field, Tom Hayes, and Craig Robinson. I was more concerned with how we utilized our players than which front we used. I wasn't concerned whether we used a 3-4 or 4-3 or a slide defense. It didn't matter as much as how we would utilize the best players we had. We had a string of safeties who came through UCLA who would really light you up and were really good run support guys. We had guys like

Ken Easley, Don Rogers, James Washington, and Matt Darby. Our defensive coaches were some of the first who utilized safeties prominently in the running game. We really tried to figure out how we could best utilize an athlete's particular talents. Utilizing the talents of a particularly good player was part of playing good defense.

We had a linebacker named Jerry Robinson. He was the fastest and most instinctive guy we had. Our defensive design was to get him covered so people couldn't get to him. He would make three-quarters of the game tackles. It wasn't so much the front we ran, but it was utilizing his talent. I always felt that if you could tackle well as a defensive team, then you always had a chance to hang in the game defensively. Tackling is a difficult skill, particularly out in the open field, and there are a lot of things you can do to make it better.

John Robinson

Most of our philosophies are products of our predecessor, Len Casanova. He was the coach I learned from and played for at the University of Oregon. He had an assistant by the name of John McKay who went to USC and became one of the great coaches. John McKay hired me. That philosophy seemed to be what I adopted.

I think defense starts with a free safety. You put him way back there, like 25 or 30 yards back, and you keep him back there until he learns to be the center fielder. You all know who the center fielder is – he doesn't have to be the fastest guy, but he's the guy who can run and catch the fly ball in baseball. You can't let the other team throw deep on you. I was recently doing an NFL game where the Washington Redskins had a free safety by the name of [LaRon] Landry and they played him at 25 yards. He could cover either side of the field. Any ball that was thrown 40 yards down the sideline, he was going to get it. Gradually, you bring that guy up. We had some of those guys who could stop the run, but we wanted to stop the deep pass first.

Also, everybody wants a corner who runs a 4.4 and can play man-to-man. Only about six of us in the room have ever had one. Those guys just aren't around and I don't know where they are. If you don't have a shutdown guy, you better teach your corners to be smart, take the inside away, take the deep pass away, and be careful so you don't get beat. The defensive back who covers the guy only seven out of 10 times is giving up 21 points, so we were very cautious there.

You also need players who will accelerate. When I was a player, and even when I was a young coach, everybody taught us to get in a football position. Len Casanova would demonstrate and he'd get his two feet planted in the ground and his arms out and say, "This is a football position." The truth was that it was a position where you stood there and the back went right by you while you weren't moving.

One of the best safeties I've ever seen is Bob Sanders of the Indianapolis Colts. That guy is unbelievable. He's about as tall as this table and he is a killer. If you give him a target, he is going to accelerate through it. His feet are always going toward the target. They don't stop. Take any film you want and look at a defensive man who widens his feet and stops. He always misses the tackle, unless he's tackling a lineman. I think acceleration is very important in college football because everybody's using the whole field.

If you're stationary, you won't make the play. You have to teach them to go after people. Terry [Donahue] mentioned Kenny Easley. We had Ronnie Lott and Dennis Smith. We had some great safeties in Los Angeles to go against each other, but they never got in football positions. They just simply tried to kill you. If they missed you, they did a great job of making a U-turn and getting you in the small of the back. They were guys who were taught to attack. It's something you have to teach.

As Terry mentioned, schemes come and go. The 3-4 is what we always played. We felt like we could get defensive tackles that were wide bodied two-gappers and use the linebackers effectively. The idea of being aggressive and tackling aggressively is crucial.

Tom Osborne

The name [black-shirt defense] kind of took on a life of its own. It was really simple and accidental. You use contrast jerseys in practice, and for some reason our first-team defense had black jerseys. There's nothing mystical or magical about it.

You want to make sure, defensively, you're simple enough that people can play and react instinctively. I had difficulty at times, because the secondary coach would want to be able to put enough check calls in there to put out every pass pattern. As a result, we began to lose our linebackers and our secondary guys. The idea of simplifying, I think, is really important, but you have to have a certain amount of complexity.

Back in the '70s, we were primarily a 5-0 defense. We slanted weak, we slanted strong, we eagled, and played mostly zone defense. The secondary guys were not particularly fast, but they were smart. Then as people began to spread you out, we had to get faster guys. The main thing we did that I thought was important was our outside backers were I-backs in high school. Some of them weren't real big, but they could run and cover. That was really critical. We began to play more man-to-man defense and variations of it. We did evolve in that direction.

Originally, Monte Kiffin, an excellent defensive coach, was our defensive coordinator back in the '70s. At that time, Monte's philosophy was bend, but don't break. He figured if you made somebody go 70 yards in 12 or 13 plays, at some place down the line they'd get a penalty. As time went on in the latter years I was coaching [things changed]. In the '90s it was more of an attacking defense, trying to force bad plays and those kinds of things. You've all seen the changes in defense, and probably a lot of you have the same philosophy today.

Joe Paterno

I really don't have a defensive philosophy. I don't have an offensive philosophy or a defensive philosophy. There was a book called *Clink*. Somebody sent me a copy of it, and I read it. I may have bought a copy for every one of my coaches. In it, the author makes a difference between the way the game of chess is played as opposed to checkers. In checkers, everybody does the same thing, you can jump or jump twice. In chess, you have different people who do different things. You have a pawn, you have a king – that's pretty much what football is. My feeling has always been, the most successful coaches are people who can take what some guy does well and get them plugged in.

If you have a lot of success, you get most of your people back, but if we have a situation where we've lost some people, we have to get reorganized. My job is to take a look at what people can do, and then put a defense together.

I disagree with my staff when they want to put too much stuff in the game plan. For crying out loud, you can't get it all done! That's the only time I really get in tough arguments. I think a kid has to have reps and feel comfortable. He has to anticipate things and be able to play fast. The first thing you have to do is establish what they can do and the best arrangement for the talent you have, then go out and don't overdo the number of things you're going to ask them to do.

Lou Holtz

These are some things I really believe strongly. Number one, give your players something they can do and insist they do it. Do not ask them to do something they can't do physically. Give them something to do and then demand they do it.

Nobody in this world ever beats you throwing and catching. Nobody. They beat you because they can run after they catch. They catch a 40-yard pass. They run for 40 yards. The quarterback scrambles. They catch a screen pass. [For example,] Texas Tech, every 400 yards passing, over 300 yards of it was run after the catch. So, don't worry about people who can throw and catch. Don't let them run after they catch. Trade them a 10-yard gain for a hitting.

Play the ball. It's unbelievable to watch college football today where people don't play the ball. How in the heck can you play pass defense without playing the ball? That's beyond me in this world.

Number two, the defensive line has to stop all five-yard passes. All these little crossing routes, etc., your defensive linemen have to get up there ahead. That will stop that. I thought Air Force did an unbelievable job of that against Houston. Disrupt the offense. That's all defense is – disrupt the offense. Don't let them fall into a rhythm. Stop the runs, stop the long plays, stop third down.

There were 10 things that I insisted our defensive coaches do. They put a report on my desk after every scrimmage and every game on these 10 things.

Number one, how many missed assignments did we have? If you had missed assignments, it's because you're too complicated.

Number two, how many missed tackles? I'm concerned about the concussions we have in football today. You know why? Because you don't teach tackling the right way. It's all this throw a head in there, a spear.

How about putting a face on the football, drive your shoulder through, wrap your arms up and knock his rear going back the other way?

Number three, I don't want any lack of effort. A lot of things don't take talent. It doesn't take talent to know your assignment. It doesn't take talent to pursue the ball.

Number four, I want to know how many times we did not have pads out. I think having pads out on defense is critical. If you can't make contact here, he's catching. You make contact. The pads have to be out. You get separation, the difference, but you have to control the line of scrimmage.

[Point number five was not covered.]

Point number six, how many times did a defensive player hit with something other than his head gear, his elbow, his shoulder pads, and his hands? A defensive player should have no pads from his chest down. Nobody should hit you in the fleshy part. Nobody should hit your leg. You play headgear. How many times did somebody make contact somewhere other than those four places?

Point number seven, how many times did we not get separation from an individual? You cannot get rid of a player unless you get separation.

Number eight, how many times were we not physical? I think you cannot play this game without being physical. Not everybody can play the game, not everybody has the courage.

Number nine, how many times did we fail to have our play-side arm free? I believe in gap control.

Number ten, how many times did we run around a block rather than across a face?

Those were the 10 things I truly believed in. Also, as I said, nobody beats you throwing and catching. You can put up a three-three-five.

You can put up a four-three. Those 10 principles apply regardless of the defense.

[My defensive approach] depended upon the personnel, but I liked a three-four better than anything else because I thought it was very adjustable. I think having four linebackers and a defensive end where they can walk out, etc., you can make the adjustments. When you go for the over, the under, the shade, etc., with a spread formation, with a four wide outs, etc., it gets a little bit harder to defend.

When we went to South Carolina – what did we have more than anything else? A six-foot, 200 pounder who ran a 4.7, 40. That's when we went to a three-three-five, which I think is great against a spread offense, but it doesn't matter what you do. It's those 10 principles.

Dick MacPherson

You know, I love defense. I think people enjoy playing defense. One of the things needed to be a good defensive unit, you must be able to stop the run. If you stop the run, there is no way they can control the ball on you, then what you have to do is stop the pass.

As [Lou Holtz] said before and I'll say again, you have to be able to tackle. There is no such thing as a bad tackle. What is a bad thing is a missed tackle, so we work really hard on exactly what [Lou] was talking about – the fundamentals of the game. The plan is to make sure we leave the field better than when we went on it, and make sure the offense has good field position so they can execute their offense.

That's what we do defensively. It's a measure I think people play-ing the game can understand. They know how they function coming in and going off the game, which is very important to us as we game manage everything for them.

I'm a lot like Lou. What is the offense we're facing? That's where the problem comes in. I think what you have to do is exactly what they are trying to do – figure out what they're trying to do against us and give the players the tools necessary to stop a good offense. That's what we had, and we enjoyed the heck out of it.

Barry Alvarez

The first thing, my background in football is being able to run the football and being able to stop the run. As a player, I was a defensive player. My last assistant job was a defensive coordinator at Notre Dame. Defense was very important to me. It was an emphasis for me. My basic philosophy was, number one, I wanted to be sound. I wanted to be sound in whatever we did. It didn't make any difference whether it was an even front or an odd front. I hear so many things said today, "Well, it's a 3-4, or it's a 4-3." It doesn't make any difference what it is. There are only so many gaps you have to cover. Make sure the defense is sound. I wanted to always be flexible. I wanted to be multiple. I wanted to be physical. I didn't want to be too complicated where my players couldn't turn it loose.

I also wanted to make sure whatever we did defensively was easily adjustable. Regardless of whatever [formation] anyone came out in, we had some basic adjustment rules where we could cover things downfield and we were going to be sound. Then, when the ball was snapped, we could play fast.

Fisher DeBerry

I think you win championships with defense and the kicking game. We'd put our best players on defense. In the springtime, when everyone was trying to get them in the right place, we'd open the personnel board up there, and I'd say "Okay, defense, you have your choice." I let them choose who they thought were the best players on the team. If I didn't think they chose one of the best players, I'd put him over there on defense.

Also, I think you have to not just give lip service to the kicking game. A lot of times, we do that. One of my priorities was to have a kick team coordinator and we spent the time it took to have what I thought was a good kicking game. I try to sell our players that, "Hey, we're going to be the best tackling football team our opponent is going to play this year." We try to take pride in that.

"Get them on the ground" is something I learned from a good friend, Dean Campbell. It used to worry me a little bit. From what I understand, today the game has changed so much that all the sled work we do in tackling is still important, but the game is played too much in space today, the mantra is to "get them on the ground," any way you can. It's certainly the turnovers in the game. We're not going to let a day go where by we don't do a lot of strip drills and use two whistles in our practice. One to hold up the guy, the second one to strip, and then we blow the whistle and it's over. I think leverage is the most important thing in playing defense. You can keep everything in front of you, everything inside of you, an outside arm, a leg free, and then I think you have a good place to start from there.

However, I think your personnel dictates the situation to a great extent, as well as the team you're playing and what you do. I think the key to playing great defense is to line up correctly. Have no question in your mind about what you're going to do and why you're going to do it. If you're thinking too much, you're certainly not going to react. Of course, the key to the game, today, is the speed of the game, but I think you have to stop the run first. You have to react to the past, then plan.

I believe you have to take the four best run plays and the three best players, and rep them, rep them, and rep them day in and day out. On Sunday, the first thing I wanted to know from the defense was how many tackles we missed in the ballgame on Saturday. Then, I made a big deal about that with our team whenever we got together. Second, how many assignments did we miss? That told me a lot; if we were doing too much on defense, or maybe not doing enough.

The last thing I'd say is I really believe the success of tackling is playing football with your eyes. I didn't realize that until the last four or five years. I believe you throw with your eyes. You catch with your eyes. You tackle with your eyes. A lot of times, when you don't have those eyes open, that head goes down a little bit and you're putting yourself in a position for an injury. When you open those eyes, the head comes up, the neck muscle sticks up a little bit and you can certainly see what you're getting done. Most importantly, you're protecting an injury factor there. When we coach, we're creatures of habit, so a lot of the time, we get in one spot and stay there. Move around so you can see if a player has his eyes open.

Lloyd Carr

If you want to learn defense, go find great defensive coaches and watch their practice. There are people in all of those colleges who will spend time with you if you show passion for the game and you are there. Just being here and listening to all the great coaches, I see coaches in every cranny of this hotel, sitting around drawing X's and O's, those are the ways you learn the game.

I really began my coaching career in 1969, the year that Coach Schembechler was hired at Michigan. He had a defensive coordinator, Jim Young, who was a great defensive coach. He brought the angle defense to Michigan, which was based out of the 3-4 front, and he had unbelievable success in defensive football.

When I became the defensive coordinator in 1987, we had a bad start. That winter I went up to the New York Giants, who were running the 3-4, to learn from them, and Bill Belichick was good enough to spend time with us. I think the best defense I have experience with is a 3-4 defense, because you can play a seven-man front. If you can play a seven-man front, you can control a passing game and force the ball east and west, and that is what we tried to do.

Tubby Raymond

I would hate to be a defensive coach today, these one-back offenses and all of the spread offenses, that is a little bit beyond me. The one thing I would want to do is go odds spacing up front, so I would get a lot of linebackers that are uncommitted.

The one thing I didn't like was the bend-but-don't-break philosophy. A coach is going to start the ball on the 20 yard line, then works it all the way down the field and kicks a field goal, the defense is all jumping around and they don't realize they've given up six or seven minutes of possession time. I always felt that I wanted [the defense] attacking and being aggressive. I liked a lot of man, a lot of zone-man, but I really wanted an aggressive defense, I wanted to turn the ball over.

It is not just the offense out there. It is not just the defense out there. They have to work together. So, if the defense can set up field position for the offense, then we have a team and we are moving, and we have a chance at winning.

Phil Fulmer

I go back to my background when I asked to be a GA on defense. We had a great staff at Tennessee at that particular time. I had coached two years of defense at Wichita State and probably my biggest lessons were much like what Dick [Vermeil] was saying. I look back to when we made it to the Southeastern conference. As a coach I was 28 years old and am looking at these Auburn defenses, these great defensive front people, and that made up my mind. When I got my chance I was going to coach some guys that look like that. When I did get my chance, philosophically again, we wanted to be four down with great anchor points and a chance to be aggressive, look for corners. We found those defensive lineups. If you followed us during our best year at Tennessee, we had a whole bunch of guys we recruited coming through there who were really good, who wanted to be perpetuated and coached, and [some wanted to] get to the NFL, and we had some outstanding cornerbacks. So, we were just as Dick described, we were very aggressive on defense. In our particular time, I think we were right at the cutting edge of all the zone blitz stuff that is happening out there today. It's not that offenses don't want to run anymore, they don't know where to run because of all the different kinds of pressures, and you can get away with a little bit more with all the slide projections. John [Chavis] and I sat down and said, "Okay, this is what I think we'd want and what we want to do, how does it fit in with what you're thinking?" From there it was just a fantastic run, because we were aggressive.

Dick Vermeil

I learned a lot from Marion "Swamp Fox" Campbell, who I brought to the Eagles in 1977. He was with me [the whole time I coached in Philadelphia]. He took my job when I left. [He was] a great football coach. I learned an awful lot from him about defense in his schemes. When I went back into the Rams, I brought Bud Carson out of retirement. Bud was a brilliant defensive mind and defensive coach, and just ornery enough and tough enough. I learned a lot from those guys.

I look at defenses, what I did not like to attack, or what gave me the most problems. If I was in charge of the defense, I would try to do those things I learned from other opponents that I didn't like, because they were miserable to attack and tough on me offensively. I would always figure if they were tough on me offensively, if we coach that and had the kind of players who could play it, then we might be a pretty good defensive football team. I looked at defense that way. Basically, what I hated [was] press-man coverage. At the Rams I had a couple of kids – Isaac Bruce and Torry Holt – who could get away from it, but before then, I didn't have anybody to get away from press-man – especially in the old days with the Oakland Raiders and those kind of guys with glue on their hands and no five-yard rule. We couldn't get off the line of scrimmage. I had a blocking tight end because I want someone who can block. That was my thing. So, the press-man coverage, if you have skilled people to play it and a halfway decent pass rush. There isn't an offensive coach who doesn't say it doesn't gives you problems. I would go to that, I'd be aggressive.

Nowadays, they throw the ball 55-60 percent of the time. You can't pick "well I'm going to come after, I'm going to change my defensive line tech on third and nine," hey, they're throwing the ball as much on first and ten. So, I'd be aggressive with the pressure – first applied by down linemen and secondly within the packages of my secondary. [I'm] not a big gambler in terms of weird blitzes, but enough to create problems for me. Side adjustment blitz, pickup packages made me mad they were doing them. You had to keep taking your coaching a little further. That's why I, basically to summarize, would be pretty much into pressure and man stuff.

Marino Casem

My theory is you have to put stress on stress and let weaknesses go by the board. To play defense, you have to be strong down the middle. You have to have straight lines, the shortest distance between two points, and you have to be strong down the middle. You have to have a good middle linebacker and a good free safety. You have to start out that way. I loved strong man-to-man defense. I think we put them out there on an island by themselves and said, "Man, oh, man, let them go at it, and may the best man win this game." I know you have to have talent, but when you're recruiting and being the 51 percent, I put all the strongest, the fastest, the best, the quickest, and the most talented people on defense. I start out that way. Offense will come along, but play defense, defense, defense.

You have to be known for something. When I was there, we were known for our defensive cornerbacks. We had a lot of guys drafted that way. You have to teach them the techniques of playing man-to-man defense. There are a lot of techniques, there are different ways of doing it – you have to know them all. You have to be slick. You have to be good, but you don't have to be the best, you just have to be the fastest. If you have to know how to play it, you know what angles to take. Be quick or be dead. You have to be physical and sound and all of that. You have to be able to adjust and be flexible. You have to be able to stop on a dime and change directions.

My philosophy about defense is to be unorthodox. Don't just line up the people the same way all the time. Master the theory, master the system, then adjust it to fit the needs of your ball club. If you have some good guys, play to their strengths. Put strength on strength and let weaknesses go by the board.

Bill McCartney

When I was at the University of Michigan, I was the defensive coordinator for four years under Coach Schembechler, then I was hired at Colorado. I was really coming in with a stronger emphasis on defense. What I learned is, defense is morale. Defense is also discipline. You have 11 guys and every time the ball snaps, they have to take the right angle to the ball. As the ball changes direction, they redirect. Those 11 guys taking the right course to the ball will prevent big plays by and large in the running game. Now, here's the key – if you get knocked down, get up; don't lay there, get in the chase. There are 11 guys in the chase. I think that kind of morale is fundamental.

When I coached at Michigan, Jack Harbaugh was our secondary coach. He was a tremendous motivator, teacher, and disciplinarian. I mean these guys got it from him, in my opinion. Defense is morale. Defense is guys wanting to tackle, not ducking their heads. There's a right way. The rules are changing all the time, but it's still the same thing. Defense is all about guys who have a tremendous desire to get to the football, but they're willing to take the right course to the ball. That's how I see defense.

Bill Curry

I thought I was a linebacker, but Don Shula decided I was not. He was right. He was right about everything. I only coached a little while in the NFL. Offense and defense was so much simpler in the NFL. Now, this was the late '70s, but systems are still relatively simpler than they are in college football. College football was an absolute mystery to me, as my assistant coaches quickly learned, to their horror. Don Lindsey came to us at Georgia Tech. He was a great defensive coach. He had the flexibility in his system that he could, if he had a special leader, create an elite unit. Now, that's dangerous because that can be divisive, but it worked because he had the instinct to know when we had a good leader.

If we had a great player, an exceptional player – like Derrick Thomas at Alabama – he would use that exceptional player in such a way that he would have him lined up in exactly the right spot, at exactly the right time to absolutely destroy opponents' offenses. The stat that mattered was points allowed. Like good offenses, defenses have to have an answer for things. So we tried to subscribe to that flexibility and not be locked into one system. It was Don Lindsey's thinking that influenced me most.

Jerry Moore

We looked for kids who had speed and were aggressive, then we put them where they could help the football team the best. I always wanted guys who could tackle well. I see lots of missed tackles. I know some of it is related to concussions. It's a little bit different right now than what it was. We looked for guys who could run well. I'm not talking about somebody who could run a 4.2. I'm talking about guys who played across the street, played pickup games, and stuff like that. They just seem to have those kinds of tools. Those are the things that we looked for as far as defense was concerned.

Ken Sparks

Offenses are spreading out all over the place, and you have to defend 70 yards because the game is played in space. You have to get defensive people to make a call. Usually they have to decide on what they're going to run in four or five seconds and get it communicated within seven seconds, because that other team's on the ball ready to go.

I used to think I had a defensive philosophy. I don't have one anymore, but I need to find one that works because the game has changed a lot. Back in the day, you had a tight end, two running backs and a quarterback under center. You could say, "Line up in that 5-0 defense and get after them," but that's not the way it is anymore.

I'm not sure I have a defensive philosophy, and I apologize for that. We've evolved because you used to say you're a 5-0 defense, a 4-3 defense or a 4-2, but none of that applies anymore because you're making so many different adjustments. You're getting all kinds of different looks. That's the reason you have to try to put your kids in all kinds of situations in practice, so they have confidence when [certain situations] happen because we get a lot of surprises. When we line up in a ball game, we see things we hadn't seen on video. We have to be ready for all those things.

Grant Teaff

It is very interesting to look back on how philosophies are developed. I played both offense and defense in high school – a linebacker on defense and a center on offense. I don't remember much about the high school philosophy on defense, but I do remember I liked to tackle and be aggressive. Those two traits became the basis to my defensive philosophy.

In junior college, I played linebacker in what is referred to as "odd-front." There was no spread during those years, which was also true when I entered senior college. Again, I was a linebacker, now weighing about 190 pounds, and the defensive coach liked my physical toughness and my tacking ability. His defensive philosophy was a seven-man front, which means with two tight ends the defense had a player lined up on every offensive player. That defense was referred to as the seven-diamond. I was the bottom of the diamond – middle linebacker who lined up behind the nose guard who lined up on the center. There were three defensive backs, two corner backs and a safety in the middle.

Those years at McMurry were the formative years of my overall defensive philosophy. Coach D.V. Marcum literally turned the defensive front over to me as the middle linebacker. He kept a close eye on me, but I set up slants to the right or left. I also learned to slide my front seven in the gaps as well as head up and short, which allowed me as the middle linebacker to read the flow of the backfield and go to the ball. I liked making tackles. Filling gaps on flow in the offense's backfield was the basis of the defense I would run at McMurry, and again at Angelo State. I used four down linemen and three linebackers.

The middle linebacker had two down linemen and the two outside linebackers had a defensive end each. I set up a system whereby each of those individual linebackers could call a stunt based on their gap responsibility and flow. A high school coach in South Texas named Bum Phillips started using a similar defense about the same time; the defense itself was known as the numbers defense.

At McMurry, and later at Angelo State, that defense was extraordinarily successful. Of course, you have to remember that most of what we saw was two tight ends.

When I came to Baylor, the wishbone used by the University of Texas had reached a high level of prominence. I could not figure out a way to defend the option with the numbers defense. We decided to go to an odd-man front and employed stunts based on flow. We were quite successful against the wishbone. In 1980, we held the very productive Texas wishbone to less than 100 yards. Of course, we won the game.

Through the years, I've seen every offensive concept as they come and go. I believe right now the spread offensive concept is here to stay for a while; however, historically defenses have caught up eventually to every offense. This one may be different.

Chapter 5

Discuss your offensive philosophy.

Don Nehlen

I don't think you win consistently if you can't run. In my first coaching job, I didn't have to call a formation because I only had one. I had two tight ends and three backs. We ran the ball and that was our offense. Now, that's still not too bad. As I got a little older and a little more mature, I still believed the same way. If I were coaching today, I would have six to seven running plays and I would run them from every formation known to man. I would boot and waggle and throw play action passes off of it. When I had to throw it, I'd spread it out and go ahead and throw it.

I don't think that there have been very many great football teams – former BYU head coach LaVell Edwards and I argue about this all the time – that can win consistently always throwing the football. You're going to make that mistake. I think it's important when you coach offensive football to make sure your players understand how you lose on offense. I think they have to understand about those penalties. I'm a lot better coach on first and 10 than I am on first and 20. I don't have many plays for third down and 18. Make sure they understand what it takes to win. Also, the punt is a pretty good offensive football play. I didn't gamble a whole lot on fourth down. When you make it, you're a hero, but when you don't and you're in a field position battle, it can really break your back. Right now, coaches are much further ahead than I was on punting the football. It's amazing what some of these younger coaches are doing with the kicking game. I always believed the punt was a good offensive football play.

R.C. Slocum

Once, I heard Darrell Royal say – "In every game there comes a time when you have to be able to make third and two, or you're behind and you have to keep the ball and advance it, or you have the lead and you're trying to keep the ball away from them." To me, you have to be able to run the ball, which gives a physical nature to your offense. If I were to design an offense, I would want to have some good run formations on first down, and I'd want to have play action passes off of those runs. I'd want to throw the quick game. That would be my passing game on first down. We're going to run the ball on first down, but we're going to have play action. We are going to make you defend the run, then we're going to have a chance to hit some big plays in a play action. If you're loading a block box on us, we're going to throw a quick passing game.

Now, when we get into long yardage situations, we're going to have a great screen draw package to try to slow the rush down. We're going to put in receivers and spread it out, and get to where we can throw the football. We wanted to mix in a great screen and draw package and make our opponent defend the whole field. If you're going to be good on defense, your offense will have a lot to do with it, and vice versa. I think you have to be able to throw and throw effectively. If you're going to throw those play action passes on first down, you better hit about 65-70 percent of them. You don't have to have a lot of them and a lot of different routes. Have a few simple things that come off of your run that are actions, and have something where you move the ball doing that. Even at the professional level – I go back to the Pittsburgh Steelers with Terry Bradshaw and Franco Harris, or the San Francisco 49ers with Bill Walsh as head coach, just to name a few – those great teams were all able to run the football.

We always looked to have some type of gimmick play every week. When we would see a gimmick play on tape, we'd just take it and put it in a file. We had a whole notebook of gimmicks. Every week we would practice one that didn't take a whole lot of extra practice time to put in. As you go through the year, defensive coordinators have to get ready for all that stuff. You may not have worked on it for five weeks, but if they're on top of things, they have to go make sure they're sound on the double-reverse pass or halfback pass. We may look conservative, but we have a few tricks up our sleeve. The players like those things, especially when they work.

Bobby Bowden

My offensive philosophy hasn't changed down through the years. It's one of those philosophies you look at sometimes and you'll say, "He doesn't do that." My philosophy would be to be able to run the ball as well as I can throw it. That's what I would like. People say, "Well, you threw it 50 times and only ran it 20." Well, our opponent might have made us do that because it's going to be dictated by the defense. You know if they're going to bring a few people, then we're going to run the ball. If the defense is going to bring a lot of people, then we're going to throw the football. So, you can determine whether we're going to run or throw.

John Gagliardi

We go along with the trends. We won early with a kind of a single wing. When I played ball, I played with the old Notre Dame box and shift. We can still get out there and use that Notre Dame shift. We went to a veer offense as soon as I heard how they were doing it, then we expanded on it and went to a quadruple offense. We won our third national championship with a quintuplet option, which no one else ever used; we ran the pass off of it. We run the fullback right off of that, double read and option off of that for the quarterback or the slot back coming around. We were very good with that, but I found out you couldn't teach very many quarterbacks that offense, so we switched over. The thing I like now is that everybody can throw the ball. Every kid can throw the ball and we like to throw it.

We're always in helmets and shoulder pads. We're always on the same practice field. Our problem is how to have 180 players practice on one field. We have the defensive guys on one end and the offensive guys on the other end. You have to be careful to not get killed at midfield.

Terry Donahue

We had to be balanced on offense, the reason I say that goes back to my experience with Pepper Rodgers. We were a wishbone team here in '72 and '73. We set every Pac-10 rushing record there was. We were 8-3 and 9-2, but we didn't beat USC. Pepper took a tremendous amount of criticism, not because the offense wasn't effective, but because it wasn't entertaining. What guys like Barry Switzer could do in Oklahoma, you might not be able to do in Los Angeles. So, we had to adjust to our environment. In Los Angeles, we not only had to win, but we also had to entertain, as well as beat USC.

We tried to be balanced on offense. We wanted a good running game. We felt the running game made you physical. We felt running the ball helped you coach good defense. We thought you needed to throw the ball to try and offset some physical disadvantages you might have against a superior team. We wanted to be able to run and throw as we wished. I watched Texas Tech, Hawai'i, and Navy play. Those staffs and coaches do an unbelievable job with what I call extreme offenses. That is a great way to play. We just didn't play that way. We played with a theory of trying to be balanced.

One of the things we did while trying to survive against John [McKay] and his USC teams was take one or two plays USC ran very well. For example, the toss sweep or the weak side isolation play. We would always make sure we had those plays in our offensive scheme. We wanted to practice against those plays in spring practice and in two-a-days, because we didn't want just three or four days to get ready for them. We wanted to have worked on those particular plays.

John Robinson

We wanted to get five big, mean, dirty, rotten SOBs and play them in the offensive line. We wanted to put the best runner we could find behind them, get a tight end who was of the same temperament, but could catch a little bit, and find a fullback who didn't care anything about the ball. That's how we played. We tried to wear the other guy down. It helped that our guys were big, but from a philosophical standpoint, it's really valid.

The most important part of the game is the last six minutes. When you come down to any of your important games, whether you're ahead or behind, the last six minutes is where the power part of the game is the most valid. It's when you're ahead and need those three first downs to close it out, or you're down and you need to get that field position to make a score.

We had coaches who looked like the linemen and saw football as that kind of a game. Those guys coached that area. These days, we have some good-looking coaches. Those guys coached the passing game. They coached the quarterbacks and the wide receivers. If you said, "All the line coaches stand up in this room," then you would see an ugly bunch of guys. If you ask the passing coaches to stand up, then you would see nice, good-looking guys who aren't fat with nice mustaches. We tried to have some of those on our staff, too. We actually had a rivalry going. I controlled the rivalry. This is why I've never been able to get any kind of option going. We felt the quarterback could pass the ball all day and our running backs could run all day.

Our offense was quite similar to Terry [Donahue's] – physical, yet we had the ability to throw the ball. We always wanted to have that guy who will carry it a lot in a game. We gave the ball to Ricky Bell 53 times in one game. We won the game, but I don't think we would have if we had given it to him 52 times. We were extreme in that way.

Now, speed is good. I watched West Virginia on TV the other night and I thought, "Those are the fastest people in the world." It's great the way they coach offense and speed. I just don't think I'd ever want to get away from the power though.

Tom Osborne

We were very fortunate, because at Nebraska we had a lot of walk-ons. Some people didn't understand that. We have only one Division I school in the state, and most of those kids grew up wanting to play at Nebraska. We would have a lot of kids who would walk on who might, in other schools, take a scholarship. We had pretty good numbers, and as a result we always ran two offensive stations and, much of the time, two defensive stations. In the course of a practice, we'd get about 90 snaps to the first team, and we'd get 90 snaps for the second team. That repetition was really important.

The turnover was a big deal to us. If a guy was flagging the ball, wasn't carrying it high and tight, or the quarterback forced the ball, we made a big deal out of it in practice. Sometimes it resulted in some laps. When you have two good teams out there, the turnover factor is huge. You don't ever want to be casual. You don't ever want to back down on the turnovers, and penalties. We had some goals, maybe a maximum of 20 yards in offensive penalties and about 20 on defense. You see over and over guys taking a swing, doing something crazy, and that lack of discipline is what can really do you in. Those things are all important, I think.

We live in a part of the country where the weather isn't always very good. We knew we were going to see two or three games a year where we had a 30- or 40-mile-per-hour wind. This was before some stadiums were completely enclosed. You'd go to Kansas State or Oklahoma State, places like that, and the wind really affected the football. We figured we'd better be able to run it, because you can always run the ball, no matter what the circumstance.

That was our point of emphasis. We were going to have a great running game. We're going to run power football. We're going to run option football. We'd have three or four different kinds of options, and we were going to play very physical football. One of the things we tried to emphasize with our players was that we'd get one-and-a-half knockdowns per play. That means an average of one-and-a-half players knocked off their feet every play, so if you had 80 plays, that meant 120 in a game. Our receivers weren't going to catch 60 balls.

They'd be lucky if they caught 30 or 35, so they knew they had to be down blocking every play.

We built a mindset that was going to be very physical football. I think it's important, however you do it, that your team has an identity and that everybody understands. The receiver coach knew what our philosophy was, the backfield coach knew, everybody knew. As a result, you didn't have people thinking different things when you went into a game. It was articulated what our philosophy was – we wrote it down together.

Joe Paterno

[Coach Paterno indicated in his answer to the previous prompt that he did not have an offensive philosophy.]

Lou Holtz

My philosophy on offense is not complicated. Number one, control the line of scrimmage. I don't care what else you do, control the line of scrimmage. I believe in running the football. There comes a time when you have to be able to run the football when everybody in the stadium knows you're going to run it. You have to be able to pass the ball when everybody knows you're going to pass it.

Let me tell you something: You get the ball on your 31-yard line; you're up by one point. The other team has two timeouts, and there's two minutes and 20 seconds left to go. You want to make them use their timeouts, yet you also want to be able to get a first down. If you throw the ball and it's incomplete, then that stops the clock. You have to be able to run it.

How many times do you get down on the goal line because you're unphysical? If you can't run the football, you cannot score. To get inside the 20-yard line and not score is like playing golf. You reach[ing the green on] a par five in two, then using seven putts. What good did it do you to reach it inside the 20 unless you utilize it?

To me, everything starts with the ability to run the football. Any time I had an offense, we're going to run an iso; we're going to run a power-off tackle; and we're going to run a sweep. I want our team to have to practice against those because the teams that are going to win on a consistent basis are the ones that can run those three plays.

I also believe that the greatest thing that's happened is a shotgun with a quarterback who can run and throw. I started out in high school playing in a single wing. Then we went to the split-T, and then from the split-T we did the wishbone, the wishbone to the veer, the veer to the I-back, the I-back to the West Coast offense. Now we're back there to the single wing. I don't care what you do, you have to be able to make that goal, third-and-one, third-and-two.

No matter what plays you run, all plays must have three things. Either you have to have a collection of plays or you have an offense. Let's take a power-off tackle or an iso. Number one with that play, you must have a counter or a reverse off of it. The second thing you have to do is have a pass off of it. The third thing, you should have a screen off of it. If you run a power-off tackle, you run the fake power-off tackle, the back and the flat. You run the fake off tackle, you bootleg away, drag the end. You run the fake power-off tackle, screen to the backside, whatever, but if you don't have all three facets of it, you really and truly have a conglomeration of plays.

I think, more important than what offense you run, it's about how you execute it and it's about calling plays. I had a folder that I always folded in my back pocket. People would say, "What do you have in that folder?" I had the game plan and what we wanted to do on first and second down. These are the things I wrote on the game plan every week.

Number one, get a first down. That's all the game is. Get a first down. If you get a first down, do it again, but get a first down.

Number two, when in doubt call a base play. If I wasn't sure what we were going to do, I called a base play. We run a play on first down, we get six yards, I'm going to tell you right now, we we're going to run the ball that next down.

Number three, learn something every play. Every time I called a play I wanted to learn something about the defense and what they were doing.

Number four, have a reason to call a special play. We all have special plays as a game plan, but don't just call it to call it. We have a reverse pass. We'll call the reverse pass because the safety is biting on the reverse, we aren't just going to grab it out.

Five, don't risk six yards versus six points. In other words, don't throw the out cut before you throw the out and the up. They say, "Well, they intercepted the out cut. We'll hit them with the out and the up now." No, we're going to run the out and up first, because, to me, I felt that was important.

Also, forget who you're playing. I don't care who's on that other side, we're going to run our offense. I only care about our team.

Last, make them beat us. Do not beat ourselves.

When I called plays, I wanted to make sure I had a game plan we followed. Many coaches follow it to this day, and it's infallible. I'll give it to you very quickly. There are five points.

Point number one, we must out-physical them and we must out-hit them. Point number two, we have to be the best fundamental football team on the field.

Point number three, we have to win the seven commandments. What are the seven commandments? Thou shall not turn the ball over. Thou shall not give up big plays. Thou shall not have foolish penalties. Thou shall not have stupid penalties, foolish penalties, missed assignments, big plays, turnovers, score every time we're inside the 20-yard line, win the kicking game, etc.

Point number four, we have to be better and closer as a family than the other team. The last point? Don't flinch.

When I'm calling plays I'm going to make sure we don't turn the ball over and that we don't make mistakes. That's just our philosophy. I always believe you should have an option in your offense, because I'm telling you – if they have to defend the option, they can't do it. You have an option in it, and I'll tell you right now, the first thing that scares defensive coaches is the option. I'm talking about you have a dive, a pitch, a quarterback, a pass, etc. That keeps people honest. When you can't block them, then finesse them. What an option does is the same thing as if the quarterback blocked the end.

The same thing when you're in the shotgun and you run an option with him, it's just unstoppable if you do it. I believe you can move the ball on anybody in this country. On offense, you're as strong as your strongest pursuit. You have a strong right tackle, you run over them. You have a weak left tackle, you don't.

On defense, you're only as strong as the weakest part of your football team. If you can't stop the run, they're going to run the ball. If you can't stop the pass, they're going to throw the ball. But offense, I love offense. It's bringing everybody together. I believe in little things. Huddle. We used to spend all kinds of time on the huddle. You lined up Nike on Nike. You're in the gap. You lined up. You broke the line of scrimmage. You checked your lineup, your splits. Do little things the right way. I believe in doing little things. The big things take care of themselves.

Dick MacPherson

Why do I love Lou Holtz? He was running the Houston Veer at North Carolina State, and we were running the same thing at UMass. We couldn't quite get it together, so I drove all the way down to New Jersey to listen to him speak at a clinic. He said he had about an hour for me – he had his family there – and after he got done, we went up to the place where he was staying. I don't think his wife was very happy he was going to spend an hour with me when she had the kids, so I was trying to get the heck out of there as fast as I could. To show you how tough he is, he told her, "Go down to the beach, have a good time. I'll see you in an hour." When I think of Lou Holtz, he's a heck of a guy. If I ever did that to my wife, I wouldn't be here today.

To me, when you're talking about offense and defense, and you're talking to a bunch of young people, they, I have no doubt, are going to get excited about moving the ball. You [have to] get the encouragement out of the Houston. With him, we were able to move the football. When you're able to do that, you control the football game.

By the same token, what you have to remember is this: the most important thing on a football team are the players themselves. Now, the assistant coaches are very, very important, but I'm telling you right now, the guy who somehow finds a way to get football players to come to his school, and be dedicated to football and academics, makes your job easy and it makes your job fun. I'm telling you right now if you listen to guys like Dr. Lou, you can't go wrong.

Fisher DeBerry

I believe in and I love option football. We felt like it was the system that gave us, and the type of talent we had at the Academy, the best opportunity to compete. I felt like we had a system, not just a bunch of plays. It was based on a system. My whole philosophy of offense is that I think you have a chance to win more consistently if you're a good running football team. You look at Penn State and what they've done year to year running the football. Being the Air Force, they always say, "Why don't you throw the ball more?" I used to try to tell them, "We throw the ball every doggone play. It's just behind the line of scrimmage." At the same time, I used to tell them, "Do they give you more points on the scoreboard when you score by pass or by run?" Of course, they can't argue with that. They still give six points. I believe fans and everyone would just as soon see a 50-yard run as they would a 50-yard pass play. The end result is the same thing. Lou Holtz influenced me a little bit back in the mid-'80s. I was at a clinic and he said, "You know, I did a little research. This past year, of the top 20 running football teams in the country, 19 of them had a winning season and no head coach was fired. So, I looked at the top 20 passing teams in the country. That particular year, 14 of them had losing seasons and four head coaches were fired."

That made a pretty big impression on me as a young coach. The predication upon what we did was, we didn't make a decision about what we were going to do with the football until the defense actually made its commitment. I thought that gave us a really good advantage. I do believe, if you're going to run the option, you have to read it. I think you're cheating yourself if you don't read the option. It takes a lot more time to do that, but I think you have a heck of an advantage whenever you can execute 9 against 11, and that's what it basically amounts to.

Bottom line is, it's an offense people are not seeing much of today. It's tough to get ready for. It's tough to get opponents to have a quarterback assimilate with the speed that you're doing the option and attacking. I felt like that gave us a good bit of advantage right there.

In contrast to what a lot of people think, I think the option is a good passing formation and a good passing attack. Having been an old secondary coach, I think play action passing is the most difficult to defend.

Barry Alvarez

I think one of the things that is important as you devise your offense, and you come up with a plan on how you're going to attack people, is what can you consistently recruit? You heard Fisher [DeBerry] talk about all the service academies. Because of the type of athletes they recruit, the best scheme for them is option football. When I took the job at Wisconsin, I had to take a look at the type of athletes we could recruit year in and year out. We don't have a lot of skill players in Wisconsin, but we have some of the biggest palookas you've ever seen in your life. I told my first staff, "The one thing we're going to start with is we can always have a good line. We're going to start with good lines. Particularly a good offensive line. That's what we're going to hang our hat on. We'll get the best skilled players we can. I like to be balanced on offense, but we're going to start by running the football first."

We've run the option, but we didn't hang our hat on it. We're a zone team. Having been a defensive coach, I want to give it a lot of window dressing. I want to use a lot of formations. I want to change strength. I want to see how the defense adjusts and changes strengths, and see if they communicate well in the back end. Did they line up properly? Are they sound in how they adjust to the strength change?

Lloyd Carr

Bo [Schembechler] always said his philosophy defensively was based on one thing: beating the teams he had to beat in the Big Ten to win the championship. He wanted a defense that would give him the best chance to beat the best team, and he wanted an offense that would have to attack that offense so that he could develop a tough team, a disciplined team, and a team that was well conditioned.

Bo ended up with a quarterback named John Wangler, who had major knee surgery and had very, very little mobility. Up until that time, Michigan's offense was option oriented, but Wangler was a guy Bo had a lot of confidence in because of his leadership. Essentially, what happened that season was that we had two tight ends and one flanker, and occasionally we would go to two wide outs. They'd call a couple of plays in the huddle. So, defensively it forced us to try to learn how to disguise our coverage's, because when we scrimmaged, which we often did in those days, if you didn't disguise it, they just ate you up. We had great backs, we had great linemen. We won a Big Ten championship and – that more than anything else – changed the offensive philosophy at Michigan.

It was no longer considered necessary to have a quarterback who could run the ball. By the time I got to be the head coach in 1995, I believed we had had enough outstanding quarterbacks and receivers that we could recruit a great quarterback to Michigan. If we had a great quarterback, we felt like we could really run a pro-oriented offense.

For a great offense, you have to be able to run the football. You have to be able to run the football when they know you are going to run it and when you know you want to run it. The second thing a great offense has to do is be able to score quickly. If you are ahead, you need an offense that can buckle it up, run the clock out, and win the game.

If you are behind, you need an offense that can use the clock and do all the things it takes to move down the field quickly.

So, that is the thing that motivated us offensively. From a recruiting standpoint, we wanted a guy who could stand in the pocket; he did not have to be a guy that could run.

Tubby Raymond

We are very, very fashion conscious these days. We see somebody do something, then we try to do it ourselves. Unless you have a great player, then I certainly wouldn't advise passing the ball directly back to him and letting him do everything, because it isn't going to work.

So, what we tried to do early is to devise an offense that would work even if we didn't have good football players. We did have some [good] players, but at the same time, we prepared for the time when we weren't going to have them.

The idea was we were going to take the ball from the center at the quarterback. He was going to handoff mostly, but he threw the ball occasionally. The quarterback was going to direct the offense and he was going to share the running responsibilities with the other three backs. If we found a guy who was real hot, we ran him. If we found two guys, we would work them together.

We continued to hide the ball, [use] misdirection, and do those things that we could teach people. That is really the basis of our offense, the basis of the wing-T.

Phil Fulmer

If you watched the National Championship Game last night, you know, if we had a perfect world we probably would want to be most like Alabama – be able to run the football, control the clock, and throw the play action pass. We adjusted as we needed to in '89 and a lot of it was just on whatever the defense was like. I was the offensive coordinator and our defense was really young, not very good, and hadn't grown very much. So, we ran the football 70 percent of the time, even though Carl Pickens and Alvin Harper and a bunch of really good receivers, and we helped our football team win games. We won 11 games because, from a philosophical standpoint, we ran the football, took care of the ball, and protected our defense. The next year we signed a couple junior college guys, our defense grew up and had a whole bunch of better players. We used those wide receivers and we ended up being very balanced, probably a little bit more to the passing, 60/40 to the passing game that particular year, and we still won 11 ball games.

So, I think running football, controlling, and being able to help your defenses anyway you can if you need to, and then being able to throw the football as your personnel will allowed to. Obviously when we had Peyton Manning, Peyton wasn't really that good, he was just well coached, but four MVPs later, nobody buys that too much. He was outstanding when he got there and he just got better. When you have him you leaned to the pass and surrounded him with players who could help you win games that way. I prided myself [that I was] able to have those conversations at any position, even though I'd been a line coach. As a young coach, I paid attention to how the quarterbacks and the receivers were coached and how to best get off-bump man, you know all those things. I think it's paid off for us at different times, that we could talk on the same level and come up with a philosophy.

You don't have to do it out of two backs either, there are so many ways to run the power play, or the down sweep, and all those kinds of things that are the same plays we all ran back in the day out of two backs. It really makes it much more difficult for the defense of a team to want to line up, to make adjustments, and you're still hitting them in the mouth. As long as you can hit them, and it doesn't just have to be the zone play, you can hit them in the mouth with power and a lot of different looks.

Dick Vermeil

[When I] started I thought you had to run the ball. If you threw the ball, you were a sissy. That was my basic thinking. I started out that way. I was head coach at Hillsdale High School for three years, and in my second year we won a conference championship and gave up, I think, seven points. Then I lost my senior class – my quarterback, my running back, my left tackle, and my all-conference linebacker. The next year I was not nearly as good a football coach. I realized then, players win games, not coaches. There are certain players on each team who are more critical to winning than others. You're never going to win if you don't have a quarterback, a good left tackle, a good running back, and somebody on defense who sets the tone and gets it all going.

We started using movement – shifting, including up down with the offensive lineman. We started doing things in the passing game. We were one of the very first ones to run the outside quick screen, now everyone is running it. We were running it in the NFL in 1978-79. We started these kinds of things that picked up the offense, and it started changing my thinking to be more aggressive. Yes, you have to run the football. There isn't any question in my mind about it. If I ask this room how you can move a ball offensively, most people will say by running it and throwing it. That's not true. It's by running and throwing a completed pass. Where guys get in trouble with the passing game, and get enamored with it, is they throw it 55 times, but they only have a 65, 60, or 55 percent completion quarterback. [You] can't throw it that many times with that guy, because it doesn't give you enough legitimate opportunities to move the football. The better the quarterback, the higher percentage of your offense, you would use with him throwing it. Fortunately, I ended up with Kurt Warner. I brought Trent Green in and he gets hurt. So, we put Kurt Warner in charge and he throws 65-70 percent complete and some games at 80 percent complete. So, you throw the ball a little bit more, but we always wanted to be able to maintain the ability to run the football in relationship to the quality of our quarterback. If you decide you're just banging your head on the wall in a game to try to beat these guys running the football, then you give that 65-70 percent quarterback an opportunity to try to throw the ball a little bit more. So, we opened up the whole scheme.

Al Saunders did a beautiful job for us in Kansas City within that philosophy of attack, movement and shifting. In the NFL it's amazing how many times we could break leverage using our shifting mechanics of a defense and exploit them. We hold the NFL record right now with the most rushing touchdowns scored in one game – seven times rushing the football in one game. It never happened before and it may never happen again, because all of a sudden the shifting mechanics broke down the mechanics of an NFL offense – a team that was undefeated at the time – and put 57 points on them.

So, a lot really depends on your quarterback. If I had it my way, I'd love to have a quarterback throw at least 65 percent of the time and run the ball 30 times a ball game. You don't get enough work in training camp against the run because you're working against yourself. You don't have scout teams. You're working against yourself and you have it do some things offensively to help your defense, and your defense has to do things that help your offense, as you look towards your first three games of the season.

I don't know if I've answered that question, but I know this, it all started back when Sid Gillman and I spent a lot of time with Don Coryell. You learn from everybody. I'll tell you this, if you think you're going to throw the ball 65 percent of the time or 60 percent of time, and the guy's only going to complete 50 percent or less, unless you have a heck of a defense, you aren't going to win many football games.

Marino Casem

I liked the old [David Nelson] wing-T system, the trapping system. Trapping has its mystiques. If you get a good trapping game, all the tall guys on the other side of the line are protecting their knees all the time. They don't know where you're coming from. I like the old wing-T system. Then it was something you could put your book on, the rules of the system told you what to do. If they changed the defense in front of you, the rules say if a man on your post block down, no man on your post block away. They told the guys, "If your number is called, you know what your assignment is." All they had to do was master that. You didn't have to go around making up plays.

I also believe in making it simple. They added one through nine across the front, having the same thing, one through four, right, one through four left. The technique is, left, you're going to run left. Right, you're going to run right. Keep it simple, but master it. Have something that is basic in style, but will understand the pressure of the game. You have to be known for something to be a builder. I wanted to be a builder of the trapping game. It sort of intimidates the defense, but it also has them always looking down. Again, you have to be strong down the middle. With a good center, good quarterback, and good fullback, you can win ball games. That's the reason I liked the trapping game.

Bill McCartney

My first three years at Colorado we won a grand total of seven games, but they were patient with us because it looked like we were recruiting well. Then, in the fourth year, we won seven more. Everybody was optimistic and believed we had turned the corner, then in my fifth year, we started the season 0-4. We had to die to get better. Everybody around the program was more than disappointed.

This was a key moment in my coaching career: It's Monday and things are gloomy. I put six chairs in the front of the team meeting room and I asked the starting offensive line to sit in those chairs, along with one of our tight ends. I should have learned faster from Coach Schembechler and his philosophy, but I really didn't. At this point, everything he taught me, we put it on the line. I turned to the team who was sitting in the chairs facing these six guys and I said, "What we're going through is a nightmare, but these guys right here are going to take us out of this, and here's how they're going to do it. Every time we snap the ball this week, they're going to SURGE." I won't do it to you, but I wore that word out. Your offensive lineman, by and large, are not well known names in the community. These are guys who put the team first. There's never been an offensive line who didn't want to run the ball.

So, here's what happened: All week long, we told our guys they were going to take us out of this nightmare. Sure enough, we win and we weren't overly impressive, but we turned a corner. Do you know what happened from that time on? With the philosophy "we're going to hit you in the mouth and create a new line of scrimmage," from that day on we won over 80 percent of our games. In other words, the whole program changed. When your offensive line dictates, your defense learns how to play against the run. Particularly in spring ball and early fall ball. It toughens up your entire program.

I would say to any of you out there – I realize there are many effective concepts that are very popular today, but when your offensive line takes over the line of scrimmage, your play action passes; there's more room to throw the ball, there's more time to throw it. Everything improves. I believe it all starts and stops with the offensive linemen.

Bill Curry

It'd be nice if you could line up and run the Green Bay Packer power sweep, and have guards like Fuzzy Thurston and Jerry Kramer, but, again, the NFL was basically a seven-man front. I confess that when I went into college football, I was very simplistic about what you had to do. I was strongly influenced by two guys, Dwain Painter, who worked with us at Georgia Tech, and Homer Smith at Alabama. They were incredibly flexible, and they had the capacity to teach a quarterback and give him absolute command of a football field. They had the capacity to make changes based on surprises the defense might present and to feel confident about executing those things constantly. I give credit to Dwain and Homer for educating me as I gradually learned what it was like in the complex world of college football. It's much more complex now than it was then, but we tried to live with that kind of flexibility and have quarterbacks who could, within the limits of their capabilities, run anything we needed to run on a given Saturday.

Jerry Moore

Like anybody else on offense, we were looking for skill guys. Up until around 2004, we were pretty small up front. We weren't as large as we probably should have been. We would make the playoffs and schools with larger offensive linemen were beating us. We had good skill kids, and we started getting a little bit bigger offensive linemen.

That's when we really got more into our off-season program, getting our guys bigger and stronger. We also wanted a quarterback who could run and throw; we didn't want a one-dimensional quarterback.

We wanted to be able to make critical situations. We'd put the ball at the nine-yard line. It'd be first-and-goal at the nine, then we'd put the ball at the three, first-and-goal at the three. We'd practice it over and over [until] we felt confident about scoring from the nine and putting the defense in a bind. We wanted to build confidence, and we wanted to build toughness. We scripted everything, and we'd have 16 or 18 plays. I'd tell our running back coach, "I want that running back to touch the ball 12 to 14 times." I wanted to see what he would do when he was tired.

Ken Sparks

My offense is a little bit different. We have an option identity. Sometimes it's one back, but a lot of times it's a two-back, split-back veer, and with a lot of motion and formations. We end our practice, at least early season and pre-season, with our guys running the option and try to read ourselves into a good, regardless of what the defensive does. On post-snap reads, we try to make sure we have every kind of option under the sun. We're basically a triple-option football team, and we make sure that we have a three-way option. We have two-way options because the defense is constantly making adjustments, so you have to keep up with the adjustment and be flexible in how you attack people.

Grant Teaff

In high school and college, I was exposed to the wing-T offense, which was a combination of power and option, but mostly power. I determined early on, if I was going to win football games, I must have a way to maintain possession of the football, use the clock, and ultimately score points. Ideally, you would get points every time the offense has the ball, but it just doesn't work that way. So, if you can't score, leave your defense in the best field position possible. Because the kicking game determined field position, specialty teams were always a vital part of my offensive philosophy. Honestly, field position can be the defense's best friend.

I had one other trait that concerned my coaches: I was very reluctant to give up the football once it was in our possession. Therefore, we developed short-yardage offenses designed to do that exactly – keep the football when you have a short-yardage down and score anytime you get inside the 10-yard line. The foundation was two tight ends and a power backfield with a setting halfback always to the right. We always ran the option and power plays with passes designed off the fake of the power play or the option. All plays were called at the line of scrimmage.

The tandem offense, as we called it, had a 93 percent conversion record on third or fourth down with two or fewer yards to go. However, there were a couple of times when that remaining seven percent was devastating. In 1985, playing Texas A&M at College Station, we lost the championship conference game 31-30. At the end of the first half, we were leading by 17 points. We were fourth and one on the goal line. We had taught our players to believe we could make a yard with that offense any place on the field. On that play, however, we did not. It is a regret that has haunted me throughout the years. Had I kicked the field goal, it is probable that we would have won by two points rather than losing by one.

At Texas Tech, we ran the veer out of the "I" formation with two split ends and a slot back. At Baylor, we went with the split backfield and ran the veer both directions. We were blessed with great running backs, one of whom was Walter Abercrombie, who still holds the career rushing yardage record at Baylor. The option pass to the split wide receiver was like gold. In my very last game, we played against Dick Tomey's "Desert Swarm" in the Sun Bowl. His great defense gave us fits with the option, but we scored on the option pass to wide receiver Melvin Bonner, which gave us the lead. We held the lead and went on to win 20-15.

Emory Bellard – the former great high school coach, assistant coach at the University of Texas, and later a head coach at Texas A&M – invented the wishbone with other staff members while at Texas. It propelled the University of Texas to a national championship. Emory once told me that his idea for the wishbone stemmed from the fact that we were running the veer out of the "I" formation while I was at Tech, and we beat Texas two years in a row. Emory experimented with the idea of using three backs and presented it to Coach Royal, who bought in, and the rest is history. Two other national powers – Oklahoma and Alabama – won big with it, as did hundreds of high school and college programs across America.

Chapter 6

Discuss your philosophy of discipline.

Don Nehlen

First of all, I think it's important when you recruit a guy that you know where he is on the discipline ladder. You may recruit a guy from the inner city, and you know you're recruiting a little bit of a problem because he hasn't had a good environment. On a scale of 1 to 10, he may be a 2 or a 3. Then you may recruit another young guy who has a great home and has been very well disciplined. He may already be a 6 or a 7. I think you have to understand where all of your players are on that ladder. You can't coach a football team or run a business without a code of conduct. You have to have one.

I think the more rules you have, the more trouble you're going to run into. I borrowed my rules from Lou Holtz: do what's right, treat other people like you want to be treated, and give me 110 percent. Those were the three rules that governed our football team at West Virginia. I remember we had a player on our team who was driving me crazy. I was looking for a way to get rid of this guy and he gave it to me. He went out and got in some trouble, so I called his mother and told her that I was sending him home. I'd already told my coaches I was getting rid of him. I'd already told the team. I called and talked to mom, and his mother says, "Coach, my sister's husband just died and they moved in with me. She has four kids. We have two bedrooms. We're in the inner city. If you send him home, he's either going to be dead or in jail in six months. I don't know which, but you can rest assured that's going to happen." So, I talked to my coaches and asked, "What do we do?" I talked to the seniors and I told them, here was my phone call, and I said, "I told you guys I was getting rid of him. I told him. I told everybody." You know how players are, they're sympathetic to a degree for sure. They said, "Hey Coach, we don't want him on our team, but let's make him practice. Suspend him for the next seven games, but let him be eligible for the last one. Make him come to practice every day and make him come to every meeting so we can keep track of him."

A lot of times, discipline takes a lot of different twists on you. In my particular situation, I handled my freshman a little bit different than I did my second-year players. I handled the third-year players a little different than I did my second-year players. I feel a kid who has been in your program for three years, he ought to be very special. He should not cause you any problems. The first-year player, you may have to give or take a little bit. I don't think the answer is just to get rid of them. If you're a coach, you don't just get rid of players, you want to try and make them better people and better men. Through your discipline program, you can do that. Now, you may have to work a little harder with certain guys. Some of my best players I wanted to strangle during the first year or two. Two or three of them came up and gave me a hug today, the very ones I wanted to strangle.

R.C. Slocum

One thing I think is really important is that the players have a very clear understanding of what you're all about, what your expectations are, and what your behavior expectations are. I tried to explain my rules in the homes when I went recruiting, so the parents would know and the young man would know. As Don [Nehlen] said, they don't all come in at the same level. You try to get the behavior you want and you constantly reinforce what you want.

We had a couple of recruits come in to visit one time. One of the things I would always do after the weekend was ask my players, "What about those guys? What do you think? We're not taking them." The players said, "We knew that, Coach. We talked and said, 'Coach is not taking those guys.'" It made me feel good that I had expressed my desire in terms of what we were all about so well that my players knew those guys wouldn't pass the test.

There are some coaches who have the philosophy of giving a lot of discipline to some players who don't play a lot, while letting the star players have a lot of slack. I always felt the opposite. If I could get my key players doing the right things, then the young guys coming up would have great examples and they would tend to follow along with the leaders on your team. The young guys will say, "If he doesn't let Johnny Holland get away with that, he's not going to let me get away with it."

I didn't [have any set rules]. I didn't want to paint myself in a corner that far because players are all individuals. My players knew that if they did something that would make the papers or embarrass themselves, their parents, or the school, they shouldn't be doing that sort of thing. If whatever they were doing would be okay with their parents or a member of the coaching staff, then it was probably all right to do. We wanted our players to have the character and courage to do the right thing. I think recognizing good behavior is an ongoing thing with your players. I don't think you can give them a rulebook and say, "Here are the rules. Anyone who breaks them is going to be punished." I think it's a daily thing of you setting the example with your behavior and the kind of conduct that you and your coaches have.

Also, I always felt like assistant coaches needed to handle the discipline of their players. If I'm coaching linebackers and I'm taking pride in my job, the head coach should never have to talk to one of my guys because I'm going to see if there's any problem coming up. I'm going to see it and get it worked out before it ever gets to the head coach.

Bobby Bowden

Have as few rules as you can. There's no sense having a hundred rules and not be able to enforce them. Cut it down, have as few as you can and enforce them. If my players break rules, then I'm going to discipline them. I'm known down in my part of the country as the second-chance coach because I do give my boys second chances. I don't want my boys out on the streets. I want them in the program, trying to help them. I have rules. If they break those rules, they're going to have to pay. A lot of fans and press think that, if you don't kick them off the team, you haven't done anything. I don't want to kick them off. There are some I have had to let go, but I sure don't want to. When a guy makes a mistake, the easiest thing to do is to kick him off the team. The press loves that, and you know the fans love a good hanging. I try to keep my guys in the program, but if somebody thinks I don't discipline, they're crazy.

I want my assistant coaches to handle the little problems. If a kid misses a meeting or he's late for a meeting, don't bring that to me unless you can't handle it. In other words, don't bring them to me unless you might be ready for them to get kicked off the team. Now, if you're about ready for him to get kicked off the team, then bring him to me, because I'm going to really back him into a corner. If it involves taking a scholarship away, taking them off the training table, or suspending them, then that has to come to me.

John Gagliardi

I think I come from a different planet completely. We say we want people who don't need rules. The only rule we have: treat everybody the way you like to be treated. The Golden Rule has served mankind pretty well. The kind of guys we get are very good students. They can't get in school unless they're a good student and they can't stay in unless they are a good student. I think that solves a lot of problems. They come from good families, so we don't have many problems.

When we go to the playoffs is the only time we stay overnight. We tell our guys, "We're not going to set any curfews or have bed checks." If you are high maintenance, then we have the wrong guy. We want the kind of guy who the teachers and custodians will come back and tell me, "Boy, the football guys are the nicest guys on campus." That's what we want to hear. The best ball players we've ever had were usually tremendous guys. I think that helps, to have your best players who are top-notch people. I don't have any discipline problems, but they're college guys. I'm sure they're not perfect.

Terry Donahue

I had what I referred to as on-the-field discipline. This kind of discipline was being on time, practicing at a certain tempo, being at your meetings, conducting your off-season program, being at the pre-game meal, and all the football things that go into your program. In regards to that kind of discipline, I really wanted our coaches to be firm, consistent and as fair as we could. That was an important kind of discipline.

There was also off-the-field discipline. That kind of discipline related to the player and how he integrated into the community and university. I wasn't as firm in that realm. I had a general rule that said you had a responsibility to conduct yourself in a positive manner and always represent the university, the team, your family and yourself properly. It was very vague and generic. I wanted it to be vague and generic, because off-the-field discipline isn't as consistent. On the field, I wanted the players treated the same. It lacked consistency if the quarterback coach chewed out the first-string quarterback one way and then he chewed out the third-string quarterback a different way for the same mistake. I wasn't comfortable with a lack of consistency in on-the-field discipline.

Off the field, I don't think you treat everybody the same. I don't believe you raise all your children identically. Your children are unique. They're individuals. So, off the field, I wanted to have the flexibility and freedom I needed, and use common sense in trying to make disciplinary decisions. Discipline's a hard thing. You have positives and negatives. As long as the negatives don't outweigh the positives, then you could stay. If the negatives begin to outweigh the positives, at some point in time, you have to cut your losses.

I had a player come in who had screwed up as bad as you can screw up. He wouldn't go to class. He destroyed our relationship with our professors on the hill. He wouldn't work out hard. He did all kinds of things wrong, so I called him into the office to kick him off the team. Before I kicked him off, I thought I would read him the riot act one last time. I gave him my best shot and my closing line to him was, "You've never done one thing here at UCLA to help us." I was really upset with this athlete. The kid leaned forward to me and he said, "Coach, I agree with everything you've just said, except that last statement." I said, "You tell me what you've ever done to help us win here." He said, "Coach, I'm one of the best recruiters on this team. I've hosted week in and week out, and I've hardly ever lost a guy. I've recruited a lot of good football players here for you." I started laughing. I didn't know what to do. He had totally disarmed me in this situation. I was looking at his negatives, and in my mind his negatives had outweighed his positives. I kept him on the team and he ended up being a good football player for us.

John Robinson

I think there are some similarities in our approach. As Terry [Donahue] said about another subject, it's environmental. I think your discipline approach on the West Coast or in the inner city is different from other parts of the country.

On the field, we had standards for certain positions. We didn't want the offensive linemen to run wind sprints the same as the corner-backs. If we asked him to, we wanted the tailback to carry the football 20 times in a row in practice. He couldn't raise his hand and say, "I'm going out." He had to measure up to that standard. We were very intolerant if you didn't measure up to that standard. If you were an offensive lineman, we tried to make it clear that you had to do the things the offensive linemen did. We confronted a player quickly on that standard and tried to teach them what the position required. We tried to talk to them about what the team requires and we weren't very tolerant if you didn't have what it took for the team. If you were tailback and you rush for 300 yards the game before, you had to get out there on time because you were the leader. If you were any kind of a star, you could probably date the best-looking girls and all of that, but you had a standard on the field that we expected.

You had to love football. We all know who those guys are. They'll play forever. When the game is over, they say, "Let's play more." Those were the guys we would go to the ends of the Earth for. For the guy who didn't love football, it's a different kind of thing.

There is respect for other people. Sometimes the physical kid can grow up to be a bully. When you get him out of high school, he is a bully. He's immature and he does stupid things. You have to begin to change those things before, because after the fact you're in a difficult position. There was always a balance with, how good is this guy versus how severe is our punishment. I think if you do too much of that, you wind up with a lack of trust by your team.

What you have to figure out is if this guy is survivable. Can this guy help us and can he help himself? One of the last things I remember Bear Bryant saying at one of these AFCA Conventions was, "I'll give a guy a second chance and I'll give a guy a third chance sometimes, but once I make up my mind that it's over, then it's over." I think he always said if he decided this guy wasn't going to help us, then he had to get rid of him. I made that mistake several times, I gave a guy one more chance and it didn't turn out well.

Tom Osborne

You always have to be consistent and make sure that somebody isn't getting by with something that somebody else is. I think everybody here understands that. The thing that was always a concern to me was that somebody would be picked up for a Minor in Possession and you'd suspend him for one game. Then, another guy would be picked up for a Minor in Possession, and you'd kick him off the team. The players wouldn't know the second guy – who you had trouble with two or three other times – was told the next time [he stepped out of line] we would have to get rid of him. So, the players would perceive that as being unfair.

I remember one time in a meeting someone said, "You not only have to be fair, you have to appear to be fair." I thought about that, and we thought, "Well, maybe what we ought to do is give the players some ownership in this thing." We had a team sports psychologist who helped us a little bit. He said, "Why don't we do something called the Unity Council?" So, we had each area of our team elect two representatives – two defensive linemen, two offensive linemen, two secondary guys, two running backs, and so on. We ended up with 16 guys who were chosen by the players. I got them together and I said, "Okay, I want you guys to do two things. One, I want you to let me know anything you feel is going on with this team that's interfering with team unity. Two, I want you to devise a disciplinary code, which I will oversee and I'll make sure I agree with it, but I want it to come from you guys."

They came up with a point system. If you missed class, that was one point. If you were late for practice or a meeting, that was two points. If you missed practice, that was three points. A misdemeanor offense was four points and a felony was five. Anytime a player got to five points, they didn't play. It could be one game, or it could be permanent, depending on how bad it was. If they had a perfect week and did everything right, they earned back a point. Once they were back to three points, they had to meet in front of the Unity Council, and those guys would rake the player over the coals. It wasn't long before every player understood who was consistently goofing off, missing practice and being late. So, players understood when discipline occurred. They were a part of the system. I don't think you want to totally give them the whole deal, but whatever they came up with, I approved it and then I enforced it. Once a player had four points, they met with me, and I would call their parents and tell them he was on the verge of not playing that week. Once a player had five points, he was gone.

I think giving the players some ownership, at least in our case, worked really well. Whether it would work for you, I don't know. They'd meet on Tuesday night, then on Wednesday morning I'd get a list from our strength coach, who had met with them. The list might say they didn't like the movie we saw last Friday and didn't like the food on the training table on Wednesday night. I'd get up in front of [the team] the next day and say, "We'll let you choose the movie this week, and we'll talk to the person at the training table about the food." I'd say 90 percent of those things were easily handled, but none of them would have ever come to my attention, because [an individual] player wouldn't walk in and say, "I didn't like the movie we saw last Friday." A lot of things were addressed that didn't become big problems, simply because we had the Unity Council in place.

Joe Paterno

I go back to years ago when George Welsh was an assistant coach. He and I were both assistant coaches together. When I got to be the head coach, he stayed on as an assistant until he took the Navy [head coaching] job. We'd start talking about rules, and George would always say, "Hey, let's not be like the Navy. Let's be like the Marine Corps. The Marine Corps only has rules they can enforce, and if you broke the rules, you're in trouble." That's been the way we've approached it. As soon as I get organized, we'll have a squad meeting. The first thing we go over is the rules: You have to go to class. You have to do this and that. We're going to monitor your class attendance. I have certain rules about the length of hair, earrings and things like that, that may be a little bit obsolete. If you don't like the rules, you guys get together and come see me, but if we decide what we're going to do, it's what we're going to do. If you don't want to go along with it, that's your problem, not mine.

We start out with rules I think are enforceable. Enforcing the rules off the field, to me, is the toughest part. Somebody on the staff [might say], "You can't do it, it's not fair, some kids have a different lifestyle." When they're on the field or in front of you, [you can say], "Hey, be on time."

Years ago, I had Franco Harris on our team. Franco would always be the last guy [to arrive] on the field. He'd meander out, and the kids would give him a little applause. I said, "Now, the next time you're late, I'm going to sit your rear end on the bench." I made a mistake. I embarrassed him in front of the whole football team, and he's a very sensitive man. I should have brought him in the office, sat him down in front of the coaches, and said, "This is what we have to have, Franco, and you have to do it." We were playing at the Cotton Bowl in Texas, and sure enough during one of our practices, Franco is two minutes late. Now what do I do? I benched him for the Cotton Bowl. I didn't start him. We had a really good player behind him, which influenced me a little bit.

Don't make rules you can't enforce. Don't make them for the sake of making them. Pick out the things that are important for you to have the kind of football team you want to have. The discipline you want to have is different. What I want may be different than what you want. I try to pick out rules I think are going to help us be a good football team. I want rules that will help our kids get an education, be an influence on our campus and be people who will fit into the social environment on the campus. If a guy goes around and he's a hotshot all the time, I don't like it.

Lou Holtz

I think discipline is essential to success. Most of our discipline was done through academics, as far as going to study hall and things along that line. Discipline is not what you do to somebody. It's what you do for somebody. Life is a matter of making choices. If you choose to do something, you have to understand what the ramifications are going to be.

When I was at Arkansas, we went down to play Oklahoma in the Orange Bowl. I had to suspend three athletes who scored 78 percent of our touchdowns. We were a 24-point underdog in the game, the largest underdog there's ever been in a major bowl. Nobody thought we had a chance to win because they were focusing on what we lost, whereas in coaching you focus on what you have. We won the game 31-6. I didn't discipline anybody. All I did was enforce their decision.

[In 1988, Notre Dame was] playing Southern Cal [in our last regular season game]. We're number one, 10-0. Southern Cal's number two, 10-0. The morning of the game I put the number one rusher and the number one pass receiver on the airplane and sent them home because of decisions they made. Now, I didn't choose to do that. They chose that because I said, "If you do this one more time, your fault, my fault, bus driver's fault, a heart attack, you're going home." They did it. They chose to go home. I enforced their decision. They said, "Oh, let us play." Just because you didn't honor your word, don't expect me to break mine. We put them on that airplane. When that plane took off I thought, "I'm not going to do that anymore. The next time I put them on the bus." They got home in four hours. It should have taken them four days. We ended up winning that game 27-10.

I think people have to understand what the parameters they can operate on are. It's like if two guys each got puppies. The first guy loved his puppy. All he wanted that puppy to do was love him, so he let that puppy do anything he wanted because he wanted that puppy to know "I love him." The other guy got a puppy, and the first thing he did was put a choke collar on that sucker. And every time that dog would go left or right, the choke collar grabbed it. Everybody said how mean and nasty that guy is to that dog. A year later the guy takes that choke collar off the dog. The dog runs the neighborhood. Everybody loves it, enjoys it. Why? The dog knew what it could do, what it could not do, what parameters [it had]. The guy who loved his puppy and let it do anything it wanted could never give it any freedom, because he didn't know what was right and what was wrong.

We get athletes at a very formative time in their lives. I think it's our obligation as coaches to make sure they understand the parameters. I told you I had three rules: Do the right thing, do the best you can, show people you care. That's it.

Now, when somebody violated those rules, whatever it is, academically, football-wise, this is how I had the conversation: "Jim, I'm often wrong, but I don't want to go through life being wrong. I don't believe you're doing the best you can in Spanish II. Here's why. You got an A in Spanish I, and you got a D in Spanish II. You missed class twice. You missed study hall once. You missed two to three times. I know that's not the best you can do, and I want to know why." I did not attack the performer, but I did attack the performance. I asked you to do the best you can.

If somebody has difficulty with the waiting lady in the dining hall: "Is that the way you'd want to treat your mother? Is that the best way to treat people? Is that the way to show you care?" When they walk in the room, is their attitude, "Hey, here I am. Look at me. It's all about me," [or is it] "There you are. Tell me about you. How can I help you?"

Now, by having those three rules, that's where all our discipline came in. I never attacked the performer, but I always attacked the performance. I never suspended a player where I didn't give him a road map of how to get back. Before I ever suspended a player, I drew up a contract. The contract said: I already have ample reason to remove you from the football team. This contract is not to remove you from the team, but to give you one last chance to become an integral part of the team. To do so, you will do the following, and we addressed whatever the problem was, whether it be academic, going to class, etc. He signed it and his parents came in and signed it. Usually that was enough, but if I did have to suspend them, I would always say, "You can get back, but here's what you're going to have to do academically, socially and football-wise."

I think our obligation is to get to the point where your seniors put pressure on the younger people. I expected very few problems from sophomores. I expected no problems when you're a junior. I expected you to solve problems when you're seniors. We also had a big brother. Every freshman who came on campus was assigned a big brother who took them aside and told them how we do things. They had to have a meal with them at least once a week their entire freshman year. At the end of the year, we had them evaluated as a big brother. It all goes back to trying to get people to understand the importance of doing the right thing, doing the very best you can and showing people you care.

Dick MacPherson

I just think that we tied [discipline] in with winning. If we're going to be great winners, we have to be disciplined people in all places of our lives. That's exactly what we constantly reminded them. To be honest, with these kinds of things, meetings with assistant coaches every day mean an awful lot. The greatest ability a head coach can have is to select people of ability. I think that's what we did at Syracuse.

In 1987 our football team took a pledge. They thought they were going to be a good football team and they policed it themselves. There was no drinking at all during the football season. That's what I talk about – leadership from within, from the staff and the football players. We ended up going undefeated that year, and what happens is the young people learn from it. The only way they learn from it is because people take on this pledge, and they commit to being successful in doing it.

So, it's the business of handling staff. It's the business of handling players. I just make the kids do it. If somebody's stepping out of line, the seniors get on them. This is the way we worked our whole football program. Peer pressure, in my opinion, is a heck of a lot better than coach pressure, because they have to determine themselves that they're going to have a legacy of excellence in everything they do. I think that's the way you accomplish it.

Barry Alvarez

The first thing we talk about with our players is accountability, responsibility, and what we expect from them. We tell them how we expect them to act, what's acceptable and what's not acceptable. They all know the difference between right and wrong. I'm also not one for a lot of rules. I think the rules should be fair. I used to sit down with our team, particularly our seniors, and we'd talk about setting up team rules. If the team set them, that is what we were going to do. I'll give you an example.

Wisconsin is a big beer drinking state. Kids in northern Wisconsin are drinking beer at the local pub at 12 years old. So I asked my players, "What about drinking?" My line tells me, "Coach, on Monday nights, we're going to have pizza and beer. That's what we're going to do." We adjusted and said this is when you can and can't have a beer, this is when you cut it off, but do it in moderation. I think just be reasonable and know that when you make a rule, you have to be strong enough to enforce it regardless of if it's your best player or your worst player. Be consistent with the rules, consistent with what you ask for day in and day out, and then live by it. Once you make rules, and live with a disciplined program, then you live by it.

Fisher DeBerry

They're young people. I'll agree, they have built-in discipline systems somewhat, but they have choices they have to make, too. I think the most important thing in discipline is being able to be consistent. We only had one rule and that was to do what was right. If you didn't do what was right, then you certainly suffer the consequences. Be consistent. I always wanted to put the discipline back on their shoulders, to not let each other down and to be accountable to their brother.

I used to ask them, "When you're out, and you have to make some decisions, ask yourself, 'If I do this, will it help us have a better football team? Will this be what my brother would expect out of me?' If it is, fine. If it's not, then don't do it and you will make the right decision."

Whether we won, lost or tied, I used to tell the team three things after every ball game as soon as we went through our little ritual of going around and hugging up our teammate's neck, and getting on the knee and thanking the good Lord for the opportunity of playing. I used to tell them, "Tomorrow is the Lord's day. Go to church." Second, "I want you to call your momma and family and tell them how much you love them, because a lot of the time, we fail to tell the people who mean the most to us in life how much we love them and, if it wasn't for them, we wouldn't be having the opportunity we have." The last thing I tell them is, "Remember who you are and remember who you represent. Don't go out tonight and do anything you'll regret. Always keep in mind who you represent." I think it's important we do that, but I do think in the

2006 Master Coaches

Don Nehlen

Bowling Green State
West Virginia

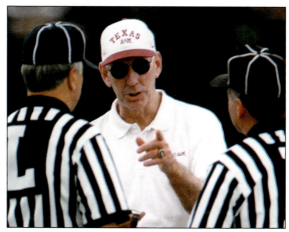

R.C. Slocum

Texas A&M

L to R: Grant Teaff, R.C. Slocum and Don Nehlen at the 2006 AFCA Convention in Dallas, Texas.

2007 Master Coaches

Bobby Bowden

Florida State

Pictured: Bobby Bowden (L) with fellow Master Coach Joe Paterno at the 2006 Orange Bowl.

John Gagliardi
St. John's

L to R: Grant Teaff, John Gagliardi and Bobby Bowden at the 2007 AFCA Convention in San Antonio, Texas.

2008 Master Coaches

Terry Donahue
UCLA

John Robinson
USC
UNLV
Los Angeles Rams

L to R: Grant Teaff, John Robinson and Terry Donahue at the 2008 AFCA Convention in Anaheim, California.

2009 Master Coaches

Tom Osborne
Nebraska

Joe Paterno
Penn State

L to R: Grant Teaff, Joe Paterno and Tom Osborne at
the 2009 AFCA Convention in Nashville, Tennessee.

2010 Master Coaches

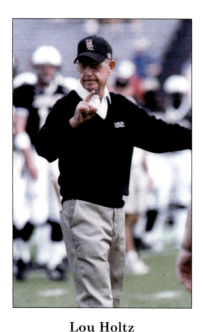

Lou Holtz

*William & Mary, North Carolina
State, Arkansas, Minnesota,
Notre Dame, South Carolina,
New York Jets*

Dick MacPherson

*Massachusetts, Syracuse,
New England Patriots*

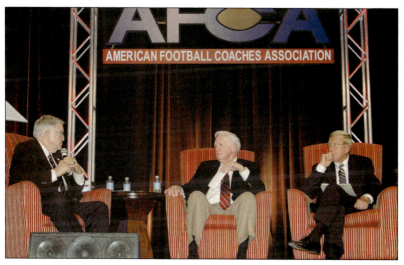

**L to R: Grant Teaff, Dick MacPherson and Lou Holtz at
the 2010 AFCA Convention in Orlando, Florida.**

2011 Master Coaches

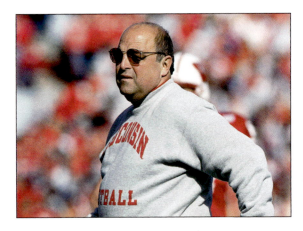

Barry Alvarez
Wisconsin

Fisher DeBerry
Air Force

**L to R: Grant Teaff, Barry Alvarez and Fisher DeBerry
at the 2011 AFCA Convention in Dallas, Texas.**

2012 Master Coaches

Lloyd Carr
Michigan

Tubby Raymond
Delaware

L to R: Grant Teaff, Lloyd Carr and Tubby Raymond at
the 2012 AFCA Convention in San Antonio, Texas.

2013 Master Coaches

Phil Fulmer

Tennessee

Dick Vermeil

UCLA
Philadelphia Eagles
St. Louis Rams
Kansas City Chiefs

L to R: Grant Teaff, Dick Vermeil and Phil Fulmer at the 2013 AFCA Convention in Nashville, Tennessee.

2014 Master Coaches

Marino Casem

Alabama State
Alcorn State
Southern

Bill McCartney

Colorado

L to R: Grant Teaff, Marino Casem and Bill McCartney at
the 2014 AFCA Convention in Indianapolis, Indiana.

2015 Master Coaches

Bill Curry

Georgia Tech
Alabama
Kentucky
Georgia State

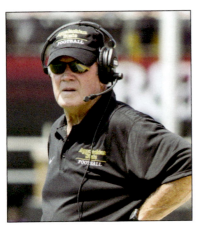

Jerry Moore

North Texas, Texas Tech
Appalachian State

Ken Sparks

Carson-Newman

**L to R: Grant Teaff, Ken Sparks, Jerry Moore and Bill Curry
at the 2015 AFCA Convention in Louisville, Kentucky.**

AFCA Executive Director Portraits by Tubby Raymond

Clockwise from top left: Tuss McLaughry, Bill Murray, Grant Teaff, and Charlie McClendon.

Left: Portraits on display in the boardroom at AFCA headquarters.

The Coaches' Trophy
The Symbol of Supremacy in College Football™

Master Coaches who have won the Coaches' Trophy:

Bobby Bowden, Florida State – 1993, 1999
Paul Dietzel, LSU – 1958
Vince Dooley, Georgia – 1980
LaVell Edwards, BYU – 1984
Phil Fulmer, Tennessee – 1998
Lou Holtz, Notre Dame – 1988
Don James, Washington – 1991
John McKay, USC – 1962, 1967, 1972, 1974
Johnny Majors, Pittsburgh – 1976
Tom Osborne, Nebraska – 1994, 1995, 1997
Joe Paterno, Penn State – 1982, 1986
John Robinson, USC – 1978
Darrell Royal, Texas – 1963, 1969, 1970

AFCA Awards Received by Master Coaches

The Tuss McLaughry Award

The Tuss McLaughry Award is given to a distinguished American (or Americans) for the highest distinction in service to others. It is named in honor of DeOrmond "Tuss" McLaughry, the first full-time secretary-treasurer of the AFCA and one of the most dedicated and influential members in the history of the Association.

1993
Tom Landry

1996
Eddie Robinson

2008
Tom Osborne

The Trailblazer Award

The AFCA Trailblazer Award was created to honor early leaders in the football coaching profession who coached at historically black colleges and universities. The award is given each year to a person that coached in a particular decade ranging from 1920-1970.

2013
Marino Casem

2015
Eddie Robinson

The Amos Alonzo Stagg Award Recipients

The Amos Alonzo Stagg Award is presented to the "individual, group or institution whose services have been outstanding in the advancement of the best interests of football."

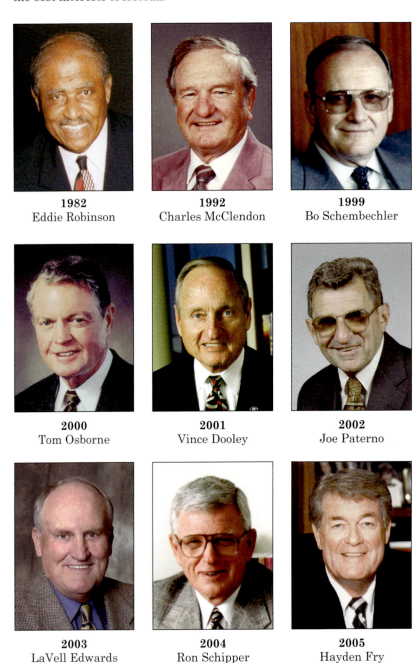

1982
Eddie Robinson

1992
Charles McClendon

1999
Bo Schembechler

2000
Tom Osborne

2001
Vince Dooley

2002
Joe Paterno

2003
LaVell Edwards

2004
Ron Schipper

2005
Hayden Fry

The Amos Alonzo Stagg Award Recipients (continued)

The Amos Alonzo Stagg Award is presented to the "individual, group or institution whose services have been outstanding in the advancement of the best interests of football."

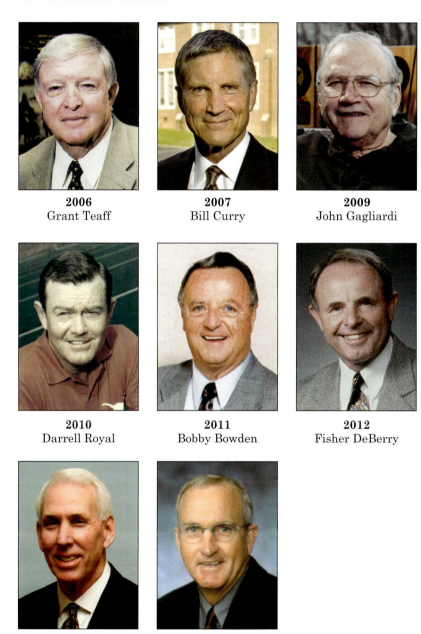

2006
Grant Teaff

2007
Bill Curry

2009
John Gagliardi

2010
Darrell Royal

2011
Bobby Bowden

2012
Fisher DeBerry

2014
R.C. Slocum

2016
John Cooper

Grant Teaff

Coach Teaff and Mike Singletary

Coach Teaff at Floyd Casey
Stadium in Waco, Texas

Coach and Donell Teaff at his
induction into the College Football
Hall of Fame in 2002

Coach Teaff being carried off
the field by his players

game, self-control is critical. You need to talk about self-control a lot. If they couldn't control themselves and it really hurt our football team, they were accountable to me for the rest of that week.

Hayden [Fry] told me something that I thought was pretty important: We all have to face some discipline problems at times. Kids make bad choices at times, but sometimes you want to make an impression on them. When you decide what you're going to do, just have that guy to come around and sit in your chair, and you go over there and sit in his chair. Say, "I'm you and you're me. Tell me, what would you do with you?"

Lloyd Carr

As coaches, it starts with the fact that we are educators. Part of our job is to educate our players. I brought in the FBI. I brought in the U.S. Attorney's office. I brought in the local police department, the university police department. I tried to educate our players on all of the dangers out there, all of those career-killing things you can get involved with if you are not careful.

I didn't have a lot of rules, because you can't keep up with all of the changes. You would be adding new rules every single day, and pretty soon it would look like the NCAA rulebook. So, what I try to say is this: "You embarrass this the integrity of the university, the integrity of our program, then we have a problem. I am going to deal with that. I am going to ask you this question: Do you want to be here? Do you want to stay at Michigan?" I never had a player who said, "No".

My basic way to deal with them, as they don't like to get up early in the morning, was to have them at Michigan Stadium at 6:00 in the morning walking steps. I went with them, because I wanted them to know they were going to have to prove to me that they wanted to be there.

I believe in second chances, but today, we are under scrutiny like never before. The job is tougher than ever, and you have to get their attention. You have to make them understand that you are going to do what you say you are going to do. That is really what we tried to do at Michigan.

Tubby Raymond

There are many [uses of] to the word discipline and I'd just like to take a look at [one]: discipline makes the world go around. Great discipline does a lot of things in this world and one thing it does is make great football teams. I talk about it often. We have to do the right thing, always, whether you want to or not.

The first aspect of discipline is being on time, which is a team thing, a respect thing. As far as the other kind of discipline goes, I never bought into the two-week suspension discipline, either you're in or you are out. Sometimes I was a little bit brisk with it, but our coaches just said to me once, "We need one of those dramatic firings." A dramatic firing is when you get in the middle of the field and say, "George, you are outta here. Leave the equipment in the locker." That sounds unfair, but we had a kid who was a fine player, defensive player, who was never paying attention in group work. He would make mistakes on the field and goof off. The night before a ball game, in our walkthrough, he had his helmet on sideways looking out the earhole. It was a dramatic firing. "John you are outta here, and I hope I never see you again." A good dramatic firing lasts about five years and will take care of a lot of discipline.

Phil Fulmer

I don't know how many of [you] guys were listening to Bill O'Brien a while ago. The Penn State story is one of the most impressive stories of this year's football season – all they came through, and for that staff and that team do that well. I thought he laid out his principles very well; from the time he spoke everyone eventually got around to understanding the expectations. You set those through the verbalization, but more through actions.

With the coach[ing staff] we used to talk about rat turds and elephant turds. Don't bring me back a rat turd to deal with. You manage those things. If something's bad out of whack, and I need to obviously handle it, then we'll get to it. Get them to a place they can find their role. I am very important part of that, or was a very important part of that, from a motivation and understanding of those expectations for kids. Buy into the family. You have a place here. You might be the best player on the team or you might be the third team left guard, but when it's all said and done you have a place here if you'll do things in the proper fashion.

You also have to be able to cut your ties. It's hard to do. I think Bill used the example of somebody stealing in the locker room. When they get into a bad place, you better make sure the team understands that you're going to stand up for what the expectations were.

Dick Vermeil

Over the years my philosophy of "discipline" sort of changed. I used to invest too much time, and waste too much time, disciplining things that made no difference in winning and losing. If you're on somebody all the time, they only hear you part of the time. So, I started boiling down what I thought was important to discipline. I started disciplining at least verbally and critically the things that made a difference in the outcome of a football game. If a guy walked into a meeting a couple minutes late you fine the kid making $3 million year $5,000. What difference does that make? He doesn't care, he spent that much last night at the bar. It's a different mentality. I really think it takes a good staff to zero in and discipline those things that make a difference in winning and losing.

Since retiring, I've read over 34 military books, all nonfiction, all starting with World War II or written by somebody there. It is amazing. I wish I would have started a reading them a long time ago. The things you find out, like in World War II they tried to determine what produced a Medal of Honor winner. What produced the greatest guy at Iwo Jima. You know what they found out? It wasn't the guy who had the shiny boots and never had any discipline points against him. A high percentage of them were the guys who drove everybody crazy in Boot Camp and all these other things, but put a gun in their hand and let them go to war and they were the best. It's amazing.

The other thing I learned about is that some guy was in a foxhole in Iwo Jima and somebody gets killed. They're disappointed that one of their guys got killed, but he was one of those guys who browbeat everyone, he called them stupid SOBs and thought that's what made him a great Marine. What really bothered them is when somebody who really cared about them got hurt. It made all the difference in the world, how they fought from then on. You took the life of somebody they really cared [about] and they were going to get you.

It's an overtone to all [the books I read]. Read the Navy SEAL books, read *Lone Survivor* or *Service* [by Marcus Luttrell], read Medal of Honor [by Peter Collier]. If you read those, you're going to find out that there's a big difference, but what makes the difference is true discipline.

Some people think discipline is when you call them an SOB and all those kind of things, which I'm totally against. I hired a coach one time who had been fired because he didn't do enough of that on the staff he was on. To me that's not discipline. If you can't communicate in a way to get the kid to care enough about doing when he's asked to, to the best of his ability, so he can make a contribution to winning and to the guy who lines up next to him, then I don't care what kind of rules you have, they aren't any good. I firmly believe that.

When I went to Kansas City I was there for five years. The president of the team, Carl Peterson, was a great administrator and a guy I raised in coaching. He said, "Dick I don't know what's wrong. You don't have any fine money," – because they collect fine money throughout the year and they'll turn 25, 30, 100 thousand dollars into the charity thing – "we're not raising any charity money." I said, "You know why? These guys care." Get them to care. If the discipline comes from them, it's a heck of a lot more important than some guy standing by the door waiting to see if a guy is going to be a minute late. It's a different mentality.

Plus, you're talking to a different kid today than you were [back] when my dad was talking to me. My dad invented verbal abuse. I worked hard in that freaking garage. I knew I was not going to be a mechanic and work in my dad's garage. I learned a lot from him, very simple common sense principles.

Marino Casem

You have to be a disciplinarian and you have to mean what you say. You have to set down the law of the land and they have to know it. It has to be simple. I didn't have a lot of rules, but everybody had to know them. Discipline comes from trust and education. They have to know and trust that you're going to do what you're saying you'll do. Then, you have to teach them about what you don't want them to do and what you want them to do.

Every assistant coach has to be a part of that discipline. Not only his position people, but he has to discipline everyone. We had what we call a squad list. Every coach has it. I don't care how many coaches you have. You go alphabetically and start at the first. They should end up with 11, 12 or 13 guys on their squad list. Now, I don't care what this kid does, this coach, be he the offensive coordinator, the defensive coordinator, the quarterback coach, the line coach – he's responsible for that squad list. They have bed check, they have to check if he's going to class. They have to monitor what he's doing in class and what he does in his social time. The kid doesn't have any spare time. He's part of the system. The assistant coach has to be on top of him.

If I ask a coach about a player, "Coach, number two, what is he doing? How is he in class? What about his discipline problem? Who is he going with?" He has to know everything about this kid. You have to be educated about the kid. Everybody on your staff has to be responsible for somebody. The squad knows that. You have to monitor them. Discipline will determine your eligibility. As I said before, you're responsible for getting that kid on the field on Saturday. If you have the best All-American in the world and he's not eligible on Saturday when you have to play, you don't have anything. That assistant coach has to be able to deliver that kid.

Bill McCartney

A lot of times, kids come from high school programs and they've had a lot of success, but there isn't necessarily a lot of discipline in those programs. Some kids come from homes where there's very little discipline. That first meeting, when the players come back, before we ever put the pads on, I think it's important to lay down the rules that are non-negotiable. In other words, there's no give and take here. If this happens, this is the punishment. When kids would break major rule violations, everybody knew you would not play in the next game. If you did it again, you would not play for the rest of the season.

Keep in mind, we were recruiting kids who were highly recruited from all over the country. Boulder is the kind of place where [the city] is alive. There's a lot to do. If you want to, you can pretty much get involved in anything. I think it's incumbent upon the head coach to understand what those rules need to be. If it's a minor rule infraction, then we're going to run you after practice, but if it's a major rule infraction, there's no compromise, there's no discussion. I will talk to your parents and you will not play in the next game. If anything like that happens twice, [you're not] playing for the rest of the season.

We were in Miami going to play for the national championship. Keep in mind, we wanted the game to be a reward. [Being] in Miami around the first of January is a great break in the weather for a Colorado kid. We had no curfew until two days before the game, then we tightened it up. I made it real clear. There are no exceptions here. Sure enough, my starting fullback, who was an outstanding player and a great kid, comes in after curfew. I put him on a bus. He lived in Los Angeles. Do you know how long it takes a bus to go from Miami to L.A.? He had a lot of time to think about it. It broke my heart. I'm telling you the truth. It broke my heart and I loved this kid.

Although I haven't coached in 20 years, I don't believe the way discipline works has changed. I believe you need to set clear boundaries and not compromise them. Those boundaries need to be fair, but you don't compromise.

Bill Curry

I had some coaches who were not in very good shape who were great coaches, and we somehow got past that. I think it starts with what [players] see in you, your work ethic and your personal habits. If you think you have some sneaky personal habits or some addictions, and you think players don't know about it, you're kidding yourself. They know.

I always come back to this same [example] when people ask me a question like this. I was in my fourth year at Georgia Tech. I had never gotten to play. I went to an assistant coach and said, "Coach, maybe I don't work hard enough." He said, "No, you work very hard." I said, "Why am I not playing?" He said, "Because you're not good enough and you'll never be good enough. So, get your education and help us recruit. Good luck." At the same time, there was another assistant coach named John Robert Bell, who eventually became the head coach at East Tennessee State and won a national championship, he came to my locker and said, "I know you can play. Would you come down to our practice field with me? Coach [Bobby] Dodd and I have been talking. We know you can play, and I'm going to work on your foot work."

Now, who do you think I was thinking about when I was in my tenth year in the National Football League? I owe everything to John Robert Bell. I did not have the discipline. I had not been a great player, had not learned to push myself really hard. When he took me down there and spent that time, he didn't have to hit me in the mouth. He didn't have to design sadistic drills. The fact that he loved me and showed me a few things, and then helped me practice them every day, was one of the things that changed my life, but first it changed my football performance.

Jerry Moore

We're in a great sport. I don't see why you have to have a lot of rules if you have respect for the game. We didn't have a lot of rules. At first, I had a list of rules. When I went to my first clinic, I heard Bud Wilkinson speak. He said, "Know what you want to do, work harder than your players, be fair, and discipline a hundred percent." Those are the four things I've tried to do.

We've tried to talk to them enough everyday in meetings, after a good practice, or even a bad practice, about respect for the game and the discipline it takes to be a good team, to be the kind of man you want to be. I think it is all related, discipline and motivation.

Ken Sparks

I think you have to be very consistent with discipline. They have to know your expectations for them. There can't be any guesswork. That doesn't mean you treat all the kids exactly the same, because some of them may need a kick in the butt and some of them may need a hug around the neck. There are times they need both. If you have rules, then you have to make sure you live with the rules. Don't make rules you're not going to enforce. Don't say anything to the kids that you're not going to do, because now you've torn up your whole discipline system and there's not trust there anymore. If they can't trust the coach, that will snowball into a whole bunch of things.

The thing that bothers me more than anything else is the entitlement kids have nowadays. They have their own brand they've worked on. It's all about me, me, me. I call it the disease of "me-ism." Meism is awful. If we don't beat meism, then it doesn't matter what kinds of rules we have or what kind of system we have. It's not going to work, because everybody is doing their own thing. In everything we do, we're trying to build an opportunity to give and earn what you get. It's changing really fast, but I think it's still the American way – earn the breaks you get in life. Consequently, we're trying to teach life. It's not just football. It's life. Football's the learning laboratory. There's not a better laboratory of learning than a football field, but if we don't execute our classroom the right way, then we're not going to teach the things that win in life. I'm going to stand before the Lord one of these days and he's not going to ask me how many football games I won. I wish he would, maybe I'd have a chance. He's going to ask me, what I did to teach life to those kids in my care and winning eternal life.

I can have rules, and I can enforce the rules, which I do. I'm the bad guy. One of our seniors stood up this year in senior week when we were giving testimonies. He said, "None of us like Coach Sparks." It punctured my heart. The reason for that is because I'm the disciplinarian. He disagreed with some of my discipline, but you have to have a structure where everybody understands how it works. Of course, the goal is to make it theirs. It has to be an inside-out deal. I can do the outside in. I can do the rules. I can run their fannies off. I can keep them from playing in ball games, but until it becomes theirs, it's artificial, and it doesn't really work.

Grant Teaff

Don't create rules just to have them. All guidelines should have a specific purpose and rationale behind them. Discipline involves the total person. Sometimes, just to clarify my own thinking on certain subjects, I go to the dictionary to get a clear definition. Discipline is defined as "the practice of training people to obey rules or a code of behavior using punishment to correct disobedience."

I'm not a big fan of the punishment part of that definition; however, I am a disciplinarian and there are times when punishment must follow disobedience. Personally, I would much rather teach the value of becoming self-disciplined and the importance of being within the guidelines of the team or the law of the land, as well as team rules. I am also a great believer in peer pressure.

I think I was the first coach in America who used the concept of a player's council. Players must buy into the total concept of a winning football program, which includes following the guidelines and rules laid out by the coaches and the team. Each class elected three representatives to serve on the player's council.

I always enjoyed the time set aside each year to personally meet with the freshmen to lay out the importance of why they were in school and how they could be successful getting their education. Class attendance was most important, of course, but also completing assignments on time, using the library, and creating a positive relationship with each professor. We taught players the fundamentals of leadership and the importance of self-discipline. At the end of our time together, we asked them to select three of their teammates to serve on the player's council. The player's council nominated the candidates for captain each year, and then the entire squad would vote. Our captains did not have to be seniors. A great example of this was Mike Singletary, who served as a captain for three years beginning with his sophomore year.

Many incidents that needed disciplinary action never got to me, because the player's council would deal with the individual or individuals to settle the situation. On one occasion, a player was caught stealing from his teammates. The leaders of the player's council met with that person and told him he needed to leave school. I did not disagree with this decision, because I am sure I would have made the same call.

Teaching self-discipline and self-control was the foundation of our discipline. If a student-athlete learns to be self-disciplined and self-controlled, he has a high percentage chance of having a very successful life, whether on the football field, in his marriage, or in his chosen profession.

As an example of what can be done with personal discipline, let me cite something that took place in our program. Baylor's offensive line coaches, F.A. Dry and Bill Lane, were emphatic with their offensive linemen concerning penalties. The offense can execute a play flawlessly for a touchdown, and then one of the eleven can have that play called back, plus/minus yardage for the penalty, because of a lack of discipline. These coaches emphasized that so much, and their players bought in so completely, that Baylor's offensive line in the mid-80s went for two years without a penalty.

Self-discipline is essential in the classroom, for personal relationships, and for husbands and fathers. Ultimately, self-discipline can play a strong role in the student-athletes' chosen life work.

Chapter 7

Discuss your method of motivation.

R.C. Slocum

We always tried to emphasize the pride factor of who we were. When you watch game tape, you have a number and a name. If a stranger watches that tape, he could tell a lot about you by how you played. He could tell the pride in yourself, the pride in your name and about the effort you gave. We tried to sell the team atmosphere – guys caring for each other and pulling together for team goals – which turned into a pride factor.

I always felt it was important to have some team settings. We would put the game tape on and watch with the entire defense and coaches. Different position coaches would be with their group of guys. I would run the tape and if I had a guy who was not chasing the football, for example, I'd stop that thing. I would run it back four or five times and say, "We're all in this thing together. Tell this group, why are you not chasing the football, son? Everybody else out here is knocking themselves out trying to get to the ball. Are you hurt? If you're hurt, tell me and I'll get you out of the game." One of my former players was Ray Childress and he played hard. When he was on the team, I would run the tape and say, "I want you all to look at this guy. He got knocked down, but he got up and saved a touchdown." I would also point out things that were undesirable behaviors. I would do it from a personal standpoint with off-the-field behaviors or maybe a quote from the paper. I would make a point in front of the whole team and say, "Joe, that was a great quote. I want to read you all what he said about our team's performance, and how that makes our whole team look, and how that's good for all of us." See, you try to build pride in a team. The next time a guy gets an opportunity for a quote, he's thinking about the point I made in that meeting.

Whether it was on offense or defense, we had a standard of expectation. With the Wrecking Crew defense, we got to the point where I wouldn't even have to tell them it was a bad performance, they knew. If we'd given up a bunch of yards or a bunch of points, those guys were saying, "Man, that's not us." I think you have to build on the pride aspect as a group, not as an individual, because there's not a guy in this room who can win a championship [alone]. If we're willing to put all of our talents in one pile, then you have a chance.

[With offense, it's the] same kind of deal, every player can't be quarterback. We don't have enough balls. Then you have a tailback who wants to carry the ball and a fullback who wants to carry it. I believe we're born selfish. If you don't believe me, take two or three kids who are two years old and put them on the floor with two or three toys. They will start fighting because each of them wants all of the toys. As you get older and become more mature, the logical thing is to give each kid their own toy and they will play with it for a little bit, then get tired. Then you switch the toys around so everybody gets a chance to play with all the toys. Same thing for a football team, we can't all carry the ball. We can't all catch the ball. We have to all work together and do what's best for the team. When we do, the byproduct will be players who will earn all-conference and all-America honors, but it's only as a byproduct. We don't start off saying that's what we're shooting for.

We start off with a hope that our guys will turn into a cohesive unit. We're looking for guys who want to be a team. We don't want some guy who's putting his shirt wrong side out in practice. I made our team dress alike. I would say, "Son, why are you trying to be different from your teammates? I want you to fit in. This is a unit we're trying to build. We're not trying to build a bunch of individuals."

Every coach decides who gets on the field. The one thing every player can do, regardless of ability level, is play hard. [The rest] is up to a coach. I've had coaches say, "Well, we're not too good this year. We don't have this." I said, "You know what? If you don't get your guys playing hard, you're not going to be good anyway." You decide who gets on the field and it's a starting point for motivation. The first requirement to get on the field is to give all-out effort. It sounds simple, but you see teams who don't play like that. Just give me some guys who will play hard all the time and as I get better players, the team will get better and better. If I don't get that established, it doesn't matter what kind of talent level our team has, we're not going to be very good.

Don Nehlen

I agree totally with R.C. When I think of motivation, if all the things in your program are special – if the locker room is clean, if the coaches dress sharp, if everything you do is first class – I think that's the kind of performance you get. There are a lot of little things that work towards motivation. I remember early in my career, we were playing Florida in the Peach Bowl. It was the mismatch of the year. They had a particularly great football player who was a defensive tackle. I had a player named Keith Jones who was a pretty good offensive lineman, but he was no match for this kid. When I gave the scouting report, I said, "You know, Keith, you're a senior. Maybe we can tell the newspaper that you got the flu and you won't be able to play against this guy. This is big time. They're going to have television cameras and they're going to zoom in on this All-American from Florida. I don't want anybody blaming me for you getting hurt." He looked at me and kind of snorted. Anyhow, that was how I talked to him all week and he played a fantastic football game. That was one way I used to motivate certain players.

If the coach is honest, consistent, and fair, and everything is classy in the entire program, [players] have a tendency to play that way. I always told my coaches: "After practice, if Johnny gets on the telephone and calls home and says, 'Mom, Coach thinks I'm special,' do you think I could motivate that kid? You bet I could." On the other hand, if that kid calls home and his dad says, 'Johnny, how you doing?' 'Well dad, I don't know. I don't know where I fit. I don't know what my role is.'" I'd say to my coaches, "Do you think I could motivate that kid?" I think it's a combination of what [that and] R.C. said about being a pride thing. We would do the same thing on the film. If some kid is loafing. I don't say a word, I just run it back and back. When I worked for Bo Schembechler, he was beautiful at that. His players hated to go into that meeting on Sunday. If one player didn't do something, the old man would sit there and hit play back for 20 minutes. Then he'd get up and say, "This is Michigan football? You have to be kidding me!" He may never even say the kid's name, but they all knew who he was.

There is an expectation level you can get, just by expecting. You know, kids love it. They want to be good and they want their coach to establish rules. So many coaches don't tell their team, "Hey, you're expected to win." That's what we're teaching. You either teach winning or you teach losing. There isn't any middle. There's a million ways to motivate, but if [the kids] feel like they're special, and they know what their role is on the team, chances are you're going to be able to motivate them.

Bobby Bowden

If you want to have a motivated team, then recruit self-motivated players. Recruit players who are motivated so you don't have to worry about it. I tell my coaches, "Men, we have to recruit guys who are motivated to play, who want to pay the price." All week, I let my coaches coach. All I do is sit and watch, I get up on the tower so I can see everything. If I get on the field, then all I can see is what's right in front of me. When I see something going wrong, I'll write a little note on my pad. I'm not going to yell at a coach and embarrass him. I'm going to write a little note saying, "You're not teaching that guy to stay low. You're not teaching that guy to do this. You're missing this. How come you're not doing this? Watch No. 37 because he is loafing when you're not looking." The next morning at our staff meeting, I read my notes to those guys. It's their job to get all that stuff corrected. As I write notes, every now and then a thought will come to mind of what I have to do to win on Saturday. A thought might occur to me like, "we have better speed than our opponent, so let's utilize it." I'll write that down. I saw in the paper this morning where they said we were not tough, so I write that down.

I compile a bunch of notes, and when I talk to the team the night before we play, I have all those notes and I try to read them all to motivate them, to make them want to go out there and play. I've always felt that you're going to play 12 games and you might have only three fire-ups. You might fire them up three times, but you're not going to fire them up every Saturday. So, you better recruit kids who are self-motivated. As we know, they're not all like that so get good followers. Get guys who will follow those guys who are motivated.

John Gagliardi

I think motivation comes from being well prepared. We say we have no goals, we just have high expectations. We don't fool around with goals. We've been good for a long time, and we expect to continue to be that way. We want our guys to be very confident but not cocky. I think if you're successful, then it breeds success. We don't holler and scream. Our halftimes are very calm, we just talk about a few things. We say things like, "We just have to execute better. Things are going okay, we just have to do it a little better." I don't know what you can do after Friday. It's a little late. I think it's all in preparation.

Terry Donahue

There are a lot of different kinds of motivation. Obviously, the best kind is self-motivation. Having people who are self-motivated to accomplish goals is by far and away the best kind of motivation. There are lots of other kinds. There's authoritarian motivation where you say, "You're going to do this, because I said and I'm the parent and I have the authority." There's a way to motivate with reward. For example, "If you'll do this, you'll get these good things." You can motivate with fear, "If we don't do this, then this is going to happen to us."

I've had all of those either work on me or work for me. The most important thing about motivation is surrounding yourself with people who understand the objective. One of the greatest thrills I ever had in athletics was doing the Army-Navy game as a commentator. I did three Army-Navy games and it was one of the most emotional experiences that I've ever had. It was an experience where I had a chance to go into a football program way different than the ones I had been associated with and see how people look at an objective. They have a job to do in the Armed Services and their players approach [football] like that.

They approached it [as though it was] their job and that was how they were going to do their jobs. I have always marveled at the Army-Navy players, for what they are able to do and how they are able to accomplish things.

Making sure that everybody understands the objective and what we want to get accomplished is all a part of motivation. There are many ways to motivate. When I was a player, they all worked on me. I wasn't a very good player and I was in fear of my coach. I played for a huge man named Tommy Prothro. He was very standoffish. We had three starting defensive players on our defense – Dick Donald, Erwin Dutcher and me. There were many occasions when I'd be walking down the hall of the athletic department and I'd pass by Coach Prothro and say, "Good afternoon, Coach." He'd say, "Good afternoon, Donald." The next day I'd walk by him and he would say, "Good afternoon, Dutcher." He wasn't sure if I was Donald, Dutcher or Donahue. That motivated me because I wanted to prove to Coach Prothro who I was so he would know me. He used that to motivate me and it worked. Now, you couldn't motivate Mel Farr or Gary Beban, our Heisman Trophy winner, like that. That wouldn't work on them. You have to use motivation specifically designed for the kind of people you're trying to influence.

When I look back, we had a lot of games we were not expected to win; the 1984 Rose Bowl against Illinois was one. We went to the Rose Bowl with a 6-4-1 record. We had started off 0-3-1. We found our sea legs and somehow won the Pac-10 conference. We were up against a very good Illinois team. They were a heavy favorite over us. They were the fifth ranked team in the country. The night before the game, half of our team got food poisoning and didn't come to the pre-game meal. Some how, our coaches were able to pull that football team together.

Our starting quarterback, Rick Neuheisel, was in the back seat of a car, throwing up. We couldn't put him on the team bus, because I didn't want the players to see that the quarterback probably wasn't going to play. We had three starters who didn't play in the game because of food poisoning. Our football team was able to go out and win that game [45-9]. I think it was because they were motivated out of fear that we were going to get the dickens beat out of us if we didn't play faster and quicker than we ever played.

The players today need positive reinforcement. So many players come from split or fatherless families. Today they really need a pat on the back. They need positive reinforcement today more than athletes have ever needed it in the history of football. I don't think you can motivate the way you did 25 years ago. I don't think it's just the modern-day athlete. Society as a whole is different.

Let me go back to Tommy Prothro to reinforce this point. We were going to play the University of Missouri during my junior year. Missouri was a very good team; they were undefeated. I'll never forget that day. Tommy Prothro stood up in front of our team and said, "Now fellows, this week we're going to play Missouri and they are a really good football team. I'm not sure that, even if you play your best, you can beat Missouri. Next week, we're going to play Cal-Berkley. It's really important that we beat Cal-Berkley because it's a Pac-10 team. I think if we play our best, we might be able to beat Cal-Berkley. If you want me to get you ready to play Missouri, we'll get you ready to play Missouri, but I don't want you flat for Cal-Berkley." He told a group of players that he didn't think we could win. We didn't beat them, but we tied them. I don't think you could do that today. It would probably be received negatively by today's athletes.

John Robinson

I've always believed in you-can-do-it motivation. I would walk up to a guy and say, "You can do it. I know you can do it, and I won't accept anything else." Then I would find things he did on the practice field that I could point to and say, "Yes, you did it." If there was a good play or a guy did something good during practice, I would have our film guy put it on tape for me. When I'd see the guy coming down the hall, I would ask him to come to my office. In the office, I would turn on the play and say "See, you can do it." We tried hard to have those visual and verbal plans to make a guy believe he can do it. You also have to put in the bad play and ask, "That was you, but that's not really you, is it? You're more like this other guy." I constantly confronted people with the idea that they could be great and if they didn't live up to it, then they were letting themselves down. That was my kind on approach.

As far as the game, I remember one of the most exciting games for us was in 1978. We went to Alabama, who was ranked No. 1 in the nation. We were ranked No. 7. For some reason, it was the big game of the week in the nation, but we were not considered to have much of a chance. Fortunately, the image at USC – that was there long before I got there – was we're as good as anybody. We played that up, "They don't think you're any good," and "They don't think you have a chance." We won that game [24-14] and that is a good memory.

One story that happened with the Rams was when we went to play the Philadelphia Eagles in the first round of the playoffs. Buddy Ryan was the [Eagles] coach. He was a very confident, forceful guy. We check into our hotel rooms and *The Buddy Ryan Show* is on TV. They ask Buddy, "What do you think you can do against the Rams tomorrow?" He said, "Anything we want to. This is a high school team we're playing. Our offense will crush that phony defense of theirs, and we'll take down that running game." He went on and on. It was actually funny, but it scared the living heck out of me. Our players were all watching and we were every bit as good a team as they were. Our players all came down the next morning and they had a quiet [air] about them. I was still all shook up. We went out there and smashed right through them. That's the only motivation I ever experienced from another team. I went over after the game and said, "Thanks, Buddy, I appreciate that." He didn't respond well to that.

Tom Osborne

Speeches don't do it. The fans, and sometimes the media, think it's what you said five minutes before they went out on the field, but five minutes before you go on the field those guys don't even hear what you're saying they're so keyed in to what's going to happen. It starts on Monday.

There were a few things I thought were important. I remember one time we were at a road game, and the locker room was crowded. I was standing outside, right next to the other team's locker room. The coach starts hollering at those guys. He was talking about Nebraska and tearing our heads off, and pretty soon I was scared. They were ahead 14-0 before we really even had a scrimmage play. I think they scored on the first possession, and then we got the kickoff and fumbled it in midair, and they ran it in. We hadn't even run a play from scrimmage. The final score was 48-14.

The thing that I want to get across to you is that I never tried to teach hatred and didn't pay much attention to this bulletin board stuff. I didn't tell them we had to go knock this guy out or whatever. We helped them up, and patted them on the back, but we're a very physical football team. This may sound a little goofy, but there's something called a galvanic skin response [now called electrodermal activity] that checks your emotional state. If you wire somebody up, you can't tell the difference between fear and anger. You get the same response. Sometimes a team who's motivated to hate, to be very angry and aggressive and nasty, can become a very fearful team if things don't go right. The most powerful emotion and the most effective emotion is love.

I was talking to the Commandant of the Marine Corps. He said they had to change their whole training, which used to be pretty dehumanizing. He said, "We finally, through research, figured out the reason somebody would go up a hill into a machine gun nest and risk their life wasn't because of the way they were treated in boot camp or because we humiliated them. It was because they really loved and cared about their fellow platoon members, and they didn't want to let them down." If you have a team who's very tight, who really cares about each other, it's really powerful.

I remember one time we were at summer conditioning. I was walking to my office and I saw this one guy take off. They were wearing sweat clothes out there, doing some drills. This guy – Jason Peter – took off 30 yards and tackled a guy. I called him over and said, "Jason, what in the world are you doing?" He said, "Well, the guy was loafing." I said, "Well, he might have been loafing, but you could have hurt him." But that was the kind of leadership we had from some of those guys. A lot of the motivation came from them.

Motivation starts on Monday and it translates to practice. We had 12 offensive goals, 11 defensive goals, and 7 kicking goals. We measured our performance on those goals. We'd put them up on a board and if we hit 9 out of 12 of those goals offensively, we played well. If we hit 10 out of 11 on defense, we had a great game. Those guys would win by 30 points and they'd walk out of the meeting room with pretty long faces, because the goals weren't very good. The goals would be things like six yards per carry average on offense and three yards per carry on defense. One or no turnovers on offense and three turnovers on defense. Those were things that translated into how we practiced on Monday, Tuesday, Wednesday and Thursday.

If you can break the game down to where you're not just shooting for a Friday night or Saturday, but you're shooting for how you do things every day, I think it really makes a difference in your team. They'll be ready to play by Saturday if they've done it right on Monday, Tuesday, Wednesday and Thursday.

Joe Paterno

Our motivation has to start when I meet with the squad [the first time]. It has to start with, how good do we want to be? We thought we had a shot this year playing for all the marbles. We didn't do it; we were careless, sloppy at the end. So, I think you start off with the idea, "How good do you want to be? Here's what it'll take to do it." I think the worst thing you can do – and I think Tom [Osborne] mentioned it earlier – in a relationship with players is get after kids for every mistake. I may have indicated we do that; we don't. I'll get the squad together, and I'll say, "Here's where we are. We think we have the makings of a really good football team, but that means you have to have a heck of a winter program and you have to get yourself ready for a heck of a spring practice."

In spring practice, I try very hard not to designate anybody as one, two, three or four. I move them around a little bit. I keep telling the kids, "Don't waste time when you get on that practice field." We have a blue line and when they hit the blue line they run on the field. I tell them, "Once you hit that blue line and you're on the practice field, you're mine. You're the coaching staff's, and they're going to try to make you into the best football player you want to be. You can't worry about your girlfriend, all right? Because there's nothing you can do about it. She may be downtown with some guy, but there's nothing you can do about it. You're right here. Now, let's make the most of it. How good a football team do you want to have? How good a player do you want to be?"

If you see a kid getting a little down, you don't try to be a buddy, but you try to relate to him: "Either you get better or you get worse." If I say that to a squad once, I must say it a hundred times, "Either you get better or you get worse. There's no sense going out there unless you're going to come off that field a better player," – Now, that won't work every time, but that's what your goal should be. – "Sooner or later, you're going to be a pretty good football player, and we're going to be a pretty good football team. It doesn't happen in one day. It isn't easy."

Going back to what Tom said about his unity group, that group should have a great impact if you get the right guys, because they obviously are concerned about how good their football team's going to be. They're going to grab some guy who they know can help them. He's goofing off, and he's not giving a hundred percent on the practice field. He doesn't feel like he's something. They can help you. Motivating a team is not a one-day affair. I think it's everything you do in practice. You praise your kid if he makes a second effort.

Tom also brought up something here that, to me, is one of the problems we have in our sport, which is the business about building up hate of the other guy. This is what I think both Tom and I feel, that we should be respectful of the other team and hope he plays his butt off against us. We're going to play better, and we're going to beat them.

Lou Holtz

Somebody asked, "How do you motivate a football team?" I said, "Eliminate those who aren't." That's probably the easiest way.

Motivation, to me, is nothing more than having a goal that a person wants to reach. Now, everybody needs four things in their life: something to do, someone to love, someone to believe in, and something to hope for. I felt the obligation to coach and to get athletes to set some goals for what they wanted to achieve. I listened to Gary Patterson [speak at the 2010 AFCA Convention]. He talked about goals. I wanted to know what individual goals players had and then show them how they can reach it. We had goals as a team as well, just like [Gary] did.

When you set your goals as a team, remember the word win. Decide what you want to do and ask yourself 25 times a day, "What's important now?" If you want to win a championship, you wake up in the morning and ask yourself, what's important now? Get out of bed. What's important now? Eat breakfast. You need your strength. You want to win a championship? What's important now? Go to class. Sit in the front row. You're in a weight room. You want to win a championship. What's important now? To get stronger not because somebody's looking or somebody's going to applaud you, but because you know, that's what you have to do.

When you're out Saturday night and there's booze and drugs and sex ... You want to win a championship? What's important now? You better avoid that situation.

So, you get people to have a dream and get them to believe they can reach it by understanding the word win. When you set dreams and goals, things happen. Martin Luther King made one of the ten greatest speeches in the history of mankind when he stood up in front of hundreds of thousands of people and said, "I have a dream." It motivated people and it inspired people.

One man had a dream and changed this country for the better. Let me ask you this, in all due respect to Martin Luther King: Do you think that speech would have had the same effect if he stood up and said, "I have a strategic plan I want to show you?" I'm telling you strategic plans don't excite people, but having dreams and goals do. So, we would set a goal that we want to win the championship this year.

Point number three, we want to win a championship and we want to win it this year. What talents do I need to acquire in order to have that happen? We have to be able to throw better, block better.

Point number four, who do I have to work with in order to have this happen? Point number five, what problems and obstacles am I going to have to overcome in order to do it? Point number six, what's the plan? I told you the plan about toughness and fundamentals.

Point number seven, how will everybody on this football team benefit by us winning the championship? You have to sell that third team member that, winning that championship, his rank is going to be the same size as an All-American. Everybody has to understand how they're going to benefit if you reach your goal. To me, motivation is nothing more than having a goal and a belief that you can achieve the goal.

There's a rule of life that says you're either growing or you're dying. The grass is either growing or dying, so is the tree, so is a marriage, so is a business, so is a football coach. It doesn't have a thing to do with your age. It has everything to do with you trying to get better. You're here, and I admire you people here. Other people out in the lobby are talking. You people are here because you want to get better. Why do you want to get better? Because you want to achieve some dreams. That's all it is. Get them to dream.

Dick MacPherson

You know, when I think of motivation, I think of football. I want you to know that as I look around this room, this is what football is all about, because you're going to take this back home. Wherever I have been if there was a good high school football coach, that town had a great chance for success.

I believe in football, as much as I believe in everybody in this room. You know, this is a lot of fun and it's what I like to see – there's a lot of teamwork going on here. People enjoying each other and getting away, listening to the clinic people in here, and everything along that line.

Barry Alvarez

I think one of the biggest injustices to football was the movie *Knute Rockne, All American*, when Pat O'Brien gives the "Win one for the Gipper" speech. Now, any time you win a big game, the media wants to know, "What did you tell them before the game?" Well, it's too late then. It's too late just before the game. A coach can give the greatest speech in the world, but motivation starts all week. It starts in how you go about your business and how you practice.

If we have a big game, the first thing I tell my coaches, on Sunday or Monday, as we get started for the week, I expect an extra hop in your step because players respond to what they see. Players are going to respond to how the coaches are acting. If they see you excited about the game, they'll be excited. If they see you out there doing the same routine every day, they'll be lethargic. It's about how the coaches go about it.

How do you prepare during the week? Are [your players] focused during the week? I'd spend a lot of time talking about focus, eliminating all outside distractions and taking care of all your tickets. If you have family coming in, make sure they have a hotel room. Make sure everyone is where they're supposed to be. Don't bring your cell phones to the hotel. Once Friday practice is over, you're mine until after the game Saturday, so concentrate and eliminate all those distractions.

One thing I honestly believe is, if you compete as a coach, your job is to make sure your players believe they're coached better than the guy they're going to play against. Every week we had some type of a motto and some type of a theme of why we're going to win. Your player has to believe he's going to win.

I'll give you one quick story. My last game, we were playing a very good Auburn team that was ranked very high. I think we were at least more than two touchdown underdogs. The day it was announced, we were playing the Capital One Bowl and I was at a big Wisconsin function. That's where everyone was apologizing. They felt sorry for us because we were going to play Auburn. I kept thinking to myself, my players are going to read that they're going to get beat for three and a half weeks.

I went down to the first meeting at the Capital One Bowl. We went up and had a media presentation. When we finished, my wife, who has always been very honest with me, said, "You really did a nice job today. The media likes you. You're probably going to get your butt kicked, but the media likes you."

My wife doesn't even think we're going to win! We go back home and I'm churning. I went right in the staff meeting and said, "Listen, guys. We drew Auburn. No one thinks we can win this game. We played them two years ago. They were better two years ago than they are now. They're not as good as they were then. We're a much better team now than we were then. I looked at the match, and we match up great." Now, I hadn't watched one second of film. I went down and said, "I want to talk to the team first," and I told the team the same thing, "Listen, no one thinks we can win, but let me tell you something guys, it's a great match up. We'll have an unbelievable plan." Went through the whole thing. The last workday before the bowl game, I gave them the day off and said, "You're right where you need to be." Our kids believed they could win. That was a long process. It wasn't just a great speech just before they went out. It was a process of putting it in their head – "You can win. You're better than they are. Now, follow the plan and execute."

Fisher DeBerry

I think if you expect your football team to be motivated, they have to feed off of you and the staff has to feed off of you. I don't think anything significant has ever been accomplished without a great deal of enthusiasm. I really wanted an energetic and enthusiastic team. I used to pride myself in the fact that there's no way those guys could stop us if we execute the way we're capable of doing and the way we're supposed to. That was a motivation we tried, but I do think it comes from the coach.

I hope there will be some self-motivation with any team you have. I'll never forget when I was coaching at Wofford College. We had two young farm boys on our team. We practiced at 6:00 in the morning. At 5:30, they were always in the dugout on the practice field ready to go, before any coach or our staff got there. When I saw that, it embarrassed the living daylights out of me. I started getting up half an hour earlier because I didn't want them to see me coming in and have them beat me on the field. Those guys were self-motivated. They were very, very good football players. I felt that's what you need in every one of your players.

176

I used to tell our players, "Don't you ever be outhustled. There's a difference in our teams. There's a difference in opponents. Some of them are bigger, stronger, faster and better than you guys, but the one thing the good Lord gave us all in common is our ability to hustle." I think if your team is going to be motivated, you have to be positive. You can't tolerate negative attitudes. I try to make them believe anything is possible and you can achieve anything if you really want it bad enough.

Every year, we had a motto going into the season. I think you have to have some direction for your football team and that was our motivation. Of course, that was to win the Commander-in-Chief's Trophy, win our conference, beat Notre Dame, and win a bowl game. Those didn't change in the 23 years I was the head coach at the Air Force Academy. It was a big deal to get bragging rights among the services and beat Army and Navy. The first thing I ever said to a football team – the new class coming in or the first meeting of the team that year – was, "Beat Army. Sink Navy." I wanted them to understand, and everything we talked about in our program was like that.

To motivate guys, I think you have to recognize them in front of their peers. We did the decal system. We gave them T-shirts that had some meaning to them. We had the Commander-in-Chief's Trophy [displayed] everywhere in the world where they could see it during the course of a day, wherever they would be.

Lloyd Carr

We had a coach from [1901-1923 and 1925-1926], his name was Fielding Yost, and he was a visionary. He built Michigan Stadium, he was a lawyer, and he wrote a book [*Football for Player and Spectator*]. Fielding Yost said, "No man can be a player who does not love the game. Halfhearted lack of interest will eliminate any man from a football team. His love of the game must be genuine. It is not devotion to a fad that makes men play football. It is because they enjoy their struggle." That became the kind of guy I was looking for at Michigan. I wanted a guy who had passion for the game.

I told our coaches, "Go out and recruit guys with passion." I do not believe that you can motivate a player on any long-term basis. That motivation comes from within. In my judgment, if you can build your football team around people who are passionate and love the game, then that is what you are looking for.

Tubby Raymond

When I first came to Delaware, David Nelson, who was the head coach, heard I painted some, so he wanted to make a poster for each game. I start out doing ridiculous things, trying to be funny, and when Eisenhower ran for the presidency I painted his picture along with a chicken's face, our mascot we called Dick. So, Eisenhower said, "Dick, I have a tough one coming up," and the chicken said, "Yeah, well we are playing Gettysburg."

This is 1950 and the kids started to laugh at that, so with that I started to paint pictures of the players. We are probably talking about some six hundred, but it gives us an entry into working with them. That is really the way we are going.

Phil Fulmer

I never was a "rah-rah" kind of guy. I picked my moments for that. It was more like, we're going to be better daily, we're going to be a part of the family. I think, more than anything, [you need to] establish expectations early, and [make sure] they mature and that they get to that place. Our seniors and juniors, when we had our best teams – in particular that run we had there in the late '90s and early 2000s – they managed the younger guys. They were the motivators. Now, we had all the signs on the wall and we hit them as we were going out the door and a lot of other great traditions we had at Tennessee. But, I think the fact that we were honest, tough, and told them the truth, and that we went to work every day to be the best that we could be, we were going to make them better every day if they would listen and learn. We had our fun times, but it got serious for those offense and defense line drills – the old Oklahoma or what we called Tennessee drills. Now we're an excited football team and the best thing was putting those down receivers and defensive backs in there and letting them do it as well; that makes them better and tougher and they look forward to those opportunities. From a motivation standpoint I think you set the expectations. I think Bill [O'Brien], today, explained exactly what he expects from his team. Then the relationship is day-to-day, it's not an all of a sudden rah-rah kind of thing.

Dick Vermeil

Players of all levels have unbelievable tolerance for appreciation and praise, they really do – it's amazing. I've seen many examples and had so many wonderful experiences watching kids go beyond where they ever thought they could be, because of the environment they came from. Maybe there weren't many male figures in their families, I don't know. When they start finding out what they can do by going through the process you're putting them through, it starts coming from them, and when it starts coming, from them, boy, then it goes like that.

As a coach you should be a never-ending source of encouragement. I have cut guys I cared so much about and I didn't want to cut them. I would try to find a way to bring them back if something happened on the roster later because, you know, certain guys are going to give you everything they have. To get the whole squad together, it all starts with them knowing you really care. When you're talking to them and it gets closer to game time and it's building up, I don't know if you're saying anything to motivate them. They hear what you're saying, but they feel your emotion. They feel your passion and they sense where your heart really is. It's amazing.

The best friends I have in my life really are former coaches and players whom I've coached. I have a message on my cell phone from Trent Green. He was doing the ball game Saturday on the radio and the last thing he says is, "I love you, Coach." You know, I've had a lot of players say that. You know why? Because I say it. You pick and choose. There are only a certain number of people who fall into that category on your roster. [Love] is a term you use to describe great respect and admiration beyond the normal level of respect. Don't love certain guys like you love your own kids and your wife, but the word respect doesn't do it justice. Mike Jones is sitting there, as an NFL linebacker ha has said "I love you, Coach." Now he's a coach. Can you imagine what kind of coach he's going to be? There are going to be some kids who love him. It's a two-way street, but I'll tell you this, when you discipline them, they know you mean it, too.

Marino Casem

I feel motivation is an everyday affair. It's every day, every minute. Every time you face a player, be it one-on-one or squad, that's a motivational activity for you. It's an everyday affair. It's a work ethic. They have to believe in what they're doing. They have to believe in the drills we're putting them through, the plays we're calling and the time we practice. In my time, there was no 40-hour workweek. It was an all-day thing, you worked until the lights went out and then you cranked up the cars and the flashlights. [It was daylight to dark] until you got the job done and felt that it was right. It's an everyday affair. It's a hard work ethic. They have to believe in it. It's an attitude they have that they're working harder than the other guy and that the other guy's working just as hard. I sometimes heard players grumbling about how many hours we were practicing and how long we were practicing and all that kind of stuff. I would say, "Grambling [State University] is practicing. Eddie [Robinson] is practicing right now."

It's about preparation. They have to believe and be motivated enough to know that they're being prepared better than the other guys; all the other nine teams in the conference aren't working as hard as we're working, their coaches haven't put together this kind of game plan. Practice sessions lead up to the game performance. Never be out-worked. They have to believe that. They have to have the thought that – when the fourth quarter comes around and when it's fourth and 1 on the goal line – "You have to run it by me. I'm in better shape than this guy in front of me."

[A player] has to be the one who wants to make play because he's better prepared. He knows what's coming. The scouting report told him what it is. The coaches say what we're going to do. He has to believe that will work if he does his job. It's just made in heaven. We're going to work harder, we're going to be better prepared, and we're going to do what we're supposed to do. The coaches are going to see if we're disciplined enough and, if it's possible to take this gap right here, I'm going to take that gap. I'm not going to second guess. It's just a matter of an everyday affair in everything that you do.

Bill McCartney

It's been said that the morale is to the physical as 4 is to 1. It's four times as important – your attitude – as your actual physical abilities. Coach Schembechler won more games in a 20-year stretch than any other coach. Fame can come in a moment, but greatness comes with longevity. You may be able to do it once, but can you do it again? He won the most games over 20 years. Invariably, I saw, if we were a significant favorite in a game coming up, he would prowl. He would be looking for anybody who was dropping their guard. However, if we were in a game that could go either way, he was completely different. He always had poise and he always had his wits about him. What I loved about Schembechler was, when Thursday's practice was over, the players would go shower and we'd come into a meeting room and they would announce the travel squad and then Bo would say, "Okay, men, here's how we're going to win this game." He was extraordinary at calling them out, encouraging guys who needed a pat on the back and calling out other guys who didn't always bring it the way they were supposed to. A lot of people think you give the pre-game talk the day of the game or the day before the game. Not with Schembechler. He gave it the Thursday before a Saturday game. The whole mood would change. When they walked out of that room on Thursday, they had their game faces on. They were getting ready from that point forward.

Bill Curry

What psychologists tell us is the three ways to motivate human beings are: fear, incentive, and relationship. Most coaches use all three, and so should you. There are times to frighten a 17-year-old about what's going to happen if he goes out and gets in a car drunk. Incentive – you want to win the championship and put that ring on. You want to have a chance to continue to play, get a college scholarship and maybe even beyond that. Those are temporary. Fear and incentive only go so far.

The great coaches that impacted me, and what we try to get done with our staff, is to have the staff understand [players are] going to be like us. If we holler at them about getting in shape and we're not in shape, they're going to laugh at us. I'm sorry, but that's just life.

Jerry Moore

For motivation, we always had a rah-rah staff. I like to see those guys run in there and slap one of them on the helmet. A guy makes a great catch and the quarterback pats him on the butt. Those are the things I think are motivational. Respect for the game is where so much of that has to come from.

Ken Sparks

I think you can tell if you have meism disease on your team if you have guys who are doubting the coaches, if you have guys who are doubting their teammates, if you have guys who have a bunch of doubts. Maybe something's happened in their past and they doubt who they are or what their purpose is in life. You get doubts and then pouts. When guys start pouting on you, then you have a meism problem. You have doubts, pouts, and then shortcuts. They are cutting corners on what they're supposed to do and always have their own way of doing it "better" than what they're asked to do. I call that defiance. You go from doubts, to pouts, to shortcuts and then to excuses. All of us have excuses. When you start seeing those four things show up, you probably have a meism problem on your football team.

I think you have to be creative in how you deal with it. I think you have to do all kinds of creative team functions. Get them serving in the community. Do fun things. Every fall, we start off our first day without practice. We work on our plan for life. We have time capsules outside of our building, and we work on our plan for life. In other words, "This is what I want to do with my life." We have categories – it's called the "Carson-Newman Plan for Life" – where we have speakers who will speak to it. Players fill out their plan for life and then we put it in a time capsule. We give them all an individual rock and they personalize their rock, then we build a little monument – our Monument to the Lord – and we put a time capsule in there with their plans for life. In 10 years, we open that time capsule and see how they're doing with their plans for life.

We're constantly trying to build on that. Let's make sure we know where we're headed, because if we don't know where we're headed, we don't know how to get there. That's been something that's been pretty successful for us.

Grant Teaff

I learned early on the power motivation had on my own life, and, therefore, I took it seriously as a husband, father, teacher, coach, and mentor. I read a lot about motivation and studied a lot about it. When I was an assistant coach, I began to study the writings of Paul J. Meyer, who lived in Waco, Texas, where I would later move. He was one of the modern day gurus of the concept of personal motivation. I began to read Paul Meyer and found that though coming from different backgrounds we had very similar philosophies. I had already started to employ personal motivation with our track athletes and football players at McMurry. By the time I became an assistant at Texas Tech,

I was fully attuned to the importance of personal motivation and total team motivation. I came to the conclusion that incentive motivation only lasted for a little while. I always thought of incentive motivation as the donkey with the pole tied to his neck and on one end of the pole was dangled a juicy carrot. The donkey would keep walking toward the carrot, but he never got any closer, until, finally at the end of the day, his master would remove the carrot and give it to him.

I came to the conclusion, and it was later verified by the writings of Paul Meyer, that self-motivation, goal oriented motivation, was the most lasting and, ultimately, the most successful type of motivation. As a young boy I had always been goal oriented. As I stated previously, one of the first things Donell and I did after getting married was to talk about our goals and how we would reach them. One of the things about goals and motivation is, if you know where you're going, you have a lot better chance of getting there, because the decisions you make on a daily basis are based on where you want to go.

Our goal was for me to be a head coach in the Southwest Conference. We started out making $3,000 a year, and our ultimate financial goal was to make $12,000 year. This was a very small goal compared to today's salary, but it was big to us. When Baylor won the first conference championship in 50 years, my salary was $25,000.

Time certainly changes your goals, and you must reflect the changing times when you set professional, family, financial, and spiritual goals. It is very simple: if you know where you're going, do the things on a daily basis that will help you reach your goals.

Chapter 8

Discuss your beliefs about ethics and values related to our game.

Don Nehlen

None of us should be interested in any type of a tarnished victory. In our society, I think the one thing we really lack in our schools is we do not teach value systems. We don't teach kids about honesty, discipline, accountability, and dependability – all of those things that make a guy special. I think coaches have the greatest chance of all to teach kids a value system. We live in a people's world. You have to get along with people and you have to know how to treat people. It's so important that a coach does that with his players. I don't remember my algebra class or English class, but I remember my coach. I remember everything about him. Then, I went to Bowling Green and I don't even know what I took there, but I remember Doyt Perry. I remember those guys and how great they were. There was something special about those guys. They demanded respect and it was just so great to be around them. [Coaches have] a chance to influence kids like that today. If anybody's going to turn the tide, it's going to be [coaches]. Being a high school coach is the greatest job in the world because you can influence so many kids. Those players are looking right up at you. That's why it's so important that you're a good guy. You all know what a "good guy" is. I don't have to explain that to you.

R.C. Slocum

Every coach I played or worked for were guys who I never doubted cared about me as a person. There was not a thing I was ever taught by one of my coaches that was dishonest or bad, or was bad for me as a person. I was fortunate because I played for a great high school coach in Texas named Ted Jefferies. One of the things he talked about, we all had to put our shoelaces in the same way every Thursday after we got through. We had to take our old shoelaces out and polish our shoes, then coach had to check them before we could leave. He said, "I know you all wonder about the shoelaces. They don't have a whole lot to do with winning or losing, but learning to do the little things exactly right, every time, has everything to do with winning and losing." Learning to do the little things exactly right, every time. The influence of a coach goes over into the character issues. I think coaching is almost like the calling of the ministry. You're in a different field, but you are molding young people, not only your own personal kids, but an extended family of young people. You want it to be positive and wholesome. In our relationships with other coaches, we should do everything we can, as a profession, to build up coaches. Every time you make a negative comment about another coach, all you are doing is pulling all of us down a little bit. This is all of our professions. Every negative comment you make about someone else, it's taking away from all of us. Most of us, almost everything we have in life, we owe to this game. I started out in a family where neither parent finished high school. This game allowed me to go to college and has allowed me to do some wonderful things in life. I owe a lot to those coaches who preceded me, who coached me, and the ones I coached with. That's why I'm up here today, trying to encourage you. Let's do everything we can to continue to elevate our profession. You're not going to get me to talk bad about another football coach. We can control a whole lot of what we're all about in how we react to each other. Don't miss an opportunity to brag on another coach. I have people in this state ask me all the time to say something about Mack Brown [former head football coach at Texas A&M rival, the University of Texas]. I love Mack Brown. Mack Brown's a good man and I'm so happy for the success he had in the Rose Bowl. While I was coaching at Texas A&M, I never taught my kids to hate the University of Texas. I'd go in homes recruiting and it would be a wonderful family with a wonderful young man who I'm trying to get to come to my program. The fact that he went to Baylor or went to the University of Texas, that doesn't make him and his family bad people. They're still the same good people I tried to recruit.

Likewise, coaches, you come up here and all of you are together at [the AFCA Convention], then you go back and line up and compete. When Joe Paterno and Bobby Bowden came to the middle of the field after a hard fought Orange Bowl and stood next to each other, they were both very gracious and very complimentary of each other. I said, "Man, that's sending a great message out to people all over the country about what coaching is all about." I was so happy to see that, and that's what you guys can do. Respect is a much better emotion than hate. We always had great respect for the University of Texas. I coached my guys as hard as I could to beat them. We lost to them and we beat them, but I never coached my guys to hate them. So, we need to respect each other in the profession.

Bobby Bowden

A couple of months ago, Joe Paterno and I got into the Hall of Fame. They let us in the Hall of Fame. Now, you're supposed to die first, but I wasn't going to go along with that so they changed the rules to let Joe and me in because we're so old. Anyway, Joe and I were on a nationwide radio show. They asked the question that I was ready for, have players changed? I've coached players in the '50s, the '60s, the '70s, the '80s, the '90s and now into 2000. Joe gave his answer, and then they asked me. It seems like the answer should be, "Yeah, they have really changed." I kind of shocked them. I said, "No, they haven't changed a bit. The parents have changed." If a boy walks into my office right now, yeah his hair's a little longer and he's got his mama's earrings on. I look at that young man and he isn't any different than what I had 50 or 60 years ago, but most of them don't have a daddy. A young man needs a male in the home and most of them don't have it. Coaches, that is your job and that is my job. Our job is to be the male figure for that young man who was raised by a mother, grandmother, or big sister. He's never had a male there to tell him, "Don't do this" and "Don't do that."

It's society today. In my opinion, God put me on this earth to try to be a father-figure for these young men I coach. You have the same responsibility. When I came up, I was lucky. I had a daddy and I loved that guy to death. He died a long time ago. But you know what? I loved my high school coach just about as much. I'll go back to Birmingham this summer and we'll have our reunion for our high school coach. That's how much we thought of him. We're all 75, 76, 77, 80 years of age, and yet we still honor him because every one of us was affected by him. I hope all of you, myself included, will do a better job of setting the example for these young men, not just talking, but trying to live a life that makes them want to live like you. We have to answer for these boys one of these days, that's something I believe.

John Gagliardi

I think you have to have good people. As I say to parents, "If you send us a good guy, we're throwing him in with other good guys. Hopefully, four years from now, we'll return you a good man." You send us a troubled player, we're not going to be able to do anything, because I'm not a psychologist. We get good guys and we tell them, "We're going to play within the rules and these are the rules. If you're getting penalties or doing these kinds of things, you have to understand there are rules in society and football. You have to understand what they are and stay within them because it hurts everyone – the team and yourself."

I certainly think that the coach has to be a role model. I don't drink or smoke, and I raised my kids that way. I didn't really have a lot of rules for them, but they saw that I didn't drink or smoke. I think that meant something to them, because I never told them not to do those things, and they didn't do them.

Terry Donahue

One of the most important lessons I learned about ethics and values really came from the American Football Coaches Association and my association with Grant Teaff. I was at UCLA. I was enjoying my job there and I was somewhat successful. Grant asked me to serve on the Ethics Committee. I was very hesitant and reluctant to do so and Grant knew it. I did not want to serve on the committee, because I didn't want to sit in judgment of other coaches. I realized that I have my own faults and failings and, as a member of the Ethics Committee, I would have to pass judgment on someone else in our profession. It was through leadership and education from Grant that, for the first time in my coaching career, I came to realize I had a responsibility I wasn't meeting. My responsibility was to the great game of football and to the profession of coaching I had gotten so much from. Basically, I was shirking my responsibility in giving anything back. That was an invaluable lesson for me. It's not all about rights and privileges. It is about responsibilities and obligations. I was more involved with my rights and privileges than I was with my responsibilities and obligations. Grant was a great mentor for me in that regard. That didn't mean I had to be goody two-shoes, but I had an obligation.

I'll reflect on a couple of things. A few years ago, I thought college football was at a very dangerous point because of the fighting occurring in the games. Some of the fights that occurred were street brawls. They were bad for the game. They were bad for the respective universities and the coaches. All of us were tainted by it. The AFCA got proactive on that problem and virtually solved the issue. You just don't see that many fights anymore. Fighting was wiped out by the AFCA and my hat is off to Grant, the coaches, and the athletic directors who did that because that was a tremendous job of seeing a problem in football and getting it fixed.

The area of sportsmanship is a very important area that college and high school football is really struggling with. I really encourage the membership, through Grant's leadership and the AFCA Board of Trustees, to really tackle the issue of sportsmanship. This topic, sportsmanship, is something that's been in my mind spanning back to when I participated as a player and as a young assistant coach, to where I am today. Sportsmanship has eroded in our game. Just 50 years ago, one of the pillars that it stood on was sportsmanship. That element is in danger. Values and ethics are the responsibility of every coach in the organization.

John Robinson

The game of football has so much benefit for the players, as well as coaches. It can change your life. It is one of the most meaningful experiences of your life. As you get older and talk to people who have played, you realize that it remains the centerpiece of their life. There is something special about participating in this game and that means you need to give it your all. There is always the ethical question of, "Are you trying your best?"

Ethics is primarily termed for those who play and those who coach. There are people around the game who judge us and think they know more than we know. These people set rules that we have to abide by. But within the game, there's a right and a wrong behavior. You can't cheat and be an honorable football coach. As a coach, you definitely want to take advantage of every opportunity that comes up within the rules. To straight-up cheat defeats this grand thing that we have been blessed with in playing this game. We owe something to the game. Truthfully, I don't have the words to be more specific. It is almost a reverence for it.

From the third grade, I have grown up with John Madden. He was just inducted into the NFL Hall of Fame as a coach and as an announcer. John's always had a reverence for this game and you hear it when he talks on TV. You feel it and you see it. He exemplifies it. I think the guy would sooner die than do something that hurts the game of football. Bo Schembechler epitomized that to me. If you were going to play him, he was going to try to destroy you, but the game of football was something very special for him. All of us have an obligation to live up to that kind of an ethic. We owe it to this game and to the players we coach to keep from screwing it up and give them our best.

Tom Osborne

At one time in college football, the atmosphere was pretty rough out there, and I'm talking cars, clothes, and cash in the '60 and '70s. In 1987, SMU had the death penalty, and that was kind of a watershed event because they couldn't play football for two years. I began to notice a lot of the big stuff kind of going away, but I think it persists today.

The biggest concern I always had was guys coming in and telling a 17-year-old kid he was going to be able to start as a freshman, or that he was going to be able to win the Heisman Trophy, all kinds of stuff you really can't promise. We told our coaches, "We don't make any promises. We'll just tell them we're going to give them an opportunity. We wouldn't be offering you a scholarship if we didn't think you were a good player, but you're going to have to prove it to us."

We'd lose some players because we weren't telling them what they wanted to hear and maybe somebody else would. You see all these recruiting ratings; we usually weren't ranked real high. You really didn't know whether you had a good class or not until about two or three years later. If you sign 25 four-or five-star players, but after two years, only half of them are still there, and half of those guys aren't real thrilled about being there, you didn't have a good recruiting class. Generally speaking, the guys we had came for the right reasons, and they bought into the program. They would hang with you.

I think players really appreciate integrity, and they sense if you're leveling with them. Of course, the worst thing you can ever do is to offer some illegal inducement. How are you going to discipline a guy you've given a car to? You can't do it. He has you over a barrel. He's not on the same footing as everybody else. I know you all understand this, but this is a profession, and it really lives and dies with the ethics and the public perception of this profession. I spent a little time in politics.

Politicians are held in very low regard today and a lot of it has to do with ethics. I hope that's never the case with our football coaches.

Joe Paterno

We shouldn't be in the game unless we understand that we, as coaches, are responsible for young people at a very formative time in their lives. We have to be good examples. If there are rules we're supposed to live by, we should live by them. I feel exactly the same way Tom [Osborne] does about these hotshot recruiting ratings. Some guy gets on television and says, "He's going to be a great defensive back. Look at the way he moves his shoulders and hips." They all want to sound like experts. You sometimes get kids who want to hear, "Hey, you're the greatest thing that ever happened." You have to be fair with them. You have to say, "Hey, you're a really good prospect, but you have a lot of work ahead of you, and we're hoping you can do it."

I'm talking to high school coaches more directly than I am some of you who are in college, but in high school, those kids need leadership. They need somebody to tell them, "Hey, this is right, and this is wrong. This is what can happen to you if you do it the right way." We're the same way in college. We have to understand that we're dealing with kids who sometimes don't understand what's right and wrong. We have got to show them that – it's an obligation we have.

Now, having said that, we can't be phonies with each other. Somebody called me up and said, "Do you know there are three schools that you're competing against that are cheating?" I said, "No, I don't know that." The guy said, "Yeah," and he named three schools. I said, "Hey, wait a second. Calm down. Have you broken any rules?" If anybody says to you that they haven't broken a couple of rules in the NCAA, they're lying.

I'm getting off the subject. My point is, don't point fingers. You take care of your group. You make the best of those kids and make freshmen the best they can be. If somebody is breaking the rules, try to get the thing straightened out so we can hold our heads high.

Lou Holtz

I think this is the greatest game in the world. Everything I have, I owe to the game of football. I ended up in college because my high school coach came up and told my parents I should go to college and be a coach. Nobody in our family had ever gone to college before. My mom went to work as a nurse's aide, working 11:00 to 7:00 so I could go to college. I ended up being a coach.

The influence you have on people, you know, is just doing the right thing. You talk about value and ethics. If some of the problems we have with different coaches being let go, outstanding coaches, just do the right thing. Do the best you can. Show your players you care.

If you listen to nothing else I've said today, I want you to remember this: When players need love and understanding the most is when they usually deserve it the least. You have an unbelievable influence on people. What good does it do to win if you can't do it the honest way?

The coaching profession's changed, I'm sad to say. In some respects, it's so much better than it's ever been before. My first AFCA Convention was in New York in 1959. I was still a senior in college. People got together, they shared thoughts, they shared ideas, and the head coaches got together. You'd end up in somebody's room – Bear Bryant's room, Joe Paterno's room.

Like Gary Patterson said, you hate the guy for three hours, but the rest of the year you care about one another. It's a game that brings you together. Nobody understands the sacrifice, the work, the difficulty, the excitement of victory, and the agony of defeat like coaches and their families.

I've been married for 48 years. I'm proud that my son, Skip, the head coach at East Carolina [currently the head coach at Louisiana Tech], is in this coaching profession. While he was at Notre Dame, he came in and said, "Dad, I want to be a coach." I said, "We didn't send you to Notre Dame to be a coach. I sent you to Notre Dame to be president. Heck, I could have sent you to [another college] to be a coach." He said, "I want to be a coach." I said, "Have you told your mom yet?" He said, "No." I said, "Make sure she's unarmed, because she'll shoot you." But this is the greatest profession in the world.

All I need to say is this: Follow those three rules. You won't have to worry about ethics. You won't have to worry about principles. You won't have to worry about anything. You'll have a free conscience if you just follow those three rules, and that's all ethics and morals are to me.

Dick MacPherson

Charity begins at home, and I think the ethics come from that. Always do the right thing. As a coach, that's exactly what you try to do with the players. From that standpoint, what Lou [Holtz] said is right on track. To me, the emphasis tonight is to make sure you know how important you are to this football system and how important you are to the game. There are people here who carry our system out to other places and have had great success.

I guarantee that if you give yourself to these football players who are with you, the results will show. Nothing gets any better than to see the defensive line stay together, work together; to see the offensive backs learning how to block, learning how to catch. Those, to me, are wrapped up in a the words ethics and values. What those really mean is you're a good football coach and making those players you have just as good as they can be, and that's how you win ball games, by making your players good.

Barry Alvarez

I think all of us who are involved in the game are obligated to uphold the integrity of the game. I understand all the pressure that comes along with this job, but you contradict everything the game stands for – and the things you teach – when you don't show integrity. Sometimes I think our game is tarnished because there may be one or two people who are cutting a corner or compromising on some things. That hurts. That gives us all a black eye.

There's a way to do things and there's a way not to do things. I think each and every one of us are obligated to make sure we do things the way they're supposed to be done. Our players will then follow that lead.

Fisher DeBerry

They call us Coach. I think that is the most awesome, responsible word there is. It's a word we all have so much pride in. I think when they call us Coach, that means we need to be ethical. We need to have core values. I think we have to operate a daily program that teaches character, integrity, and leadership. That will result in our guys becoming good husbands, good fathers, good officers, and certainly contributing to the betterment of our society. I was very, very proud and honored to be able to serve on the Ethics Committee, and to be [chairman] of the Ethics Committee. We're one of the few organizations in America that has its own ethical code. Grant gets calls all the time about how we govern ourselves. People are envious of us, because they don't have that in their professions.

Football is the best game, as we know, to teach life's lessons. That's why we all coach. The highlight of my Christmas was a call I received from a player's dad, who happens to be a very successful high school football coach. He said, "I just want you to know I sent you a boy, and you sent me back not just a man, but a man with values." To me, that's about the highest compliment I think I could have ever been paid. It certainly reinforced the sign I had in my office, which was my basic philosophy. I wanted people who visited in my office to know what my core values were and what my philosophy of operation was. It simply said, "The success in coaching is not measured by the number of wins and losses; but the real success in coaching is measured by the men your players become."

That's the responsibility I think we have as coaches and as an association. We have a tremendous responsibility. We might very well be the only father figure in a lot of kids' lives today. We have a real responsibility, men, to protect the integrity of this game. We are the custodians of the game, and we certainly have to respect the game. This is our profession. I know each and every one of us are very, very proud to be a part of the American Football Coaches Association. I encourage you to really, really be ethical in everything you do. I encourage you to uphold the standards of this association, and certainly to volunteer and be active in your association, and be willing to serve it in any way you can.

Lloyd Carr

I would begin by urging every man in this room to read the Code of Ethics. My career was greatly influenced by the guy I worked for, Bo Schembechler. When it came to recruiting, as assistant coaches we would say, "Bo, you could tell this kid he is going to start as a freshman, he is going to be an all-American, it is not that hard at Michigan academically."

Bo wasn't having any of that. Bo would go in and he would talk about how tough it was at Michigan, he was going to tell him the way it was. He wasn't going to make promises or mislead them. He said, "I don't want them to get here and the first thing they realize is that I lied to them." Once in a while he would run into somebody we were recruiting who wanted something beyond what the rules allowed. Bo would say, "Room, books, board, tuition. That is it. That is all we have for you. If that isn't enough, then we are going to have to go without you."

Bo was one of those coaches who had an extraordinary career, an extraordinary winning percentage, more championships than any coach in Big Ten history, but he never won a national championship. He told a group of coaches one day, "You know, I have had a chance to look back on my career and I always wanted to win a national championship. I didn't do it, but I will tell you this, I think I could have [won] one, if I had been willing to compromise or violate the rules. It would not have been worth it. No championship, nothing, is worth the cost of compromising the principles."

They had an induction ceremony down at Miami (Ohio) University this year. Coach [Ara] Parseghian, the great Notre Dame coach, was asked, "What are you most proud of?" He said, "What I am most proud of is that everywhere we coached, we never compromised the rules."

If you are a young coach out there – wherever you are in your career – you have to make those decisions, those choices. The reason I encourage you to read the Code of Ethics is because the price for not reading it is too heavy. It is too high and this game is too important. You want to leave a legacy. Make sure that legacy is one you can look back on and know you did it the right way.

Tubby Raymond

In 2008, we had a sixtieth reunion of the 1948 National Championship in Ann Arbor. I went back there and I was amazed when I saw the things [the players] had done. There were doctors and dentists, it was just wonderful.

This last year, we had a 1972 reunion of a championship team in Delaware. I was amazed at the love, respect, and care these men showed each other. It was just wonderful to see. To a man, they say, "If it weren't for football, if it weren't for the discipline of football I learned – doing the right thing at the right time – I would have never made it. I run my business exactly the way you coaches coached at Delaware." To me that was really very special.

Phil Fulmer

I think, certainly, in this day and age our problems are magnified because the family unit and the church unit have broken down. I remember the day I decided I wanted to coach was at an AFCA Convention in Chicago and Bo Schembechler was speaking on tackling. Being a college football fan, I just thought I wanted to hear Bo Schembechler speak. He started talking about tackling and the slant and angle defense and all those kinds of things, but in short order, he got off on exactly what we're talking about today. Now, this is 1972, the problems were the same then as they are now. They're just more magnified now. Those kids need us. They need our guidance, to learn temperament, and how to be a man. I was on the edge of my seat before Bo finished because he had gone a long way from tackling and into the role of the coach. Then I started thinking about all the coaches who made a difference in my life and in that moment I knew I was going to do this. Here's a guy who I'd never met, who I'd only heard about, [who made a difference in my life].

Fortunately, Wichita was close to Lincoln, Nebraska, and Coach Osborne allowed me to come up quite a bit. I'm 23 years old, at Wichita State, and Tom Osborne's invited me to come sit in a meeting and watch spring practice. He didn't talk about tackling very long. He talked about what it took to be a man to the football team in 1970, 1973, 1974 and 1975 – I went up there for several years. We have that obligation as coaches now, to take over that role of the dad who he has missed, or who didn't do his job, or whoever the male figure was and we should – you should – take that very, very seriously, because you can make a difference in our society right now. They want instant gratification. They have been brought up and recruited; all these services are telling them they're the best of all time, and asking which hat are they going to pick. It's all a show. It gets real when you line up in that program for the first-time. Those seniors have been through all they've been through, and now they have to compete with them and find their place. They'll go in one direction or the other. They'll either follow the good guys or they'll follow, if you have bad guys on your team, they'll follow the bad guys. They're going to follow somebody. There again is the role of the assistant coach, the role of the head coach, of the whole support staff. You can absolutely make a difference. That's why we went into coaching. All of us, I think. It wasn't about the money or the glory or any of those kinds of things. It's about helping kids.

Dick Vermeil

[Coaches are needed now more than any time in the history of our country,] no question. There's an old expression that describes it as well as you can describe it: "If you have integrity, nothing else matters. If you don't have integrity, nothing else matters." As a coach in the National Football League this is especially true. You lie to the troops and you are going to be gone in no time at all. All you have to do is lie to one guy. There are no secrets in an NFL locker room. All you have to do is lie to one coach. It's out of your door and into that locker room and spread all over, and pretty quick nobody trusts you. It is so important to have integrity. That doesn't mean you have to be a saint, but if you tell somebody you were going to do it, do it. For example, I'm coach of the All-Star game out here for the NFL players Association again this year and on the back page I have rookie alerts. The number one alert is, you only rent your locker. Okay, the number two alert is, if you tell somebody you're going to do it, do it. Number three, if you get a call – phone call or email or text – return that call within a matter of hours. All these fundamental things young people today breakdown on. Imagine me telling your dad you were going to do something and [I didn't let you] do it. Do you know how many kids have told people all along, until you get them on your squad, that they were going to do something and they didn't do it? I push these fundamental little things and I really think they learn that it does make a difference.

Marino Casem

Regardless of how we got into this profession, we're in the profession respected the world over. The word coach – or the title Coach – is the same in China as it is in Russia, the United States, Somalia, and Vietnam. Anywhere you go, the word coach has its own mystique about itself. If you're going to wear that title, you have to be ethically right. You have to dress the part, look the part, and be the part. A coach can relate to people others can't relate to. The profession ranks itself right there with religion. Coach means something – like he had been called from on high to do his job. Some folks say they coach and they hadn't been called by anybody, but you have to believe in what you do and really want to be the coach. It gets to you.

Bill McCartney

Tom Landry, the legendary Dallas Cowboy coach, said, "A coach is a man who requires others to do what they don't want to do, in order to accomplish all the things they dreamed of doing." Tell them how to do it, tell them again what you told them, and then tell them 1,000 times more, because that's how men learn. Don Shula won 347 games [in the NFL. The only current coach with over 200 wins is New England Patriots head coach Bill Belichick.] Shula's record won't be broken in our lifetimes. Listen to what Shula said, "Conviction driven leadership is based on a vision of perfection." Shula knew what it looked like and he wouldn't compromise it. I never watched him coach, but they said he wasn't a loud guy; he wasn't a harsh guy, but he knew what he wanted. If a quarterback's cadence was uncertain, he would correct him. If an offensive guard's stance or weight was not distributed properly, he would always make that correction. If an offensive tackle took a split that was wrong, Shula would always see it. If the tailback didn't hit the hole correctly, Shula would have them run over it again. Conviction driven leadership is based on a vision of perfection.

Bill Curry

Values and ethics are everything. If we are dishonest, the players know it. I'm not just talking about making a rule and then failing to enforce it. Most of us don't do that. Most of us do enforce our rules. Most of us have a code of discipline. I evolved to a system whereby we had a code of honor. It had a few items everybody agreed to and every player signed it, then I signed it. We sat down and we went through it. You understand what you're signing up for, you agree that you're going to do this. Where we had success that went beyond expectation was when we related to the players so that they could see in us what we expected of them. We all did it together. Those are the things that stand out.

Coach Lombardi, whether you liked his personality or not, had a unit that he called the "War Council." There were five or six guys, who we could go to, and tell them, "Go tell him he's driving us crazy," and they would. If you could get Forrest Gregg, Bart Starr and Herb Adderley to go talk to him, they would say, "Coach, you need to back off," and he would do it. He would actually respond to this. So, that was a disciplinary mechanism we tried. It works when you have the right corps to be your War Council. When you don't, if you pick the wrong guys, you have a mess on your hands. I've experienced that, too. I think discipline is a complex issue in today's world. ... It's always going to come back to, what do they see in you? Do they want to be like you? If you tell them to be in shape, are you in shape? I think those things matter more now than ever before.

Jerry Moore

I've just [adopted] with a new phrase I read in a golf magazine, "Pick your foursome." I think it's important that you pick the right people. My high school coaches were in my foursome. They gave me the leadership. Teachers in my high school and some professors in college were in my foursome. I wanted to be like them. I wanted to be able to teach. I wanted to coach since I was a sophomore in high school. None of those people are still alive, but I feel like, even today, I would not want to let them down. I don't want to disappoint them.

Ken Sparks

I think we talk about [values and ethics] quite a bit. I think we talk about it more than we do it. There are four cornerstones of a man: do what's right, do it with great effort, make sure you have the attitude that you can build your life on – humility – and make sure you have some courage. We need some coaches to stand up and be counted. If not, we're going to lose this battle. The fact is, we're losing the battle.

Grant Teaff

The founding fathers of the American Football Coaches Association first met in 1921 to discuss the need for an organization of coaches to promote, protect, and create safer playing rules. The development of the Code of Ethics was foundational and has been ever since the beginning of the AFCA in 1922. While serving on the Board of Trustees, I was asked by the chairman of the Ethics Committee, Coach Vince Dooley – at the time head football coach at the University of Georgia – to succeed him as the chairman of the Ethics Committee. I had served on the committee for a few years, so I did as he requested and served as chairman for 11 more years.

My message then, and now, to all of our young coaches is that the Code of Ethics are the foundation of our profession. Our Code of Ethics stand the test of time. It appears in today's world that money is king, but we must always keep the bottom line as one of integrity and ethics. The NCAA and the AFCA have worked together for many years interviewing coaches who were accused of certain NCAA violations. Today it is even more severe than in the past. Under NCAA rules an assistant coach or head coach

---

can be suspended for a few games or a full year if NCAA rules are broken. Ethics in coaching are the foundation of our profession. At the present time, our great game is under attack. Everyone involved with the game, especially coaches, must do everything in our power to make sure we are coaching the safest fundamentals of the game, living by the rules, and coaching "beyond the game."

Chapter 9

What regrets do you have and would you do anything differently?

Don Nehlen

I am the luckiest guy in America. I coached high school football for six years. Every job I ever took, I took saying, "I'm going to be here for the rest of my life." My first job, I was a sophomore coach and I told myself, "Wow. I'm going to be here the rest of my life. I'm going to make this the best sophomore team in America." A year later, I was a head coach at a small high school in Ohio. I said, "Wow, I'm going to be here the rest of my life." Four years later, I ended up at the University of Cincinnati, and I said, "Wow! I'm going to be the best secondary coach they've ever had." A year later, I ended up back in high school at McKinley High School in Ohio and I said, "This is a great job. I'm going to be here all of my life." A year later, I'm off to Bowling Green. My wife said, "Get a covered wagon, we're moving too much." Three years later, at 30 years old, I get the head coaching job [at Bowling Green State]. Twelve years later, I end up at Michigan with Bo [Schembechler]. That was the greatest experience I have ever had. I said, "Wow, I'm going to be here the rest of my life." Three years later, I ended up [the head coach] at West Virginia. I went, "Wow, I'm going to be here the rest of my life." Now, "Wow, I retired! I just loved coaching. I can't imagine them paying me to do what I did."

R.C. Slocum

When I got to the head coaching job at Texas A&M, I was so proud and happy. One of the first things I did was go down to the front of my church and talk to the preacher. I said, "I wish this church would take time to pray that I will do the right thing in this job. I want to coach in such a way that will be positive, which will reflect on everybody in the right way." I told my coaches, "We're not going to worry about wins right now. I want us to get off on the right track doing things the right way." I always had it in my mind that I wanted to do things the right way, so that whenever the end came, I could look at myself and look those kids in the eye and say, "You know what? I told you the right things and we did it the right way." So, I really don't have any regrets. I did not lie to any of my players or do anything dishonest. I feel good about how I did things. I wish I didn't play as many bowl-eligible teams during the season, but other than that, I don't really have any regrets.

Bobby Bowden

I could name a million [things] I'd love to change. When I look back, there were certain guys whom I was not fair to. I may have pre-judged them, but I was wrong. When you get older, like I am now, you don't do that. If I could change anything, it'd be to go back and treat some guys more fairly.

John Gagliardi

I don't have any regrets. The fact that I'm sitting here with two of the greatest coaches of all time, how could I ask anything more than that? Someone asked me when we won our last national champion-ship, "Did you think you would get to this point?" I said, "Listen, when I started, I was 26 years old. My only thought was, how could I get a date with that good looking woman?" How could I think, all these many years later, that good-looking woman would still be my wife? I have no regrets at all. The three things I have to pay attention to are: when I start forgetting to zip up, when I start forgetting to zip down, and the third very critical thing – I can't remember the third thing.

Terry Donahue

I have a lot of regrets. I think all of us do. We have regrets about certain games where we could have done a better job for our players and our coaches. My main regret is that I retired from college football so early. I was 50 or 51 when I stopped coaching. It wasn't until this year that I reconnected with college football on the NFL Network show called *College Football Now*. It was so refreshing for me to get back into the college game. I realized this year, more than any other year in the last 10 years, how much I missed relationships with friends like Rich Brooks, Dick Tomey, and different guys we battled on the football field. I missed the excitement, the variety in offenses and defenses, and all the emotion in college football. I gave that up way too early in my life, and I wish I hadn't done that.

The other major regret I have is that, if I had it to do all over again, I would have a better relationship with the players. When you're coaching, you're in "survival mode." You're just trying to survive. You're trying to win enough games to get the next contract or the next job to keep your family going. Now that I am older, I have a different relationship with players. It isn't so much about the wins and the losses. It's more about the struggles, the fun times, and the bonding. I wish I had told our football team, more often and more directly, how much I appreciated, loved, and respected them for what they were trying to do for the university, the coaches and me. I think we get so bogged down in the battle that we don't stop and just say, "Man, I really appreciate you." A lot of coaches have done that much better than I have. I admire Dick Tomey and Rich Brooks a great deal. They don't hesitate to tell their players how much they love and appreciate them. If I could do one thing over again, I'd do that better and more often.

John Robinson

The things I regret most are those players who I failed in some way. There were guys who I was indifferent toward and I didn't see them clearly enough to influence them. There are players who come up to all of us old, retired coaches and say, "Man, you meant everything to me," but there are also players who don't come up to us. Those are the players we didn't do a good job with.

My career was 90 percent of everything you dream about. There was 10 percent that wasn't so good. There were times in my career I focused on the 10 percent too much, like asking for new buildings or the selfish things you go through that take you away from what you're doing.

Another thing that sticks out in my mind relates to the last part of my career. I didn't watch film as much as I had before. I didn't focus on the details. When you're a young coach, you will stay up all night watching film, come up with the perfect plan, and then go back over it. I think as a veteran coach, you're quicker, smarter, and you can do it in less time. As an old veteran coach, you stop looking at the [details] and begin to make decisions based on inadequate information. Some of that is age and some of it, I am ashamed to say, is physical condition. I gave away one of my strengths over the last part of my career.

Tom Osborne

I'd say I really don't have many regrets. I guess one thing, if I had it to do over again, would be to live and die with my assistants. I was fortunate to have some really great people, but maybe had one or two whom I didn't know enough about them. I didn't know their character well enough. In the last seven, eight, or nine years I coached, I tried to make sure everyone I hired had some kind of a spiritual base. Now, it didn't mean they believed like I did. We didn't force our beliefs on anybody. I think my feeling was that if a coach had allegiance to something beyond winning and losing football games – that God was part of their life and they were sincere about it – you could count on him to do the right thing and be a good role model. That's one thing I might have done earlier on. But, I was privileged to have some really great people work for me.

Joe Paterno

I don't know if I have any regrets. I don't know how you can be my age, still have a good job and be able to go to work, and have any regrets. I have 16 grandkids, the oldest is 12. I have a seventeenth on the way. They're all healthy. I have a young wife, we've been married forty-something years. So, I don't really have any regrets.

If there would be anything I could have done a little bit better, it would have been dealing with the kids I lost here and there over the years. There were people we just missed. Tom [Osborne] hit it on the head – maybe kids fooled you about drugs, or you didn't pay enough attention to them. Those are the regrets I have.

I worry about our profession in the sense that money has become such an important factor, that you give up the loyalty to institutions that gave you a good start. Tom didn't go to [college at] Nebraska, he went to a place called Hastings, but when he went to Nebraska [to coach], he stayed there.

Once in a while I regret the role I'm in, because of the camaraderie I used to have with other coaches. I loved being an assistant coach. I loved being on the road. In the old days, you could take some people out once in a while.

Lou Holtz

I regret four things that come to my mind. Number one – and I'm being honest – I regret I was never asked to be on the AFCA Board of Trustees, because one of my goals in life was to be president of the American Football Coaches Association. I couldn't think of anything that would have been a greater honor than to represent the greatest profession, and the people who have the greatest impact on people's lives.

The second thing I regret was leaving the University of Notre Dame. When I left Notre Dame, I thought I was tired of coaching. You take a program and you get it on top, then for nine straight years we went to a New Years bowl: the Sugar, the Cotton, the Orange, or the Fiesta. You get on top and you say, "This is pretty good. Let's keep it here. Let's not run any risks. Let's not jeopardize everything," – because, as you know, with the internet everybody criticizes [your] coaching – "Let's just maintain it."

As I said before, there's a rule of life – you're either growing or you're dying. When I left Notre Dame, I thought I'd never coach again. Where do you go from Notre Dame? According to my mother, you go directly to heaven or you sit by the Pope, you don't coach anymore.

When I left Notre Dame, I found I wasn't tired of coaching, I was tired of maintaining. No matter how much success you've had, [you should] always look at how you can take another step.

The third thing I regret, I was unfair to a young man named Paul Failla. He's the only one I can really look at and say I really was unfair to him, although not intentionally. Paul Failla was a quarterback and a very good one. He came to Notre Dame and he was forced into action against No. 3 Southern Cal. We beat them 37-6. We also had an outstanding quarterback by the name of Ron Powlus. I'd seen enough of Ron to think he had a chance to be great. I told Paul that Ron would be the starting quarterback the next year. It was totally unfair to Ron; it was totally unfair to Paul. Ron could have earned the job, but he never had the opportunity. Paul believed he was good enough to start, but I never gave him the opportunity. – He was also a great baseball player. He stopped playing football and played baseball. – I've written and apologized to him. Just make sure you're being fair and don't just look at somebody who has talent. Ron had great talent. It wasn't his or Paul's fault, I made the decision. Let people earn it on the field.

The last thing I regret was when I was back at the University of South Carolina. We were 0-11 the first year. Records can be deceiving – we really weren't as good as our record would lead you to believe. Everybody's complaining and moaning. I'm in an airport after that year and a guy came up to me and said, "Anybody tell you, you look like Lou Holtz?" I said, "It happens all the time." He said, "It makes you mad, doesn't it?" The second year we had the second greatest turnaround in the history of NCAA football. We went from 0-11 to twenty-first in the country, and we beat Ohio State [at the 2001 Outback Bowl, 27-7]. The following year we beat Ohio State [31-28 at the 2002 Outback Bowl], and finished fourteenth in the country. We had the sixth best recruiting class one year, the seventh best the next.

In looking at it, people say you're getting too old, you have to change. You're too tough, you're not bending. Single-parent homes, hip-hop culture, you have to change. I changed and I regret it. Don't change what you believe in your heart. It's the most miserable I've ever been in coaching, when I wasn't true to myself.

Sometimes I think I'd like to go back into coaching. I still have great energy and I believe in the things I've talked about. There comes a time when you have to step aside and let the young people carry forth the banner. Whatever you do, don't compromise the things you really believe, because society has changed. I have firm beliefs. I'm not going to change them, and I'm proud of it.

Dick MacPherson

I think it's like Frank Sinatra said: "Regrets, I've had a few, but too few to mention." I am so filled with thankfulness for the game of football. I can't say I really have anything from a negative standpoint. To be very honest with you, when I was coaching at Syracuse I wasn't making a heck of a lot of money. At the time, pro people were after me to see if I'd go there. I made a mistake and went [to the New England Patriots,] because I thought I would be able to support my family a little bit better, and I thought I could get a good retirement system. I was an easy pickup, because what I didn't do was investigate who I was going to work for and just exactly what I was going to do. I wasn't there for six months before I knew I had made the wrong move.

All I'm saying to you is, try to make sure you understand that a football game is what it's all about and to make darn sure you carry it on. I also believe very, very strongly that if you, as a family, get together, you're going to win.

Barry Alvarez

I think the one thing I probably regret is I didn't take the time to tell my assistant coaches how much I appreciated them and all the hard work they did, as well as all the players for their time and effort, and buying in to the system. I don't think you ever do that enough. With the way our schedule goes, you're on a treadmill and the time flies. You just don't take the opportunity to show people how much you appreciate them. I think all of us should make [an effort] to spend more time with our own children. In my case, and I've said this several times, I feel like I cheated my own children. I can remember my wife telling me, "I wish you'd talk to your son and your kids like you do to your players. You give them more life lessons than you do your own children." Create that time for your own children.

The one thing I don't regret was my path through coaching. I started out as a graduate assistant. I was an assistant at a high school, then I moved to be a head coach in a small high school, and then to a larger high school. I got an opportunity to be an assistant for Hayden Fry. Then I moved up the ranks at Notre Dame, [before ultimately settling at Wisconsin.] To work through all those levels and pay your dues, I think it makes you really appreciate when you do have some success at a high level.

Fisher DeBerry

I would probably tell my players how much I really loved them a little more often, and how much I really appreciated them and the sacrifices they made. I'll tell you what I do. The first summer after I retired, I was trying to find my way. I was involved in a foundation my wife and I have, and I sat down and had my foundation headquarters draft a letter about what our foundation was doing and what it was all about. Then I asked them to give me some space on the letter where I could write a personal note. I sat down and wrote every kid who had played in our football program and thanked them. I also would mention something humorous I remembered about them, or if I had to get on their butt about something. I just wanted them to know, again, how much I appreciated them. We often don't realize how important the relationships are, and the influence we as coaches have. I tell you something else I would do more – read. I didn't read [enough about things not related to football], or even things about the game, as I should have. I'd probably try to stay up with the technology of the game and the changes that are going on in that area of the game. I think I would involve players from previous years more in the game.

I do know this. I'd get a lot more sleep than I did. I'd probably eat a little bit better. I'd spend a little more time with my own kids, because we spent so much time with other people's kids.

Lloyd Carr

Forty losses. When I became the coach at Michigan, I put up a sign at several places throughout our football building, which said, "Michigan football – where only your best is good enough." That was the way I tried to approach my job. I asked my coaches and our players every day they walked in that building to give their best. I did my best. If you do your best, you can hold your head high. Even after those losses – that were miserable – I tried to figure out what we could have done better. In college, you have a choice to meet and watch film on either Sunday or Monday. We met Sunday afternoon so that, whether we won or lost, we were on to the next one.

If there was one thing I would do differently, I would try to enjoy the wins. You get so busy, it is such an intense competitive profession, that you get off the field and you are thinking about the next game. Somewhere in there, there is so much fun, and we miss a lot of it.

Tubby Raymond

The first thing that I regret is that I always associated mobility with success – that if you are not moving every three years, you are not doing the job – and I think that is a horrible mistake. I was a head coach at UD, I just loved that. I should have really cared for and loved it, but I was still just waiting for the next job. I used to come to AFCA Conventions, maybe I would see somebody who would promote me here or do this, or get an opportunity. If I had to do it all over again, I think I would have enjoyed what I was doing. I might not have worked so hard and would have enjoyed my children a little bit more. Other than that, I'd probably make the same mistakes all over again.

Phil Fulmer

I regret that they fired me. I didn't like that very much, but it may be the best thing that ever happened to me. I got to be more aware of my families. I have four children and we had quality time together – my wife did a great job of making sure of that. I have since talked to some coaches who did it differently. I was one of those guys who was a grinder and expected grinders around me. Our family would come to dinner on certain nights. We had nights before recruiting calls that you could get home to see your family. I would do that differently. There's so much I'm enjoying right now with my grandchildren that I missed with my own children, like birthdays and lots and lots of things. Now, I have a wonderful relationship. I don't want that to sound bad. But I think we can do a better job of defining the game and not letting the game define us.

Dick Vermeil

I regret not listening to the people at the Eagle organization who told me I couldn't keep going the way I was going – grinding – I slept in my office. You get going and you start experiencing some success. You work until two o'clock in morning, you drive 45 minutes home, you sleep, you get up, you're back in the office at seven very little sleep. Pretty quick I was saying, "Well, why waste that time driving I'll just sleep in my office." I started doing that. Then you start saying, "Well, I might as well work until three o'clock, we're getting better." You think some of those decisions you make at three or four in the morning are better than the ones you made at nine.

I was a little insecure in my position because I was a high school coach a few years before, then a junior college coach, and now I am looking at Tom Landry and coaching against George Allen, Don Shula and guys like that. I never felt very secure in that environment, so I just kept pushing myself. Soon, I'd go to bed in my office at four o'clock and [wake up] at seven.

I love to tell a story about on Ken Iman, who played 16 years in the league. I made a coach out of him when I went to the Philadelphia Eagles, because I had so much respect for him [when he played for] the Rams. I made him a special teams coach and assistant line coach his first year. We had an eight o'clock meeting and he walked in five minutes after eight. I said, "Ken you're late." He said, "Coach, how can I be late? I slept in my office." That's what we did. We stayed there Monday night, Tuesday night, and Wednesday. I didn't go home until Thursday night at about 11 o'clock and I regret doing that. I didn't have to do that, it was my own insecurities and I wouldn't listen. You keep doing that, it's going to catch up with you, and it did. I regret leaving the Rams after winning the Super Bowl because I thought [I should go out a Super Bowl champion and an NFL Coach of the Year, and spend time with my kids and grandkids.]

Regrets in anything I did as a coach, with the staff, with the players, or the organizations I worked for? I don't have any.

Marino Casem

I actually have no regrets. When I went to college, I majored in health and physical education. I got my degree and I didn't want to teach. I couldn't stand writing essays and grading papers. That was not what I wanted to do. I went and took a course at Tuskegee in corrective therapy. I [graduated] and went home, [only to find out] my wife, Betty, had taken a job at Utica Junior College in Mississippi. She is very sharp. We went to school together at Xavier. She was so smart, she didn't have to take her final exams.

The Utica coach quit after we graduated. I was at home with mama waiting for the job offers to come from the VA, because I was going to be a therapist. Betty called me and said, "The coach out here quit. Come down and interview at Utica." I was in Memphis and I didn't want to go to Mississippi. I was a big city boy, but I said, "Well, I'll go down there to see her." I went down and interviewed for the job and was hired as an assistant coach. Betty got me the job, so every time she started complaining or started talking about the long hours or how I didn't do anything right around the house, I would say, "You got me this job!" She got me the job, but there were a lot of problems happening. We'd been together for 30 years. I was coming up on 65 and my retirement was coming due. All I'd had all these years was coaching and working in administration. My wife told me, "Walk away while they're still applauding."

Bill McCartney

When I was seven years old, I knew I was going to be a coach. Most guys at that age want to be President or a pilot or a scientist, but I knew I was going to be a coach. I studied my high school coaches early on, then I was a basketball coach. I would go anywhere to watch Bob Knight when he was at the University of Indiana.

A pastor came into our church. He was a visiting preacher and I had never seen him before or since. He said, "You want to know about a man? You want to know whether a man has character or not? All you need to do is look in his wife's eyes because everything he's invested or withheld will be in her countenance. The almighty God has mandated that every man bring his wife to splendor. Everything she could possibly be, a man's supposed to do that." I had been married over 30 years and I turned and looked at Lyndi, and I didn't see splendor. I saw torment. I didn't see contentment, I saw anguish. I tried to defend myself [to my mind.]. This was during the season, my last year in coaching, and I realized that I was exposed in my wife's face. That's why I got out of coaching. On Valentine's Day, I got a card, and it said, "I finally found the man I thought I married." I was too over the top. I was taking the game plan home with me. There's a balance. In March, Lyndi died. We had been married 50 years. I really knew, in my heart, that I had to put her first. I knew that I had to get out of coaching to do it. I'm not telling you to get out of coaching, I'm saying put her first – never let football be so important that your wife or your children take a back seat. I had to give up the game, but I have no regrets.

Bill Curry

The best person I've ever known is Carolyn Curry. I left her with the children because I thought you were supposed to work at the office

90, 100 hours a week. I was doing what I thought you're supposed to do. It caused enormous difficulties in our family, but she managed them all. Our kids are grown with children. They're fine. We're all close now, but there's been a lot of making up to do.

That regret never really leaves me at all. No matter how you justify the hours, you're not with your children. The most common phrase I hear is, "We have quality time." Quality time is BS to a four-year-old. A four-year-old spells love, t-i-m-e. My son informed me last year that I had already been to more of his son's football games than I had to his, and it killed me. It was true. I can't believe I did that. I thought I needed to be with my team. Baloney! So, I have horrific regret.

As for words of wisdom, I sat down at a leadership conference with Dr. David Abshire [Special Counselor to President Reagan and the U.S. Ambassador to NATO from 1983-87] at Washington and Lee University. He stood up, and the first thing he asked us was, "What's the difference in a great leader and a terrible leader? Twenty seconds." What does he mean by that? He said this: "Richard Nixon and Bill Clinton destroyed their legacies with decisions they made in a few seconds. You are a product of what you've been thinking about. You do what you think about. Your habits are the behaviors you have allowed to penetrate your life through the years, and you're going to do what you've been doing under the gun. When crunch time comes, you make decisions in very rapid-fire succession that will affect the rest of your life, and they're not based on rational thought unless you pre-think all of them and create habits that are worth having."

One other I would leave with you is one my father hit me with early in my life when he caught me cheating on some things. He said, "Let me tell you something. If you have to cheat to win, you didn't win." You never have a "W" when you broke a rule to get it. Were we perfect in all our behaviors? Of course not. But when you set those standards, or they're set for you by somebody you love and admire, then there's a good chance that when crunch time does come, you'll do the right thing, because you know what the right thing is.

Jerry Moore

I didn't spend enough time with my children. I had a great wife, but I didn't spend enough time with my children. My last couple of years at Appalachian State, every Thursday evening, we'd all go eat together. My kids were in their 30s and 40s by then. I really regret that, because I could have [spent more time with them, the time was there,] I just didn't discipline myself.

Ken Sparks

When I said I was going to be a coach, I wanted to be the best coach in America. I had a timeline. I wanted to be a high school head coach by a certain age. So, before I got my college diploma, I was named the head coach at a high school. I wanted to be a college assistant, and I reached that goal by the time I was 26 or 27. I wanted to be a coordinator. Dal Shealy gave me the opportunity to be a coordinator. I wanted to be a college head coach by a certain age, I reached that goal. But while I was doing all that stuff, my wife had some needs that I didn't realize she had, because I was too busy climbing my golden ladder. As a result, I lost my wife, and now have two young kids – a daughter and a son – who I raised myself. It was a great time in my life. The Lord taught me a whole lot and the golden ladder wasn't as attractive.

I have another piece of advice. The first thing you do when you get home from work, make sure you spend the first 30 minutes talking to your wife and asking, "How are you doing? What can I do to help you?"

Grant Teaff

As a football coach, you always have a game, or games, that you usually regret the outcome of. I remember in 1998 when Vince Dooley and Tom Landry were the Master Coaches. Almost everyone – except the diehard Cowboy fans, players and the coaches who had experienced it – had forgotten about the Ice Bowl. I remember looking directly at Tom asking, "Coach, do you have a regret?" His jaw tightened, and after a pause, he said, "Well, I don't think there's any question we were defeated in the Ice Bowl against Green Bay. That was probably the biggest disappointment that I had, mainly because we lost twice in that stadium. When you think about it, probably the key to the whole ball game was something I couldn't control." As Coach Landry explained, everything was fine when they arrived in Green Bay for the game. However, when they stepped on the field the next morning, it was solid ice. Someone had "accidentally" watered the field the night before. The Cowboys were ahead until the end of the game. With a few minutes remaining, Green Bay was on the one yard line and scored. Coach Landry never got over the fact his defensive players were unable to get traction on the ice and one yard cost them the Super Bowl.

We've all had games like that, the ones where we truly regret the outcome. Sometimes, as coaches, we regret many of our actions. Years after I had been a young head coach at McMurry, I received a letter from a young man. In the letter, he explained to me that I had kicked him off the team and that, at first, he resented and despised me because of it. He wrote that he finally realized the importance of what I was trying to teach him, and, frankly, didn't think he would have changed had he not gone through the trauma of losing the opportunity to be a part of the McMurry team. He wanted to let me know that my action made a positive difference in his life.

I was so glad to get that letter, because for all those years, I had deeply regretted my action toward that one player. I kept thinking it was my fault, because maybe I had not been patient enough or hadn't done a good enough job of explaining the consequences of certain behaviors that could lead to a young man being taken off my squad. Though I regretted my action, that letter verified that you still must do what you believe is right and stick to your guns.

I don't regret any job opportunity I refused. I always wanted to be head coach at Texas Tech, because I was from West Texas and had been an assistant at Tech. I was actually offered the job three times, but on each occasion, I felt I couldn't break away from the Baylor people who had suffered for many years before our staff arrived. Also, of course, I didn't want to leave my players. The same thing happened when I was offered jobs at Oklahoma State, Arizona, LSU, and Auburn. Paul Dietzel, the athletic director at LSU, came after me hard. I really liked him – and it was hard to say no – but again I was compelled to stay at Baylor.

Interestingly enough, I have never regretted those decisions, even though I would have received higher compensation and had better facilities. People could not understand why I felt Baylor was where I needed to be. I never regretted leaving my position as Baylor's athletic director to take over as the executive director of the American Football Coaches Association. Now when I step away from the AFCA in early 2016, I will once again leave with no regrets.

Chapter 10

Please, share some words of wisdom or an example of the power of a coach's influence.

Don Nehlen

I think the greatest influence on me was when I was a freshman at Bowling Green State University. At that time, freshmen played on the freshman team and I think our record was 1-9. My dad came to the homecoming game. We were playing Muhlenberg. They were beating us pretty bad and my dad said, "Don, you made a great decision. If you can't play here, you can't play anywhere." He was probably right. The next year, they hired Doyt Perry from Ohio State and everything changed. Bo Schembechler was an assistant coach, along with Bill Mallory, who was a graduate assistant, to name a few. All of a sudden, the football team took on a completely new direction because of the leader. The leader got what he demanded. He was honest and sincere. You always knew where you stood with the guy. Without him, I don't know where I'd be. He was the greatest coach I had ever been around.

Billy Graham said a coach has more influence on a young man in one day than the average guy has in a year. If I was going to pass on any information to a coach, it is, you have a great responsibility and a great opportunity to really help mold the young people in America.

I feel strongly that we don't teach values and discipline enough, but coaches can do that and make a difference in their schools.

R.C. Slocum

All of my coaches were the same kind of people. They were strong disciplinarians, but very caring people. One of my college coaches died two years ago. We stayed in close touch all the way up until his death. I remember one time when he kept me out of practice because I didn't recover a punt like I should have. I remember cussing that sucker for making me run laps after practice. I ended up loving the guy when it was all said and done. I had several coaches along the way who stressed, "I'm not as concerned about you really liking me as I am you respecting me." I can say that about every coach I had. Some of them, at that moment, I didn't like much; but I never had a coach I didn't respect. I came to love all of them the longer I played for them. I'm still in contact with every one of them who is still living.

Get up each day and be thankful for the things you have. It's been my experience that every job has some shortcomings. If you are in a rural setting coaching at a small school or if you are at a big school, there are some drawbacks to each. Some guys tend to spend all their time focusing on the things they don't have, or the things that are wrong with their job, instead of getting up every day and being thankful for all of the good things they have in their lives and in their job. I'm not worried about what's down the road; today, I am going to enjoy this situation. I'm going to enjoy those kids and enjoy the coaches around me.

I never worried about money at all. I was fortunate at the end that I made some money. I never took a job for money, never worried about it. I have young people come to me all the time who are looking for jobs, and I say, "You know what? Go find something you enjoy doing.

If you enjoy getting up every day and going to work, then stick with it." My experience was, even after some of the worst losses, I couldn't wait to get up and go in there with a bunch of coaches and say, "Man, we're going to get this worked out before next week." You can't put a price tag on that. There are guys driving BMWs and making a bunch of money, but they are miserable. They would come hang out with the athletic teams on the road because they were miserable in their jobs and they're looking for an outlet to have some fun. There was never a day in my life that I got up and said, "Oh man, I have to go to work today." So, get up every day and be excited and thankful for all you have. Whatever shortcomings there are, don't worry about them. Think about the positive things in your life. Take the players you have and make them better.

Bobby Bowden

My number one [influence] would have been my dad, but a real close second would be my high school coach.

I would like to say to [you coaches,] I really admire every one of you. I wish I knew all of you personally. I wish I could meet everybody and hear your life story. I think you and I are in the greatest profession in the world. I've always felt you could take this group of men and their influence [and they would be] as powerful as any group you could throw together in the world. I just want y'all to know that I'm very privileged to be in the same profession you're in. I'm thankful I know some of you. I wish I knew all of you, because of the camaraderie of our profession.

John Gagliardi

My father was an immigrant. He came from Italy at the age of 16 and went to the coal mines. Sometimes I think, how would I possibly go to a new land, not knowing the language and having just a third grade education? How could I possibly have done that? Now that's a hero to me; somebody who comes from nothing. I had a big head start.

Through the years, I have learned that there are a lot of great high school coaches and college coaches. Unfortunately, there are only so many big jobs at the big-time level and not so many are going to get a shot at it. I don't think you have to be at [a big college] to be happy. There are a lot of great high school coaches who have an incredibly good job. I don't know how they could be any happier. Honestly, I think you can do more good at the high school level than we can by the time we get them. At least, when we get them, they're pretty well [taught.] High school coaches are the real teachers. I hear from high school coaches all over the country, "How would you teach these guys how to tackle if you never tackle?" I say, "The kind of guys I get have made a lot of tackles. I didn't teach them." Mike Grant is a great high school coach in Minnesota. He played for me and uses our techniques. He's the guy who is teaching these guys how to do it. High school coaches are the teachers. By the time I get them, they're pretty well taught. I win and I coach a lot better with real good ball players. I'm not that good a coach where I can turn a lousy player into a good one. I have to figure out which ones are the best ones and play those guys.

I see a lot of kids coming to St. John's who want to be medical students. Well, they can't all get into med school. Amazingly, they find other careers and other things that make them happy. There's a lot of ways to get through the forest. You have to be happy with whatever you're doing. To be truthful, you might not get the credit. Offensive linemen are the guys who make a football team. They get no credit, and yet they're the first guys down after they blast a hole and let a guy run through and score. They're the first guys down there to congratulate the running back who did nothing but carry the ball. The ball wasn't very heavy. Offensive linemen and high school coaches are my heroes.

Terry Donahue

As you grow through life, you change. Your views on a lot of things change. I'm not sure that, as a young coach or even as a veteran coach, I had a total appreciation or understanding of how powerful words that come from a coach are. I wish I was as smart then as I think I might be today. Words are very powerful. How and what we say to players has a dramatic effect on them; much more than you will ever imagine at this stage of your career. It's incredible. When Troy Aikman was inducted into the NFL Hall of Fame, he thanked his various coaches. I happened to be lucky enough to be one of them. He said, "When things were going good, Coach Donahue would always say that they're not going that good, or when things are going bad, he would say that they're not going that bad. I've always taken this through my life." I never knew he even listened to it or paid any attention to it, and yet he could recite it years after he'd left UCLA.

As a coach, you have to recognize that you're held in a position of esteem and players are going to remember what you say to them. I think you have to be very careful with your criticism and with how you try to improve a player. You have to be very careful, because sometimes your words can be a very deadly instrument.

My words of wisdom to the young coaches – be very careful [of what you say,] because words can do an inordinate amount of damage and a lot more damage than you mean.

There are coaches in my life like Jerry Long, Pepper Rodgers, Dick Vermeil and Tommy Prothro. These were four people in my life who gave me an opportunity to play and an opportunity to coach.

Opportunity is one of the most important and precious gifts anyone can receive. How we respond when we receive the gift of opportunity, and how often we can give it back to others, can really define our lives. It can define who we are and what we've done. I was given the gift of opportunity from those four coaches. One was my head coach. One was my position coach who believed in me when I didn't. One was a coach who hired me as a volunteer coach when I had no experience or knowledge. The last was a coach who gave me a job when he didn't have to. Those four guys dramatically influenced my professional life.

John Robinson

For young coaches, it's important that you aspire to teach better. It's so easy to want to become the coordinator who draws up new defenses, zone blitzes, sprint formations and such. You become focused on that part of the game and ignore the chance to teach a guy to move his feet or do the basic things. The great coaches are always great teachers and think through teaching.

There were coaches who meant a big deal to me. John McKay gave me advice when I was trying to become a coach. He said, "Take a yellow pad with you everywhere you go. When you go to the can, take a yellow pad with you." It's been embarrassing to me in parts of my life, but I've always done it. I've always had a yellow pad. My wife will say, "Why do you have that yellow pad, we're going to church." I just reply, "You don't understand."

Len Casanova was my coach in college. He was a great man. He was a tough guy and demanded a lot of us. I wasn't a very good football player, but I was smart enough to know I had to do all the other things right. We were both Catholic. He was a devout Catholic and he demanded that you go to church on Sunday. It wasn't because he was the coach, it was because he was going to strangle you if you didn't. I made sure that whichever Mass he went to, I went to. I would stay and say to him, "Hi Cas, just wanted to say 'hello.'" If I missed him at Mass, I stayed after and saw him coming into the next Mass. Later on, I was at USC and we beat Notre Dame in the last game of the year. We were ranked No. 3 in the nation and we were headed to the Rose Bowl. At about midnight, I get a call from Cas and he says, "Now Robby, I know you're on top and I know you think you're big-time and all that, but you get up and you go to Mass tomorrow morning." That was something I always thought was impressive.

There is an emotional aspect, too. I don't know why I got caught up in this Michigan thing. Bo Schembechler and I ended up friends and we traveled a lot. I had a chance to speak at his memorial service and I think there were over 30,000 Michigan alumni. There were probably four or five hundred Michigan guys who had played for Bo. Being there that day, and seeing all of those guys there for their coach, made me think about how important coaching is. We will go to our grave wishing we could still be coaching. I'm 87 and I'd go back. If somebody gave me a job, I'd go back tomorrow. Now, I'd need a nap at about 2:00 in the afternoon, but I'd still love to go back one more time.

Tom Osborne

I want to say just a word or two about influence. I think you're all aware of this, but our culture has changed. I started coaching in 1962. In 1962, the out-of-wedlock birth rate was five percent. Today it's 37 percent. When I went out recruiting in 1962 and 1963, we'd occasionally run across somebody from a single-parent family, but if we did, it was usually because one parent was deceased. Today, over half of our kids are growing up without both biological parents.

The drug culture, the alcohol issue, the gangs, and the violence have shifted tremendously. The biggest factor we're dealing with is homes without fathers. About 25 million kids in our country have no father. When you don't have a dad, just about every kind of dysfunction doubles and triples.

So, in many cases, [coaches are] the dad, taking the place of something missing in a kid's life. It's a tremendous responsibility. Typically what happens is, we have a single mom who's working hard and can barely keep her head above water. She can't really discipline and pay attention to some of the kids, try as she might. So, a lot of the kids don't know much about discipline. [Coaches] have to teach them about discipline. A lot of them don't value education. They don't realize that they're not going to go very far if they don't have some kind of marketable skill. You're the only guy who, maybe, can make them do [right], because they'll go to class so they can play football. Maybe somewhere along the line, they'll begin to realize that education is worth [their time]. The best way you can [help them] is by being a role model.

There's one type of leadership called transformational leadership. I invite you to study it a little bit. A transformational leader is one who can get a group of people from here to there better than any other kind of leader. But it comes with a price, because you have to be a role model. You have to walk the walk. You have to be willing to listen empathetically, not just always tell, but really listen and try to get inside a kid's psyche and know what's making him behave like he does. You have to be able to see over the horizon. You have to anticipate the future a little bit. If [coaches] can become transformational leaders, or at least have some of those characteristics, it will make a difference in our culture.

The number one threat I see to our country today is not al Qaeda, it's not the economy. Those things are all important, but the biggest threat I see is what's happening to our young people. If we reach a critical point where we have 40, 50, 60 percent dropping out of school and so many broken families, at some point a free society will not function anymore. That's the thing [coaches] can make a significant difference in.

I hope that doesn't come off as too emotional or phony, but I really have come to believe [coaches can make a huge impact]. It's a very powerful profession. I've done some things since I left coaching, but I would have to say that certainly the years I spent coaching were the most significant years I had in my lifetime. Don't lose track of that

Joe Paterno

I would encourage you to do just as Tom [Osborne] said to. I couldn't improve on what he said. Our problem is our young people. Our problem is the temptations they have, and the environment they're in. If we don't have the ability to influence them and set the example to help these kids understand what they can do with their lives if they get their education, who's going to do it? Who has more influence on a kid? It drives me nuts when I go into a high school and they don't have the football coach teaching in the high school, which is happening a lot in our state. That doesn't mean that the fellow who's coaching football isn't a great guy and he isn't doing a great job. When I was in high school and my high school coach walked down that hall, I went around the corner. I've seen guys take high schools and turn the whole environment around. It's the same way in college. We're getting 18-, 19-, 20-year-old kids don't have the slightest idea what's important to them except football.

In 1951, I went to my first AFCA Convention. The AFCA Convention was held at the Baker Hotel in Dallas, Texas. We drove from State College to Dallas. We got into Dallas late one night and couldn't get into our rooms. There's this guy in the lobby, and he has a whole bunch of guys around him – it might have been 40 or 50 guys – because nobody could get into their room. I think his name was Woody Hayes, and he was giving a clinic on how to run the off-tackle play. He'd just won all his games at Miami (Ohio) University. I've never forgotten that moment.

It's been a great life for me, and I hope it's as good a life for you. The more you put into it, the more you're going to get out of it. I have no regrets about how much I've put into it. I've given it my best shot. Hopefully, I have a couple more shots left. You guys go get it and have a heck of a good time.

Lou Holtz

You can be successful. You can go out and make millions of dollars if you put the same amount of time in [another] profession as you do in coaching. But when you die, that ends. When you're in coaching, you have a chance to be significant. Significance is when you help other people be successful and that lasts many a lifetime.

I was tough on athletes, but when I talk about trust, commitment, and care, I believe it. It's not something I just talk about. It's something I believe and I try to live. There's not a week that goes by where I don't get a letter from a former athlete. I have a letter here from a guy who played for me at Notre Dame.

It says: "Coach, as I find myself preparing for the new year, I can't help but reflect on the influence you've had on my life. Each year that passes, I find myself quoting more and more of your words and truly understanding the importance of what you taught me, from the prayer you shared, 'What will the day bring?' to the importance of having a plan. I've truly come to appreciate all you've done for me. You made me a better husband, a better father, and a better human being. I hope you never forget the impact you had on the players, the men who have had the pleasure of playing for you, and I truly wish there was more I could do beyond saying thank you. To that end, I also hope the commitment, trust, and love that I give influences those who I come in contact with every day in some small way, and will allow me to share these great things you've given me. God bless and I hope the best for your and the entire Holtz family, and that you experience the blessings in the New Year that you so richly deserve. – Charlie Stafford, University of Notre Dame, '91 to '95."

As a coach, you have such an influence. I would give our players a questionnaire, "Who influenced your life the most and why?" Eighty percent of the athletes [would say it] was their coach – not always a high school coach or their head coach – but it was always a coach.

Remember, the great impact you have is on young people's lives. Be proud of what you're doing and understand that you're doing them a favor by setting standards and helping them to be great and to believe in themselves. Also, remember, when they need love and understanding the most is usually when they deserve it the least.

Lastly, have a vision where you want to take your program, and a plan of how you're going to get there. Hold people accountable and make sure everybody on your team shares the same core values. What holds a country together, what holds a family together, what holds a team together, are core values. You don't have to like one another. You don't have to like the same music. You don't have to like the same food. Family doesn't mean you have the same last name or the same address. It means you share the same core values: We're going to trust one another. We're going to be committed. We're going to care. We're going to close ranks. We're going to march on.

Dick MacPherson

I don't think the power of the coach's influence can be exemplified [by anyone more than it can] by Lou Holtz. He has certainly done a great job. I hope you all know that I am too darn old to coach anymore. I also want you to know that, as I look around, the message I want to leave with everybody is that I respect the heck out of each and every one of you. You are what is going to make the greatest game even better. I think when you go back to your community, your college, and you find a way to become a better football team, that day is way, way above anything you've won.

It's been a huge privilege for me, and to be honest with you, I'm going to be a better man and more fired up about this game just by being here with you people tonight. Thank you very much for the opportunity.

Barry Alvarez

I always hear, "How do I get a head coaching job? How do I get hired here? How do I get there?" Take care of your business. Work the job you have as hard as you can work it. Don't worry about your next job. How many times do we see guys go through [their contacts] when they get a new job, and they're on the phone calling for their next job? Let me tell you, when you do a good job where you are, people notice. When I was an assistant coach, I knew the [other coaches]. When I arrived at school at 7:30, I knew who was there at 7:15. I knew the guys who were out late and the guys who weren't getting up. I knew who the guys who were working were. The guys who are coaching well, you see it on film. Film doesn't lie. When you take care of your business and do your job well, people will notice. In this business, [that's the way to have] upward mobility.

Fisher DeBerry

I would like to leave you with a thought on how I believe, without a doubt, how the game has changed. That [change is in regard to] the fundamentals of the game – blocking and tackling. The team who blocks tackles the best has the best chance to win. I try to make my guys understand that and not lose sight of the four critical areas I felt were so important [in respect to] who won or lost. Number one, we had to win the turnover battle. Two, we had to be penalized less than our opponent. Three, we had to dominate the kicking game. Then, four, we had to dominate the possession game. Those were four things I thought were [critical].

We never know the seeds we sow and the influence we have as coaches or adults. Just a couple years ago, I was in South Carolina playing in a golf tournament for our foundation. I had called a couple of guys who played for me in high school and asked them to come be a part of that and help us orchestrate it.

One who came, I hadn't seen in almost 40 years. He said, "Coach, how many garden seeds did you say today?" I said, "What the heck are you talking about?" He said, "Coach, all the time, rather than cuss us, you used to say, garden seed, you could do better than that." I'd never really given it much thought, but you never know the influence you're going to have.

The greatest words I hear since I retired is when I get a call from a former player or a former coach, and the last thing he tells me is,

"Coach, I love you and I appreciate what you did for me." I think most of us here today are in coaching – whether it's high school or college – because of our coaches. The influence they had on us motivated and stimulated us to want to give back and be a coach. I think the greatest thing we could do today as coaches, if your coach is still living, pick up the phone and give him a call; tell him how much you really appreciate him. I did that myself just prior to Christmas and it made me feel good.

Probably the greatest honor I ever had in coaching was last Christmas, when I got a Christmas card from a former manager. On the front of that Christmas card, it had the cutest little boy you've ever seen in a Santa Claus suit. The boy was his first son. I read the letter and it said: "Coach, you were always there for us." – He didn't play, but he was our head manager, and I always tried to make him feel like he was just as important as any [of the players.] – He said, "I attended a lot of the meetings and I listened. I learned a lot that I'm able to use in my military assignments now. You were there for me. I got in a little pickle there in my senior year, and you went to bat for me. My wife and I decided if our first child was a little boy, we would name him Fisher." To me, that is the highest compliment and the highest honor I ever had, along with the honor of being asked by the family of my college coach to do his eulogy.

We have an awesome responsibility today to be role models. A lot of us might be the only father figure that a kid has. One out of every four kids in this nation today are products of single-parent families. We might very well be the only father figure in their life, and the team might be the only family identification some kids have. I think we have an awesome responsibility there.

In closing ask yourself this question, "As you go on day by day, what do you want your legacy to be?" As Barry [Alvarez] was saying, when it's all over, I don't think the wins and losses are going to mean as much, and the plaques and awards will have dust all over them. I think the only thing that will last is the investment we're making in young people's lives. That investment is going to last forever.

Lloyd Carr

I came across a statement I think sums up what this game is all about. Georgia Tech coach Bobby Dodd said, "We must always remember that the most important thing in the game is the boy who plays the game." What that means to me is this: if you are a high school coach, there are all kinds of college opportunities for these kids. It may be NAIA, it may be Division III, Division II, but there is a place for a lot of these kids, and if you, as a high school coach, can help them find it, you have changed a life.

If you are a college coach, I always said, "What is your goal in terms of graduation rates?" There should only be one goal and that is 100 percent. We may not get there, but we have to strive to get there. Whether you are an assistant coach or a head coach, stay after them. When their eligibility is up, check on them, call them, "Hey, if you finish this course, how can I help you?" That is putting the kid first. Education is a part of our job.

Second? Safety. I go all over the country and I am starting to run into a lot of mothers who say, "I am not going to let my son play football because of all of these issues regarding concussions." Gentlemen, when you take that field, whatever you do in your drills, the way you conduct your practices, ask yourselves, "How do we make the game safer?" That is our job.

There are a lot of things that are going to be developing here in the next few years. We have to show people we know how to coach this game in a way that is good for kids, because if we can't, what good is this game? We have to do better, and every man can make a difference.

Tubby Raymond

Learning how to focus on the job at hand is extremely important; it may be the answer to solving all the problems, or a lot of the problems, of coaches today. Before ball games, I see some coaches who are flitting around and not really paying attention, where kids are bouncing around and they are not focusing on the job at hand. I think if you focus on the job at hand, you have a chance of being the very best you can be. You have to work at it; you have to practice it. We used to say with our football games, "Give us two hours. Don't think about the chemistry test on Monday, your girlfriend, your dog, you mother, you father, just think about your assignments for two hours."

Phil Fulmer

If I were a young coach, I would try the best I could to learn the other side of the ball and learn different positions. You have to be a teacher, you have to be a teacher on a lot of levels. The more you know about the game, the better coach that you're going to be. The more fundamentals you can coach, the more opportunities you're going to have for a lot of different positions.

Being a teacher means you're a great communicator, that you're able to make a youngster understand what you're trying to get across and where he fits into the scheme of things.

Establish a philosophy about what you want [your team] to look like from a physical standpoint. I mentioned earlier that I cut my teeth on going against those Auburn and Alabama defenses as an offensive line coach. I knew when I [was a head coach], that was going to be a priority for me. Not that I wasn't trying to do it the whole time as an assistant coach, but we were going to have tailbacks and receivers of that kind. I want those guys who can control the game.

Figure out who the three teams you have to beat are and recruit to that, whoever they are. For us, after the divisional play, it was Georgia, Alabama, and Florida. We recruited to that. We coached to that. We think we were outstanding, fundamental coaches. You're not going to out scheme people and win a lot of football games. In the end, you're going to have to be able to hit somebody, and you're going to have to be able to run proper depth on a route or break or whatever and get 65 percent rather than 50 percent done to win games.

Dick Vermeil

I don't know if I can give wisdom, but I'll tell you, I believe in experience. I believe you can gain experience quicker by surrounding yourself with people you respect who have already done it successfully many, many times. You can learn from them. I learned an awful lot by having the office next door to John Wooden when I was at UCLA. – early as an assistant and then when I came back. After he retired, he still had an office there. He would eat breakfast with us in the mornings at training camp. You wouldn't believe how fundamentally simple he boiled down winning. If I tell people, it's something they think is not really true.

I'm sitting there in my office. We have to beat USC to do anything in Southern California. One day, we're at the turning table and John says, "You know Dick I hear you talking a lot about USC. Quit talking about USC. First off, you are never going to have as many good players as they have. Spend more time worrying about making the kids you have the best they can be. Spend more time helping your coaches be the best coaches they can be. Invest more time in recruiting the kids that you can get and making them better." Don't worry about winning. John Wooden never talked about winning. Your process will take care of that. It was so simple and I never ever forgot that. If I find myself in a bind, even today, I stop and think about that.

Once, I said, "John I have three pretty good running backs here. I'm going to have a hard time keeping them all happy." He said, "Don't worry about that. Just make sure you keep the best one happy." Now how simple and fundamental is that? That's how he would answer you.

I would go watch his practice. That's where I developed our fast practices. That doesn't mean you have to knock the heck out of everybody when you have pads on, but the tempo in which we practiced was very fast. When I watched John Wooden's practices, it was amazing how quickly they did everything. It was always a direct carryover to how well they played. I've gone in and watched Phil [Fulmer's] teams practice and seen how hard they worked, and with Bill Snyder at Kansas State, you can see – yes, they have talented players – the practice tempo and the quickness in the movement. It is a game of movement and you can get used to moving extremely quick all the time.

Tommy Prothro taught me – and it was especially true in the old days – you only scrimmage when you don't know what else to do. Stop and think about it. He taught me more about breaking down an offensive team, a defensive team and units, and to coach them and make them better without being a full team, than anybody I was ever around. He was really good at putting up practice. There was no routine practice. Every practice was totally different. We did that at the Rams my first two years. One day, we added a period to practice the next day. Sure it made practices longer, but you know what happened? They got better.

Marino Casem

"Ask not of your neighbor's birth, nor the way he makes a prayer, ask only if his game is square." I believe you have to believe in the worth of every man. I don't care what his makeup is, "ask not of his birth, nor the way he makes a prayer, just treat him squarely." I believe, ethically, you have to choose your words wisely. You have to mean what you say. What you say has to have meaning to the person you're talking to, whether it's your squad or an individual. We are very fortunate to be called coach.

Bill McCartney

How many of you know that 211 degree water is hot? At 212 degrees, water boils. At 211 degrees, a steam engine's not going anywhere. At 212 degrees, a steam engine can pull a mile-long freight train around a mountain pass. One degree changes everything. That's the way it is with young men. The lights go on. You never give up on them. You're always bringing out more in them. I believe everything rises and falls on leadership. I believe coaches are in the best position to bring that kind of leadership.

Bill Curry

I had a very complicated relationship with Coach Lombardi because I had just left Bobby Dodd at Georgia Tech. Under Coach Dodd, who was the epitome of the Southern gentleman, profanity was used maybe once every five years when we just went off and went crazy, then he might use a few words of profanity. Otherwise, that just wasn't part of the process. When I got to Green Bay, we had this guy who was not Southern, and his vocabulary was considerably saltier than Coach Dodd's. All he talked about was your religion, your family, and the

Green Bay Packers. Those will be your priorities. You'll think of nothing else. As soon as we got on the practice field, he got really confused about the order of the priorities. I didn't like him. I did not play well for him. I hated his guts because I thought he was a hypocrite. Somebody said, "Coach goes to church every day." I said, "Ain't no way this guy's a Christian. There's no way." Naturally, I was being judgmental. He was a Brooklyn native. He was Catholic. He was different from us, and you weren't supposed to like anybody different from us, so I bridled at all of that.

I was traded to the Baltimore Colts where Don Shula had an entirely different approach – equally great coach, entirely different personality. I was openly critical of Coach Lombardi. I was downright dishonest. When we got to Super Bowl III, I was the only player who had played for both Lombardi and Shula, so the press descended on me, wanted to know the difference between them. I said, "I love Coach Shula. I don't respect Coach Lombardi. Coach Lombardi's abusive."

I had gone to Bart Starr, who was the only veteran who would talk rookie. I said, "There's no way Coach goes to church every day." He said, "Oh, no, he does, goes to Mass every morning. He's a very devout Catholic. You're going to realize, after you work for this man about three weeks, this man needs to go to church every day."

I was accosted by Paul Hornung not long after that Super Bowl. Paul wanted to fight. He said, "You trashed the old man in the press. You made his mama cry." I had never thought about Vince Lombardi having a mom. I felt bad then. Paul wanted to punch me out for saying the things I said; we argued back and forth, and I defended myself. He said, "I'll tell you this. If the old man saw you, he would treat you like his long-lost son." I said, "If the old man saw me, he'd treat me like dirt, like he always did." They pulled us apart, and that was the end of that.

I was at the National Prayer Breakfast in Washington, D.C., a month later. I was walking up a narrow staircase at the Washington Hilton and guess who's coming down the other way? No escape. Vince Lombardi sticks out his hand. He greets me like his long-lost son, which made me feel about an inch high.

A few months later, he was on his deathbed, and one of my teammates, Bob Long, called. He said, "You and I are going to go see Coach." I told him, "We are not going to see Coach, because I wouldn't be allowed in the room." He said, "If I have to come drag your big rear end out of that hotel room, I will, but you're going to go see Vince Lombardi."

We get off the elevator, and the person I was really scared to see was Marie [Lombardi's wife]. She was standing right there with Sonny Jurgensen – Coach Lombardi had gone to Washington to be the head coach. – Marie escorted me into the room. I stood there shaking like a leaf with tears in my eyes and apologized for shooting my mouth off. I said, "Coach, I really came here today to tell you that you've meant a lot to my life." He stretched out his left hand, his right arm was full of tubes. I took his left hand, and he said, "You can mean a lot to my life if you'll pray for me."

So, what had the great man done? He had forgiven me when I least deserved it. In that moment, it changed my life. That's what the Christian faith is about, and I saw that he was true to his value system. Yes, he had the greatest play-off record, and he was an incredible football coach, but he was so much more. I had not been mature enough to see it. I was deeply humbled.

Coach Lombardi's greatest attribute as a coach was that he would not tolerate racism. In 1965, other teams in the NFL had quotas, so they had one or two African-American players. Vince Lombardi had 10 African-American players on a 40-man roster. Other teams bragged about having quotas and that they only had one, two, or no African-American players, and we beat them every Sunday. That was his greatest attribute as a human being, and his spiritual fiber was his greatest attribute as a Christian.

Jerry Moore

Don't forget what it really takes to be the kind of man you should be. There are so many good examples.

Ken Sparks

God called me into coaching. I wasn't a Christian until I was 18 years old. Right at the end of my senior year, I became a Christian and accepted Christ into my life. All at once, I wasn't getting put in jail, and I wasn't doing some of the crazy things I'd been doing, because he changed my life. I was asked, as a 19-year-old, to coach a 12- and 13-year-old little league football team. I coached them, and it was unbelievable. We won the Knoxville City Championship. All at once, I understood the power of influence a coach has.

I have cancer, but cancer doesn't have me, the Lord has me. So, my words of wisdom are along those lines. I was fired at Carson-Newman once. I've been the head coach there for 35 years, but when I was assistant coach, I got fired. Coach [Dal] Shealy went to Baylor, and the guy who replaced him fired me. I've been through a divorce. Now, I have cancer, but the promises of God have not let me down.

So, here's my advice: leave the results up to him. He's never made a mistake. Honor him with the way you live your life. Jeremiah 29:11 says, "I know the plans I have for you." They're plans for good, not for bad. They're plans to give you a future. I'd like to paraphrase Jeremiah 20, verse 9, which we don't hear much about: If I say that I'm not going to mention the Lord anymore or call on his name, his message becomes a fire burning inside of me, even consuming my bones. I can't contain it, and I cannot hold it in.

The greatest hope this country has is for you guys to take a stand for the things you know are right. If we did, we probably wouldn't be staying in the office till 10, 11 o'clock at night. We would probably take at least one day off, to spend quality time with our family. If God created the world and all that's in it in six days, then we can get ready to play a football game in [that time] and we can take a day off, and go to church. We can spend time with our families. We can spend it in personal growth. We can spend it in doing things that are critical for us.

Grant Teaff

I have written and spoken throughout the years about the impact my high school and college coaches had on my life. Somehow, I knew they loved me even though that word was never mentioned. That love caused me to be open about my love for my players. I always encouraged my teams to find ways to care about each other.

One other thing my coaches taught me is that the coach-player relationship does not end with the last ball game. I believe it behooves all of us to make sure we prepare ourselves to mentor, coach, and lead those we are responsible for.

My final words of wisdom have been spoken and written many times. This is my strong conviction: "If we, as teachers, coaches, and parents, preach a sermon, we need to make sure we live what we preach."

Biographical Sketches

Barry Alvarez
2011 Master Coach

Barry Alvarez was born in Langeloth, Pennsylvania, in 1946. Alvarez attended the University of Nebraska-Lincoln, where he played linebacker from 1965-1967. He accepted his first coaching position at Lincoln Northeast (Neb.) High School as an assistant from 1971-1973. He then accepted a head coaching position at Lexington (Neb.) High School from 1974-1975 and served as the head coach at Mason City (Iowa) High School, from 1976-1978.

In 1979, Alvarez coached linebackers at the University of Iowa, then moved on to coach linebackers at Notre Dame in 1987. He was Notre Dame's defensive coordinator from 1988-1989.

In 1990, Alvarez accepted the head coaching job at Wisconsin. During his time there, he lead the Badgers to a 119-74-4 record, three Big Ten conference championships (1993, 1998, 1999) and nine bowl victories, including three Rose Bowl wins.

Alvarez became the Athletic Director at Wisconsin in 2004 and currently serves in that role. He was inducted into the College Football Hall of Fame in 2010. He was the AFCA Coach of the Year in 1993, the Bobby Dodd Coach of the Year in 1993, and a two-time Big Ten Coach of the Year in 1993 and 1998. Alvarez was also an AFCA Regional Coach of the Year in 2004.

Bobby Bowden
2007 Master Coach

Bobby Bowden was born in Birmingham, Alabama, in 1929. He attended the University of Alabama and played as a quarterback his freshman year before transferring and playing for Howard College (now Samford University).

He graduated from Howard College in 1953 and served as an assistant football coach and head track and field coach. He left his alma mater to become athletic director, as well as head football, baseball and basketball coach at South Georgia College from 1956 to 1958. Bowden then returned to Howard as head coach, where he compiled a 31-6 record between 1959 and 1962. In 1962, Bowden went to Florida State University as an assistant coach. Bowden left Florida State in 1965 to go to West Virginia University as an assistant. In 1970, Bowden became the head coach of the Mountaineers and compiled a 42-26 record. Bowden returned to FSU as head coach in 1976, where he compiled a 304-97-4 record, led his teams to two National Championships (1993 and 1999), 12 Atlantic Coast Conference titles and 2 ACC Atlantic Division titles before retiring in 2009.

Bowden was inducted to the College Football Hall of Fame in 2006. He also received the Bobby Dodd Coach of the Year Award (1980) and the Walter Camp Coach of the Year Award (1991). He was the 2011 AFCA Amos Alonzo Stagg Award recipient and received AFCA Regional -District Coach of the Year honors in 1977, 1979, 1992 and 1995. Bowden served on the AFCA Board of Trustees from 1993 to 1998.

Lloyd Carr
2012 Master Coach

Lloyd Carr was born in Hawkins County, Tennessee, in 1945. He attended the University of Missouri from 1964 to 1966, where he played both football and baseball, then attended Northern Michigan University in 1967 and played quarterback for them while earning his Master's in Education Administration.

Carr began his coaching career as an assistant coach at several high schools in Michigan from 1968 to 1975. At the collegiate level, he made assistant coaching stops at Eastern Michigan (1976-1977), Illinois (1978-1979), West Virginia (1980) and Michigan (1980-1994). Carr became the head coach at Michigan in 1995 and led the Wolverines to a 122-40 record, five Big Ten Conference championships (1997, 1998, 2000, 2003, 2004) and a National Championship (1997) before retiring after the 2007 season.

Carr was inducted into the College Football Hall of Fame in 2011. He has received several honors, including the AFCA Coach of the Year (1997), the George Munger Award (1997), the Paul "Bear" Bryant Award (1997), the Walter Camp Coach of the Year Award (1997), the Bobby Dodd Coach of the Year Award (2007), and an AFCA Regional Coach of the Year in 1997. Carr served on the AFCA Board of Trustees from 2003-2005.

Marino Casem
2014 Master Coach

Marino Casem was born in Memphis, Tennessee, in 1934. Casem attended Xavier University of New Orleans where he played as a center on offense and as a linebacker on defense. Upon his graduation in 1956, Casem got his first coaching job at Utica Junior College. He was drafted into the Army in 1957, where he served for three years. Casem got his Master's degree from the University of Northern Colorado in 1962 and went straight to Alabama State to work as head coach for a year.

It was at Alcorn State University where Casem truly made a name for himself. Made head coach in 1964, with athletic director responsibilities added in 1966, Casem won his first Black College National Championship in 1968 and repeated the endeavor the next year. Marino would go on to add two more Black College National Championships while at Alcorn State, making his biggest statement with his squad in 1984. It was the team in 1984 that finished its season as the top team in Division I-AA with a 9-0 record, the first black college to achieve that honor. Casem maintained a high drive in his football program while with the Braves, ending his time there with a 132-65-8 record to become the all-time winningest coach in program history. Casem was awarded the Southwestern Athletic Conference's Coach of the Year award seven times while at Alcorn State.

In addition to receiving the 2013 AFCA Trailblazer Award, Casem was inducted into the Southwestern Athletic Conference Hall of Fame in 1992, the Alcorn State University Hall of Honor in 1993, the Mississippi Sports Hall of Fame in 1994, the Alcorn State University Sports Hall of Fame in 1996, the College Football Hall of Fame in 2003 and, finally, into the National Association of Collegiate Director of Athletics Hall of Fame in 2006, not to mention a plethora of individual awards from several national institutions.

Bill Curry
2015 Master Coach

Bill Curry was born in College Park, Georgia, in 1942. Curry played at Georgia Tech from 1962 to 1964 and was drafted by the Green Bay Packers in 1965. He played for the Baltimore Colts from 1967-1972, and made a year-long stop at the Houston Oilers (1973) and the Los Angeles Rams (1974).

Curry's first coaching job was at Georgia Tech in 1976, he served as an assistant before moving up as an offensive line coach with the Green Bay Packers from 1977 to 1979.

Bill Curry became the head coach at his alma mater, Georgia Tech, in 1980. After seven years at Georgia Tech, Curry moved on to the University of Alabama. During his time at the helm of the Crimson Tide, Curry led his teams to an appearance in three bowl games, winning the Sun Bowl in 1988. In 1989, Curry led Alabama to an SEC conference championship title.

After Alabama, Coach Curry went on to the University of Kentucky as the head coach for seven seasons. In 2010, he was named the first head coach at Georgia State University and retired after the 2012 season.

Curry received many honors, including the AFCA Amos Alonzo Stagg Award (2007), the ACC Coach of the Year Award (1985), the Bobby Dodd Coach of the Year Award (1989) and was a two-time SEC Coach of the Year (1987, 1989).

Fisher DeBerry
2011 Master Coach

Fisher DeBerry was born in Cheraw, South Carolina, in 1938. DeBerry attended and played for Wofford College from 1956-1960. He began his coaching career as an assistant at Bennettsville (S.C.) High School in 1962 and at Florence McClenaghan (S.C.) High School from 1963-1968. DeBerry returned to Wofford as an assistant coach from 1969-1970 before moving on to Appalachian State as an assistant from 1971-1979.

DeBerry arrived at Air Force in 1980 as the quarterbacks coach and became the offensive coordinator in 1981. In 1984, DeBerry became the head coach at Air Force and served in that role until 2006. During that time, he led the Falcons to a 169-109-1 record, three Western Athletic Conference championships (1985, 1995, 1998) and a Western Athletic Conference Mountain Division title (1998).

DeBerry was inducted into the College Football Hall of Fame in 2011. He received several honors, including the AFCA Coach of the Year (1985), the Bobby Dodd Coach of the Year Award (1985), the Walter Camp Coach of the Year Award (1985). He was a three-time WAC Coach of the Year and an AFCA Regional Coach of the Year (1985), among many other honors. He received the AFCA Amos Alonzo Stagg Award in 2012, one of the AFCA's highest honors.

DeBerry served on the AFCA's Board of Trustees from 1988 to 1995 and served as the Association's President in 1996. From 2001 to 2005, he served as the AFCA Code of Ethics Committee Chairman.

Terry Donahue
2008 Master Coach

Terry Donahue was born in Los Angeles, California, in 1944. He played at UCLA as a defensive tackle from 1965 to 1966.

After graduating, Donahue became an assistant coach at the University of Kansas. In 1971, he returned to UCLA as an assistant coach before he took over as head coach. From 1976 to 1995, Donahue led the Bruins to a 151-74-8 record and five Pac-10 Conference titles. Donahue has the most conference wins of any coach in Pacific-10 Conference history (98) and also the most wins in UCLA Bruins football history (151).

Donahue was the lead college football analyst for CBS Sports from 1996 to 1998. In 1999, Donahue became the Director of Player Personnel for the San Francisco 49ers, where he later became the general manager from 2001 to 2005.

Donahue was inducted into the College Football Hall of Fame in 2000 and was a two time Pac-10 Coach of the Year (1985, 1993). He served on the AFCA Board of Trustees from 1990 to 1995.

Phil Fulmer
2013 Master Coach

Phillip Fulmer was born in Winchester, Tennessee, in 1950. He attended the University of Tennessee and played as an offensive guard from 1968 to 1971. In 1972, Fulmer served as a student coach until his first assistant coaching job in 1974 at Wichita State. After making a stop at Vanderbilt in 1979, Fulmer returned to Tennessee as the offensive line coach from 1980 to 1988 and then served as the offensive coordinator from 1989 to 1992.

In 1992, Fulmer became Tennessee's head coach and led his teams to an overall record of 152-52, six Southeastern Conference Eastern division titles (1997, 1998, 2001, 2003, 2004, 2007), two SEC Conference Championships (1997, 1998) and a National Championship in 1998 before retiring in 2008.

Fulmer was inducted into the College Football Hall of Fame in 2012. He received several honors, including AFCA Coach of the Year (1998), AFCA Regional Coach of the Year (1993), the Eddie Robinson Coach of the Year Award (1998), the George Munger Award (1998), the Home Depot Coach of the Year Award (1998), the Sporting News College Football Coach of the Year Award (1998) and the SEC Coach of the Year Award (1998).

Fulmer served on the AFCA Board of Trustees from 1996 to 2002 and served as the Association's President in 2003.

John Gagliardi
2007 Master Coach

John Gagliardi was born in Trinidad, Colorado in 1926. Gagliardi began coaching football at Trinidad High School in 1943, at the age of 16, when his high school coach was called into service during World War II. He was a player-coach his senior year of high school and continued to coach high school football at St. Mary's High School while obtaining his college degree at Colorado College.

At the age of 22, with six years of high school coaching, Gagliardi was hired at Carroll College in Helena, Montana. In four seasons as head coach at Carroll, Gagliardi compiled a 24-6-1 record, winning three Montana Collegiate Conference championships. After the 1952 season, Gagliardi left Carroll for Saint John's University. In 60 seasons coaching the Saint John's Johnnies, Gagliardi won a school and conference record 27 Minnesota Intercollegiate Athletic Conference (MIAC) titles and 4 national championships. His record at Saint John's was 465-132-10, bringing his career college football mark to 489-138-11, the most wins in college football history.

Gagliardi was inducted into the College Football Hall of Fame in 2006 and was an AFCA Amos Alonzo Stagg Award recipient in 2009. He received the AFCA National Coach of the Year Award and was an AFCA Regional Coach of the Year in 2003. He was an AFCA District Coach of the Year in 1976.

Lou Holtz
2010 Master Coach

Lou Holtz was born in Follansbee, West Virginia, in 1937 and grew up in East Liverpool, Ohio. He attended Kent State as a linebacker from 1956 to 1957.

Holtz began his coaching career as a graduate assistant in 1960, at Iowa, where he received his Master's degree. From there, he made stops as an assistant at William & Mary (1961-1963), Connecticut (1964-1965), South Carolina (1966-1967) and Ohio State (1968).

Holtz landed his first head coach position at William & Mary in 1969. In 1970, he led the Indians to a Southern Conference title. In 1972, he moved on to North Carolina State and led his 1973 team to a win in the Liberty Bowl and an Atlantic Coast Conference title. Holtz was the head coach for the New York Jets for a year in 1976 before accepting the head coach position at the University of Arkansas from 1977 to 1983. He led the Razorbacks to a Southwest Conference title in 1979.

After two years as head coach for the Minnesota Gophers, Holtz arrived at Notre Dame, where he served as the head coach from 1986 to 1996. He led the Fighting Irish to a National Championship in 1988. In 1999, he moved to the University of South Carolina until he retired from coaching in 2004. He accumulated an overall career record of 249-132-7. Holtz worked for CBS Sports and ESPN as a college football analyst in the years following until 2015.

Holtz is a two-time Paul "Bear" Bryant Award recipient (1977, 1988), a two-time Eddie Robinson Coach of the Year (1977, 1988) and the Water Camp Coach of the Year in 1977. He was the 1972 ACC Coach of the Year recipient and the SEC Coach of the Year in 2000. He also received four AFCA District/Regional Coach of the Year honors (1972, 1979, 1988, 2000). Holtz was inducted into the College Football Hall of Fame in 2008.

Dick MacPherson
2010 Master Coach

Dick MacPherson was born in Old Town, Maine, in 1930. He played center and linebacker at Springfield College (Mass.). MacPherson began his coaching career as a graduate assistant as the University of Illinois in 1958. He received his first coaching job as an assistant at the University of Massachusetts in 1959. He made coaching stops at

Cincinnati (1961-1965), and Maryland (1966) before moving up to the NFL and serving as the defensive backs coach for the Denver Broncos from 1967-1970.

Named head coach at Massachusetts in 1971, MacPherson led the Minutemen to four Yankee Conference titles in seven years. During that span, he twice claimed New England Football Coach of the Year honors. His 45 victories at Massachusetts rank him third all-time in school history, and his 28-8-1 mark in Yankee Conference games notches a .778 winning percentage, which places him fifth in league history. The first UMass coach to win eight or more games in three different seasons, his nine-win campaign in 1972 tied the school record for single-season victories first set in 1901.

After his success with the Minutemen, Syracuse gave MacPherson their head job in 1981. MacPherson ranks third all-time at Syracuse for wins (66) and most seasons coached (10). During his tenure as head coach, he led the Orange to five bowl games while posting a 3-1-1 record in post-season play. In 1987, the Orange posted an 11-0-1 record, playing Auburn to a 16-16 tie in the Sugar Bowl and finishing fourth in the national polls, earning MacPherson AFCA FBS National Coach of the Year honors. He was a two-time AFCA District-Regional Coach of the Year honoree, earning one honor in 1977 during his tenure at Massachusetts while earning his last award in 1987 while at Syracuse.

Bill McCartney
2014 Master Coach

Bill McCartney was born in Riverview, Michigan, in 1940. McCartney attended the University of Missouri, where he played for them from 1959-1961. McCartney's first assistant coaching job was at Holy Redeemer (Mich.) High School in 1965. He was also the head basketball coach at Redeemer from 1965-1969. McCartney's first head coach job was at Divine Child (Mich.) High School before becoming the only high school coach ever hired by University of Michigan coaching legend Bo Schembechler in 1974.

After eight years as an assistant at Michigan, McCartney became the head coach at the University of Colorado in 1982. During his 12 years with the Buffaloes, he accumulated an overall record of 93-55-5, led his teams to three Big Eight Conference titles (1989, 1990, 1991) and a National Championship (1990).

McCartney was inducted into the College Football Hall of Fame in 2013. He received several honors, including the AFCA Coach of the Year (1989), the Eddie Robinson Coach of the Year Award (1989), the Walter Camp Coach of the Year Award (1989), the Paul "Bear" Bryant Award (1989), was a three-time Big Eight Coach of the Year winner (1985, 1989, 1990) and was a two-time AFCA Regional Coach of the Year (1985, 1989).

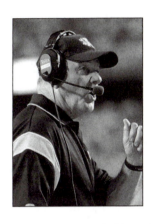

Jerry Moore
2015 Master Coach

Jerry Moore was born in Bonham, Texas, in 1939. He played wide receiver for Baylor University from 1958 to 1960. Moore began his coaching career at Corsicana (Texas) High School. In 1965, he became an assistant coach at SMU. After the 1972 season, he joined the Nebraska Cornhuskers as their wide receivers coach and served as their offensive coordinator in 1978.

Moore accepted his first head coaching job in 1979 at North Texas State (now the University of North Texas). After two seasons, he left for the University of Texas Tech where he spent five seasons with the Red Raiders from 1981 to 1985. After three years away from football, Moore accepted an assistant position with the University of Arkansas in 1988.

In 1989, Moore accepted the head coach position at Appalachian State University, where he led the Mountaineers to a 215-87 record (overall coaching record is 242-135-2), 10 Southern Conference championships (1991, 1995, 1999, 2005-2010, 2012) and 3 NCAA Division 1-AA/FCS National Championships (2005, 2006, 2007).

Moore was inducted into both the College Football Hall of Fame and the Southern Conference Hall of Fame in 2014. He received several other honors, including the Eddie Robinson Award (2006), the Liberty Mutual Coach of the Year Award (2009), was a three-time AFCA Division I-AA/FCS Coach of the Year winner (2005, 2006, 2007), was a six-time AFCA Regional Coach of the Year (1994-1995, 2005-2006, 2008-2009) and was an eight-time Southern Conference Coach of the Year (1991, 1994-1995, 2005-2006, 2008-2010).

Don Nehlen
2006 Master Coach

Don Nehlen was born in Mansfield, Ohio, in 1936. Nehlen played quarterback at Bowling Green State from 1955 to 1957 and led the team to a Mid-American Conference championship in 1956.

He began his coaching career in 1958 at Mansfield Senior High School and then served as head coach at Canton South High School and Canton McKinley High School. Nehlen later made coaching stops at the University of Cincinnati and Bowling Green State as an assistant coach before serving as Bowling Green State's head coach from 1968 to 1976, and the University of Michigan as the quarterback coach in 1977 before arriving at West Virginia. As the head coach for the Mountaineers from 1980 to 2000, he led his teams to 13 bowl games and a Big East Conference championship in 1993. Nehlen accumulated a 202-128-8 overall record.

Nehlen has received many honors, including being inducted into the College Football Hall of Fame in 2005 and receiving the Walter Camp Coach of the Year Award (1988), the Bobby Dodd Coach of the Year Award (1988), the Big East Coach of the Year (1993), the Kodak Coach of the Year (1993) and the Woody Hayes Trophy (1993). Nehlen served on the AFCA Board of Trustees from 1989 to 1996 and served as the AFCA President in 1997. He also received the AFCA Coach of the Year Award in 1988 and was an AFCA Regional Coach of the Year in 1988 and an AFCA Regional Coach of the Year in 1993.

Tom Osborne
2009 Master Coach

Tom Osborne was born in Hastings, Nebraska, in 1937. He stayed in his hometown and played football and basketball at Hastings College from 1956-1958. He graduated with a B.A. in History in 1959, and was awarded the Nebraska College Athlete of the Year.

Osborne was drafted into the National Football League (NFL) by the San Francisco 49ers in 1959 before he went to the Washington Redskins, for whom he played two seasons as a wide receiver from 1960-1961.

Osborne joined the University of Nebraska football staff as an offensive assistant in 1967 and then served as an offensive coordinator from 1969 to 1972 before becoming the head coach for the Cornhuskers in 1973.

Under Osborne's guidance, he led his teams to a 255-49-3 overall record, three National Championships (1994,1995, 1997), 12 Big Eight Conference titles, one Big 12 Conference title and two Big 12 North Division titles. All 25 of his Husker teams went to a bowl game.

Osborne was inducted into the College Football Hall of Fame in 1999, and in 2000, he received the Jim Thorpe Lifetime Achievement Award. In 1999, ESPN honored Osborne as the coach of the decade for the 1990s. He was the recipient for the 2000 AFCA Amos Alonzo Stagg Award and the 2008 AFCA Tuss McLaughry Award. He was the AFCA Coach of the Year in 1994, received AFCA Regional-District Coach of the Year honors in 1974, 1978, 1979, 1982, 1983, 1987 and 1994. He served on the AFCA Board of Trustees from 1978 to 1983 and 1986 to 1988.

Joe Paterno
2009 Master Coach

Joe Paterno was born in Brooklyn, New York, in 1926. He attended Brown University and played as a quarterback and cornerback from 1946 to 1949.

Paterno joined at Penn State as an assistant coach in 1950 and became the head coach for the Nittany Lions in 1966. During his 46 years as the head coach, he accumulated an overall record of 409-136-3, led the Nittany Lions to two National Championships in 1982 and 1986, 3 Big Ten Conference titles and had a bowl record of 24-12-1.

Paterno is a five-time AFCA Coach of the Year winner (1968, 1978, 1982, 1986, 2005), a three-time Walter Camp Coach of the Year winner (1972, 1994, 2005), a three-time Eddie Robinson Coach of the Year winner (1978, 1982, 1986), a three-time Big Ten Coach of the Year (1994, 2005, 2008) and a two-time Bobby Dodd Coach of the Year winner (1981, 2005). He was the 1986 recipient of the Paul "Bear" Bryant Award and the 2002 recipient of the AFCA Amos Alonzo Stagg Award. Paterno has the second most district/regional honors in AFCA history with 11 AFCA District/Regional Coach of the Year honors. Paterno was inducted into the College Football Hall of Fame in 2007. He served on the AFCA Board of Trustees from 1969 to 1972. Paterno passed away in January of 2012.

Tubby Raymond
2012 Master Coach

Harold R. "Tubby" Raymond was born in Flint, Michigan, in 1926. Raymond played quarterback and linebacker at the University of Michigan in 1946 and 1948. He also played baseball at the University of Michigan in 1949 and went on to play minor league baseball for the Clarksdale Planters (1950) and the Flint Arrows (1951).

Raymond's first coaching job was as an assistant at the University of Maine from 1951 to 1953, where he also coached baseball. In 1954, Raymond left to be an assistant coach at the University of Delaware. He also coached Delaware's baseball teams from 1956 to 1964.

In 1966, Raymond became the head coach at Delaware, leading the Fightin' Blue Hens to a 300-119-3 record, three Middle Atlantic Conference Championships (1966, 1968, 1969), two College Division National Championships (1971, 1972), an NCAA Division II National Championship (1979), five Yankee Conference Championships (1986, 1988, 1991, 1992, 1995) and an Atlantic 10 Conference (2000).

Raymond was inducted into the College Football Hall of Fame in 2003. He was a two-time AFCA Coach of the Year (1971, 1972) and a seven-time AFCA Regional/District Coach of the Year (1971, 1972, 1974, 1978, 1979, 1992, 1995). Raymond served on the AFCA Board of Trustees from 1974 to 1980 and served as the AFCA's President in 1981.

John Robinson
2008 Master Coach

John Robinson was born in Chicago, Illinois, in 1935 and grew up in Daly City, California. He played football at the University of Oregon from 1955 to 1957.

Robinson began his coaching career at the University of Oregon from 1961-1971. He then moved on to USC and served as an offensive coordinator from 1972-1974. After leaving in 1975 and spending one year as the running backs coach with the Oakland Raiders, Robinson returned to USC as the head coach, where he coached the Trojans form 1976 to 1982 and again from 1993 to 1997, compiling a 104-35-4 record, a National Championship and five Pac-8/Pac-10 Conference titles in 1976, 1978, 1979, 1993 and 1995.

Form 1983-1991, Robinson was the head coach for the Los Angeles Rams. Robinson is considered one of the more successful coaches in Rams history, twice leading the team to the NFC title game. His 79 victories are the most in Rams franchise history.

Robinson coached the University of Nevada, Las Vegas, from 1999 to 2004, leading his 2000 team to a victory in the Las Vegas Bowl. He spent the 2010 season as a defensive coordinator for San Marcos High School (Calif.).

Robinson was inducted into the College Football Hall of Fame in 2009. He was an AFCA District Coach of the Year recipient in 1978 and 1976. Robinson currently serves as an analyst on NFL game broadcasts for the Sports USA Radio Network.

R.C. Slocum
2006 Master Coach

R.C. Slocum was born in Oakdale, Louisiana, in 1944. He grew up in Orange, Texas, and later attended McNeese State University from 1965-1967, where he played as a tight end. Slocum began his career as a football coach at a Lake Charles high school in 1968. Two years later, in 1970, Slocum became a graduate assistant at Kansas State University.

Slocum arrived at Texas A&M in 1972, where he spent most of his assistant coaching career on the defensive side of the ball. After spending one year at USC in 1981 as the defensive coordinator, he returned to Texas A&M and served as the defensive coordinator for the Aggies from 1982 to 1988. In 1989, Slocum was named head coach at Texas A&M, where he led the Aggies to a 123-47-2 record, making him the winningest coach in Texas A&M history. During his career, Slocum won four conference championships, including the Big 12 title in 1998, two Big 12 South Championships in 1997 and 1998 and three Southwest Conference titles in a row from 1991 to 1993.

Slocum retired in 2002 and currently serves as the president for the American Football Coaches Foundation. He served on the AFCA Board of Trustees from 2001-2002. Slocum received the AFCA Amos Alonzo Stagg Award in 2014 and was enshrined into the College Football Hall of Fame in 2012.

Ken Sparks
2015 Master Coach

Ken Sparks was born in Knoxville, Tennessee, in 1944. He played wide receiver for Carson-Newman in 1967. Sparks began his coaching career at Gibbs High School in Knoxville, restarting the football program with a winning season. A year later Sparks coached quarterbacks and wide receivers at Tennessee Tech while earning his Master's Degree. He coached Morristown East High School for one season before returning to his alma mater, Carson-Newman, to serve as offensive coordinator for then-Carson-Newman head coach Dal Shealy and oversee the track program. Sparks served both teams with distinction, receiving Southern Collegiate Track Coach of the Year honors in 1977.

Sparks took over the Farragut High School football program in 1977, guiding the Admirals to a 29-5 record. After three seasons, Sparks was asked to take command of the Carson-Newman football program.

From 1980 to 2014, Sparks led the Eagles to an overall record of 325-89-2, 21 South Atlantic Conference titles (1982-1984, 1986, 1988-1991, 1993-1999, 2002-2004, 2007-2009) and five NAIA National Championships (1983-1984, 1986, 1988-1989). Sparks is currently in his thirty-sixth season at Carson-Newman in 2015.

Sparks was inducted into the inaugural class of the Division II Coaches Hall of Fame in 2010. Sparks is also a member of the South Atlantic Conference Hall of Fame, the Knoxville Sports Hall of Fame, the Carson-Newman Athletic Hall of Fame, the Tennessee Sports Hall of Fame and the NAIA Hall of Fame. Sparks has received many honors throughout his career, including the FCA Lifetime Achievement Award, NAIA Coach of the Year honors (1984). He's been voted SAC Coach of the Year 12 times and was an AFCA Division II Regional Coach of the Year in 1997.

Sparks served on the AFCA's Board of Trustees from 2000 to 2006 served as the AFCA's President in 2007.

Dick Vermeil
2013 Master Coach

Dick Vermeil was born in Calistoga, California, in 1936. Vermeil graduated from San Jose State University in 1959, where he was the back up quarterback. After serving as assistant coach for the Del Mar

(Calif.) High School football team for on season, he became the head coach at Hillsdale (Calif.) High School for three seasons, then went to Sam Mateo College as an assistant coach. In 1964, Vermeil served as the head coach at Napa Junior College. He served as an assistant coach at Stanford University for two seasons (1965-1966).

Vermeil was hired by the Los Angeles Rams in 1969 and served as the special teams coach for one season. In 1970, Vermeil served as the offensive coordinator for one season before returning to the Los Angels Rams as an assistant coach for three seasons (1971-1973).

Vermeil took the head coaching position at UCLA in 1974, and in his two seasons with the Bruins, he compiled a 15-5-3 record, including a 9-2-1 record in 1975 when he led the Bruins to their first conference championship in 10 years and a win in the Rose Bowl. He was inducted into the Rose Bowl Hall of Fame in 2014.

In 1976, Vermeil took over as head coach for the Philadelphia Eagles. From 1976 to 1982, he led his teams to a 54-47 record. For the next 15 years, Vermeil spent time working as a sports announcer for CBS and ABC. Vermeil returned to coaching with the St. Louis Rams in 1997. He led the Rams to their first ever Super Bowl victory in Super Bowl XXXIV in 1999. He joined the Kansas City Chiefs as their head coach in 2001 and accumulated a 44-36 record in five seasons.

During his career, he received many honors, including the Walter Camp Distinguished American award (2006), was inducted into the Eagles Hall of Fame (1994), was inducted into the St. Louis Rams Ring of Honor (2008), was the NFL Coach of the Year (UPI - 1978), NFL Coach of the Year (PFWA, SN - 1979), NFL Coach of the Year (AP, MX, PFWA, SN - 1999), NFL Coach of the Year (Maxwell - 2003) and was the Sporting News Sportsman of the Year (2003).

About the Author

Grant Teaff, as a player, coach, and executive director of the American Football Coaches Association (AFCA), has spent his life immersed in what he calls, "the great game."

A native of Snyder, Texas, Teaff served as the head football coach of McMurry University, Angelo State University, and Baylor University. He won 170 football games, plus 2 Southwest Conference Championships, and coached in 20 post-season bowls and all-star games, all while becoming a national leader and spokesman for the game of football.

Coach Teaff has been inducted into eight Halls of Fame, including the College Football Hall of Fame and the Texas Sports Hall of Fame. In 2006, he received the highest award the AFCA can bestow – the Amos Alonzo Stagg Award.

As a nationally known author and motivational speaker, Teaff enthusiastically shares his belief that a coach's influence should, and does, go beyond the game. He has written seven books: *I Believe*, *Winning*, *Seasons of Glory*, *Coaching in the Classroom*, *Grant Teaff with the Master Coaches Volumes I and II*, and *A Coach's Influence: Beyond the Game*.

Teaff and his wife, Donell, live in Waco, Texas. They have three daughters and four grandchildren.

About the American Football Coaches Association

The American Coaches Association (AFCA) is the only national organization solely dedicated to improving football coaches through ongoing education, interaction, and networking. Its primary goal is to provide resources for personal and professional development among the football coaching profession.

The AFCA membership includes over 11,000 members and represents coaches and several stakeholders within the game of football. Any high school, junior college, international, semi-professional or professional football coach is eligible to become a member of the AFCA.

Founded in December of 1921 by 43 coaches in a meeting at the Hotel Astor in New York City, the AFCA has continued to push the envelope in regard to the growth of the profession.

The AFCA strives to maintain the highest possible standards in football and the profession of coaching football, as well as to provide a forum for the discussion and study of all matters pertaining to football and coaching.

The flagship event of the AFCA is its annual coaches' convention, which takes place in January. More than 6,000 coaches attend the four-day event. Each year, numerous speakers lecture on topics such as concussion management, X's & O's, practice and program organization, media relations, and career development. Attendees can earn professional development hours that can help with school district recertification, salary points, and other career-related opportunities.

269

About the American Football Coaches Foundation

The American Football Coaches Foundation was established in 1998. One of the twenty major goals set by Grant Teaff for the American Football Coaches Association in 1994 was to create an educational foundation that would provide funds to assist the American Football Coaches Association in all of its educational venues.

The Foundation's financial contribution to the annual AFCA convention benefits the rank and file of AFCA membership. Fees for the convention and membership are kept at a minimum, while providing funds for publications and the educational website. The premise for intense education of coaches is simple; a trained, educated, and developed coaches will invariably have a more positive influence on those they teach and coach

The Board of Directors of The Foundation consists of men from the business and corporate world, lawyers, representatives of the NFL and the NCAA, a former governor, and a former president of the Fellowship of Christian Athletes. The Board is a strong, hard-working group who care about the game and those who coach and play.

The Foundation hosts three golf tournaments and the prestigious CEO Coach of the Year award and dinner. Anyone can contribute to The Foundation and many have in appreciation of a specific coach, and many coaches have contributed to show appreciation for the education they have received.

In the of spirit giving back, Coach and Mrs. Teaff (Donell) have given this book and its proceeds to the American Football Coaches Association Foundation.